First World War

and Army of Occupation

War Diary

France, Belgium and Germany

17 DIVISION
50 Infantry Brigade
Alexandra, Princess of Wales's Own (Yorkshire Regiment)
7th Battalion
13 July 1915 - 28 February 1918

WO95/2004/2

The Naval & Military Press Ltd
www.nmarchive.com
Published in association with The National Archives

Published by

The Naval & Military Press Ltd

Unit 10 Ridgewood Industrial Park,
Uckfield, East Sussex,
TN22 5QE England
Tel: +44 (0) 1825 749494

www.naval-military-press.com
www.nmarchive.com

This diary has been reprinted in facsimile from the original. Any imperfections are inevitably reproduced and the quality may fall short of modern type and cartographic standards.

Contents

Document type	Place/Title	Date From	Date To
Heading	WO95/2004 7 Yorks Regt. Jul 1915-Feb 1918 (Disbanded) 17 Div-50 Inf Bde		
Heading	17th Division 50th Infy Bde 7th Bn The Yorkshire Regt. Jlu 1915-Feb 1918		
Heading	50th Inf. Bde. 17th Div. 7th Battn. The Yorkshire Regiment. July And August (13.7.15-31.8.15) 1915		
War Diary	Folkestone	13/07/1915	13/07/1915
War Diary	Boulogne	14/07/1915	14/07/1915
War Diary	Remeilly-Wirquin	15/07/1915	15/07/1915
War Diary	Arques	17/07/1915	17/07/1915
War Diary	Steenvoorde	19/07/1915	21/07/1915
War Diary	La Clytte	23/07/1915	02/08/1915
War Diary	Voormezeele	02/08/1915	12/08/1915
War Diary	Voormezeele (Trenches)	13/08/1915	14/08/1915
War Diary	Reninghelst	15/08/1915	26/08/1915
War Diary	Voormezeele	27/08/1915	31/08/1915
Heading	50th Inf. Bde. 17th Div. 7th Battn. The Yorkshire Regiment. September 1915		
War Diary	Voormezeele	01/09/1915	02/09/1915
War Diary	Reninghelst	03/09/1915	10/09/1915
War Diary	Voormezeele	11/09/1915	19/09/1915
War Diary	Reninghelst	20/09/1915	27/09/1915
War Diary	Voormezeele	28/09/1915	30/09/1915
Heading	50th Inf. Bde. 17th Div. 7th Battn. The Yorkshire Regiment. October 1915		
War Diary	Voormezeele	01/10/1915	04/10/1915
War Diary	Reninghelst To Steenvoorde	05/10/1915	05/10/1915
War Diary	Steenvoorde	06/10/1915	21/10/1915
War Diary	Poperinghe	21/10/1915	21/10/1915
War Diary	Hooge	22/10/1915	27/10/1915
War Diary	Ypres	28/10/1915	31/10/1915
Heading	50th Inf. Bde. 17th Div. 7th Battn. The Yorkshire Regiment. November 1915		
War Diary	Ypres	01/11/1915	03/11/1915
War Diary	Hooge	03/11/1915	06/11/1915
War Diary	Busseboom	07/11/1915	10/11/1915
War Diary	Hooge	11/11/1915	15/11/1915
War Diary	Busseboom	16/11/1915	23/11/1915
War Diary	Ypres	23/11/1915	26/11/1915
War Diary	Hooge	27/11/1915	30/11/1915
Heading	50th Inf. Bde. 17th Div. 7th Battn. The Yorkshire Regiment. December 1915		
War Diary	Hooge	01/12/1915	01/12/1915
War Diary	Busseboom	02/12/1915	09/12/1915
War Diary	Ouderdom	09/12/1915	10/12/1915
War Diary	Hooge	13/12/1915	17/12/1915
War Diary	Busseboom	18/12/1915	20/12/1915
War Diary	Ypres	25/12/1915	26/12/1915
War Diary	Zillebeke Lake	27/12/1915	27/12/1915
War Diary	Trenches	29/12/1915	31/12/1915

Heading	7th Yorkshire Vol 5 17 Div Jan 1916 50th-Bde		
War Diary	Hooge Busseboom	01/01/1916	04/01/1916
War Diary	Polincove	05/01/1916	31/01/1916
Miscellaneous	The Officer i/c A.Gs Dept. Base	10/03/1916	10/03/1916
War Diary	Polincove	01/02/1916	06/02/1916
War Diary	Reninghelst	06/02/1916	06/02/1916
War Diary	Dickebusch	07/02/1916	14/02/1916
War Diary	G.H.Q. Line	14/02/1916	14/02/1916
War Diary	Voormezeele	15/02/1916	16/02/1916
War Diary	Reninghelst	17/02/1916	19/02/1916
War Diary	Voormezeele	20/02/1916	29/02/1916
War Diary	Polincove	01/02/1916	06/02/1916
War Diary	Dickebusch	07/02/1916	14/02/1916
War Diary	G.H.Q. Line	14/02/1916	14/02/1916
War Diary	Voormezeele	15/02/1916	16/02/1916
War Diary	Reninghelst	17/02/1916	19/02/1916
War Diary	Voormezeele	20/02/1916	29/02/1916
Miscellaneous	Entraining Programme		
War Diary	Voormezeele	01/03/1916	06/03/1916
War Diary	Reninghelst	07/03/1916	08/03/1916
War Diary	Voormezeele	09/03/1916	11/03/1916
War Diary	Reninghelst	12/03/1916	12/03/1916
War Diary	Moolenacker	13/03/1916	21/03/1916
War Diary	La Creche	22/03/1916	22/03/1916
War Diary	Armentieres	23/03/1916	30/03/1916
War Diary	Pont Ballot	31/03/1916	07/04/1916
War Diary	Armentieres	08/04/1916	15/04/1916
War Diary	Pont Ballot	15/04/1916	23/04/1916
War Diary	Armentieres	23/04/1916	30/04/1916
War Diary	Pont Ballot	01/05/1916	08/05/1916
War Diary	Armentieres	09/05/1916	11/05/1916
War Diary	Estaires	12/05/1916	13/05/1916
War Diary	Morbecque	14/05/1916	14/05/1916
War Diary	Wardrecques	15/05/1916	15/05/1916
War Diary	Mentque	16/05/1916	20/06/1916
War Diary	Heilly	21/06/1916	26/06/1916
War Diary	Ville	27/06/1916	30/06/1916
Heading	50th Inf. Bde. 17th Div. War Diary 7th Battn. The Yorkshire Regiment. July 1916		
War Diary	Trenches In Front of Fricourt Village	30/06/1916	01/07/1916
War Diary	Fricourt	01/07/1916	02/07/1916
War Diary	Heilly	02/07/1916	06/07/1916
War Diary	Fricourt Wood	07/07/1916	08/07/1916
War Diary	Bottom Wood	08/07/1916	08/07/1916
War Diary	Trenches S W of Mametz Wood	08/07/1916	11/07/1916
War Diary	Grove Town Siding	11/07/1916	11/07/1916
War Diary	Molliens-Vidames	12/07/1916	15/07/1916
War Diary	Bellancourt	16/07/1916	22/07/1916
War Diary	Conde	23/07/1916	24/07/1916
War Diary	Mericourt	24/07/1916	24/07/1916
War Diary	Near Dernancourt	25/07/1916	31/07/1916
Operation(al) Order(s)	Battalion Operation Order No. 63		
Operation(al) Order(s)	7th Yorkshire Regiment Operation Order No 53	25/06/1916	25/06/1916
Miscellaneous	Instruction in Connection with Forthcoming Operation		
Miscellaneous	War Diary		
Map	Fricourt		

Heading	50th Brigade. 17th Division. 1/7th Battalion The Yorkshire Regiment August 1916		
Heading	7th Yorkshire Regt, August 1916 Vol 11		
War Diary	Near Dernancourt	01/08/1916	02/08/1916
War Diary	Bellevue Farm	03/08/1916	04/08/1916
War Diary	Pommiers Redoubt	05/08/1916	12/08/1916
War Diary	Bellevue Farm	13/08/1916	13/08/1916
War Diary	Dernancourt	14/08/1916	15/08/1916
War Diary	Heuzecourt	16/08/1916	16/08/1916
War Diary	Bonnieres	17/08/1916	17/08/1916
War Diary	Doullens	18/08/1916	18/08/1916
War Diary	Bayencourt	18/08/1916	19/08/1916
War Diary	Trenches Hebuterne	20/08/1916	25/08/1916
War Diary	Sailly Au Bois	26/08/1916	31/08/1916
Heading	7th Yorks Regt Sept 1916 Vol 12		
War Diary	Trenches Hebuterne	01/09/1916	06/09/1916
War Diary	Bayencourt	07/09/1916	11/09/1916
War Diary	Hebuterne	12/09/1916	16/09/1916
War Diary	Sailly-Au-Bois	16/09/1916	16/09/1916
War Diary	Halloy	17/09/1916	21/09/1916
War Diary	Occoches	21/09/1916	21/09/1916
War Diary	Maizicourt	22/09/1916	22/09/1916
War Diary	Drucat	23/09/1916	30/09/1916
Map	Trench Map Scale 1/5000		
Heading	War Diary of 7th York Regt. For October 1916 Vol 13		
War Diary	Drucat	01/10/1916	06/10/1916
War Diary	Maison Ponthieu	07/10/1916	07/10/1916
War Diary	Barly	08/10/1916	10/10/1916
War Diary	Halloy	11/10/1916	11/10/1916
War Diary	Souastre	12/10/1916	14/10/1916
War Diary	Sailly-Au-Bois	14/10/1916	17/10/1916
War Diary	Trenches Hebuterne	18/10/1916	18/10/1916
War Diary	Sailly-Au-Bois	19/10/1916	19/10/1916
War Diary	Halloy	20/10/1916	20/10/1916
War Diary	Talmas	21/10/1916	21/10/1916
War Diary	La Houssoye	22/10/1916	22/10/1916
War Diary	Meaulte	23/10/1916	27/10/1916
War Diary	Mansel Camp	28/10/1916	31/10/1916
Heading	7th Yorkshire R. Nov 16 Vol 14		
Miscellaneous	D.A.G. Base	08/12/1916	08/12/1916
War Diary	B Camp S 23.d.4.4	01/11/1916	02/11/1916
War Diary	N 34 C 1.9	03/11/1916	07/11/1916
War Diary	H Camp	08/11/1916	10/11/1916
War Diary	C Camp	10/11/1916	10/11/1916
War Diary	Trenches N34.c.1.9	10/11/1916	14/11/1916
War Diary	Mansel Camp	15/11/1916	16/11/1916
War Diary	Molliens-Vidames	17/11/1916	30/11/1916
Miscellaneous	Ref. O.O 112	04/11/1916	04/11/1916
Operation(al) Order(s)	50th Infantry Brigade Operation Order No. 112	04/11/1916	04/11/1916
Operation(al) Order(s)	Operation Order S1 by Lieut. Col. R. D' A. Fife Commdg. 7th York Regt		
Diagram etc	Trench Map B		
Map	Trench Map A		
Miscellaneous	Patrol Report		
Miscellaneous	Headquarters 50 Brigade	01/12/1916	01/12/1916
Miscellaneous	H.Q. 50 Brigade	03/01/1917	03/01/1917

Heading	War Diary For The Month of December 1916 For 7th Yorkshire Regiment. Vol 15		
War Diary	Molliens-Vidames	01/12/1916	14/12/1916
War Diary	Mericourt L'Abbe	15/12/1916	15/12/1916
Miscellaneous	Map of Trenches	03/01/1917	03/01/1917
War Diary	Mericourt L'Abbe	16/12/1916	22/12/1916
War Diary	Ville	23/12/1916	24/12/1916
War Diary	Carnoy Camp	25/12/1916	25/12/1916
War Diary	Guillemont	26/12/1916	26/12/1916
War Diary	Trenches Les Boeufs	27/12/1916	28/12/1916
War Diary	Carnoy Camp XXII	29/12/1916	31/12/1916
War Diary	Guillemont	31/12/1916	31/12/1916
Map	For War Diary 7th York Regt.		
Heading	War Diary For January of 7th Yorkshire Regiment. 1917 Vol 16		
War Diary	Guillemont	01/01/1917	02/01/1917
War Diary	Trenches Near Les Boeufs	03/01/1917	04/01/1917
War Diary	Carnoy Camp No XXII	05/01/1917	05/01/1917
War Diary	Carnoy Camp 22	06/01/1917	07/01/1917
War Diary	Guillemont	08/01/1917	08/01/1917
War Diary	Trenches Near Les Boeufs	09/01/1917	10/01/1917
War Diary	Carnoy Camp No 22	11/01/1917	13/01/1917
War Diary	Meaulte	14/01/1917	14/01/1917
War Diary	La Neuville	15/01/1917	16/01/1917
War Diary	Corbie	17/01/1917	25/01/1917
War Diary	Fregicourt	26/01/1917	26/01/1917
War Diary	Sailly-Saillisel	27/01/1917	27/01/1917
War Diary	Trenches Sailly-Saillisel	27/01/1917	28/01/1917
War Diary	Combles	29/01/1917	30/01/1917
War Diary	Trenches Sailly-Saillisel	31/01/1917	31/01/1917
Diagram etc	Trench Map		
Heading	War Diary For February 1917 7th Bn. Yorkshire Regiment. Vol 17		
War Diary	Trenches Sailly-Saillisel	01/02/1917	01/02/1917
War Diary	Bronfay Camp	02/02/1917	05/02/1917
War Diary	Combles	06/02/1917	07/02/1917
War Diary	Trenches Sailly-Saillisel	08/02/1917	09/02/1917
War Diary	Bronfay Camp	10/02/1917	13/02/1917
War Diary	Trenches Sailly-Saillisel	14/02/1917	15/02/1917
War Diary	Combles	16/02/1917	16/02/1917
War Diary	Bronfay	17/02/1917	19/02/1917
War Diary	Meaulte	20/02/1917	27/02/1917
Operation(al) Order(s)	52nd. Order No. 136.	05/02/1917	05/02/1917
Map	Trench Map		
Map	A 2. Scale 1:2,500		
Map	Map No. 1 Diary		
Miscellaneous	Operation Order by Lieut. Col. R.D' A. Fife. C.M.G. Commanding 7th Battalion Yorkshire Regiment	06/02/1917	06/02/1917
Miscellaneous	Artillery Barrage. (Reference Para: 6 17th Div. Operation Order No. 109) Appendix "A"		
Miscellaneous	Further Instructions	06/02/1917	06/02/1917
Heading	War Diary 7th Yorkshire Regiment March 1917		
War Diary	Meault	01/03/1917	01/03/1917
War Diary	Warloy	02/03/1917	14/03/1917
War Diary	Beauval	15/03/1917	15/03/1917
War Diary	Bonnieres	16/03/1917	16/03/1917

War Diary	Vieil Hesdin	17/03/1917	23/03/1917
War Diary	Ivergny	24/03/1917	31/03/1917
Heading	War Diary For April 7th Yorkshire Regt Vol 19		
War Diary	Ivergny	01/04/1917	05/04/1917
War Diary	Maizieres	06/04/1917	07/04/1917
War Diary	Izel-Les-Hameaux	08/04/1917	08/04/1917
War Diary	Montenes-Court	09/04/1917	09/04/1917
War Diary	Bivouack West of Arras	10/04/1917	10/04/1917
War Diary	Arras	11/04/1917	11/04/1917
War Diary	East of Arras	12/04/1917	12/04/1917
War Diary	Feuchy	13/04/1917	14/04/1917
War Diary	H.19.c	15/04/1917	15/04/1917
War Diary	Fauberge St Sauveur G 29.d	16/04/1917	19/04/1917
War Diary	Front Line H 26-H 23	20/04/1917	22/04/1917
War Diary	Railway Triangle	23/04/1917	23/04/1917
War Diary	Now German Support Line H.28.a.5.8	23/04/1917	23/04/1917
War Diary	H 29.b.6.7	24/04/1917	25/04/1917
War Diary	Railway Triangle	26/04/1917	26/04/1917
War Diary	Fosseux	27/04/1917	30/04/1917
Map	G "D" Coy Sane		
Miscellaneous	Sane		
Map	Cavalry Corps H.Q.	08/04/1917	08/04/1917
Heading	War Diary May 1917 7th (S) Bn. A.P.W.O. (The Yorkshire Regt) Vol 20		
War Diary	Fosseux	01/05/1917	02/05/1917
War Diary	San Nicholas Arras	03/05/1917	04/05/1917
War Diary	Y Hutments Agnes-Lez-Duisans	05/05/1917	09/05/1917
War Diary	Trenches North of Roeux	10/05/1917	15/05/1917
War Diary	St Nicholas G.17.a.	16/05/1917	21/05/1917
War Diary	H.10.d.4.6	22/05/1917	23/05/1917
War Diary	H.11.b.0.4	24/05/1917	26/05/1917
War Diary	Heron Trench	27/05/1917	27/05/1917
War Diary	St Nicholas	28/05/1917	28/05/1917
War Diary	Halloy	29/05/1917	31/05/1917
Operation(al) Order(s)	50th Infantry Brigade Operation Order No. 142	10/05/1917	10/05/1917
Operation(al) Order(s)	50th Infantry Brigade Operation Order No. 143	10/05/1917	10/05/1917
Map	Maps		
Miscellaneous	behind C in the left	11/05/1917	11/05/1917
Miscellaneous	A Form Messages And Signals		
Miscellaneous	For 100 Yards York of Cam On The Night 1 of 10th May	10/05/1917	10/05/1917
Miscellaneous	A Form Messages And Signals		
Operation(al) Order(s)	Operation Order 51		
Operation(al) Order(s)	Operation Order 53		
Miscellaneous			
Heading	War Diary June. 7th Yorkshire Regt. Vol 21		
War Diary	Halloy	01/06/1917	19/06/1917
War Diary	St. Nicholas C.17.a	20/06/1917	20/06/1917
War Diary	Railway Cutting H.7.d.	21/06/1917	24/06/1917
War Diary	Hurrum Trench H.6.c.1.5	25/06/1917	26/06/1917
War Diary	Chili H.12.b.2.8	27/06/1917	29/06/1917
War Diary	Camp St. Nicholas C.17.a	30/06/1917	30/06/1917
Map	Detail And Trenches Revised	04/05/1917	04/05/1917
Map	Detail And Trenches Revised	19/05/1917	19/05/1917
Heading	War Diary July 1917 7th Yorkshire Regt. Vol 22		
War Diary	St. Nicholas Camp G.17	01/07/1917	07/07/1917

War Diary	Cadiz Trench H.18.b. 50.75	08/07/1917	10/07/1917
War Diary	H 11.a.6.1	11/07/1917	15/07/1917
War Diary	Battn. H.Q. Cadiz H18.b.50.75	16/07/1917	16/07/1917
War Diary	Cadiz. H.18.b.50.75	16/07/1917	21/07/1917
War Diary	Railway Cutting H.7.d.	22/07/1917	24/07/1917
War Diary	St Nicholas Grimsby Camp G.17	25/07/1917	31/07/1917
Map	Plouvain Parts of 51 N.W. & S.W. Detail	03/07/1917	03/07/1917
Miscellaneous	A Form Messages And Signals		
Miscellaneous	In Operation for Raid No 2		
Miscellaneous	Operation Details by Major R C Cotton Comdg 7th Bn Yorkshire Regt	18/07/1917	18/07/1917
Miscellaneous	58th Infantry Brigade Report On Raid	20/07/1917	20/07/1917
Miscellaneous	50th Infantry Brigade Report On Raid	21/07/1917	21/07/1917
Miscellaneous	Additional Orders for Raid	19/07/1917	19/07/1917
Miscellaneous	O.C. D. Coy	20/07/1917	20/07/1917
Miscellaneous	Barrage Table	18/07/1917	18/07/1917
Miscellaneous	Instruction For Raid No1	19/07/1917	19/07/1917
War Diary	Civil Trench H.6.G.3.3	01/08/1917	06/08/1917
War Diary	Helford Humid Trench H.6.c.	07/08/1917	12/08/1917
War Diary	Civil Avenue H.6.b.3.3	13/08/1917	17/08/1917
War Diary	Grims by Camp	18/08/1917	24/08/1917
War Diary	Right Support Gavrelle French Sub Sector	24/08/1917	31/08/1917
Map	Plouvain Map Scale 1/10,000 51 NW + NE		
Heading	July War Diary		
War Diary	Right Front Battn. Chemical Works Sector H.Q. Corfu. Avenue	01/09/1917	04/09/1917
War Diary	H.Q. Pudding Trench H.16.b	05/09/1917	09/09/1917
War Diary	Gavrelle Fampouy	09/09/1917	09/09/1917
War Diary	Grimsby Camp G.17.c	10/09/1917	17/09/1917
War Diary	H.Q. Chili Avenue H.12.b.2.9	18/09/1917	21/09/1917
War Diary	Gavrelle Switch Line H.Q. H11.b.6.5	22/09/1917	24/09/1917
War Diary	Arras	25/09/1917	25/09/1917
War Diary	Izel-Les-Hameau	26/09/1917	26/09/1917
War Diary	Lignereuil	27/09/1917	30/09/1917
Map	Greenland Hill Trench Map		
Map	Map For War Diary For		
Miscellaneous		20/09/1917	20/09/1917
Miscellaneous	17th. Division	27/09/1917	27/09/1917
Miscellaneous	Adjt 7th Yorkshire Regt.	28/09/1917	28/09/1917
Map	Schaap-Balie		
Map	J. Corps T.S. No. 69.		
Map	51b (Part of) 1:40000 Reference		
War Diary	Lignereuil	01/10/1917	04/10/1917
War Diary	Saulty Station	05/10/1917	05/10/1917
War Diary	Piddington Camp Proven	06/10/1917	09/10/1917
War Diary	Dragon Camp A.15.b	10/10/1917	10/10/1917
War Diary	Harrow Camp B.7.d.8.5	11/10/1917	11/10/1917
War Diary	White Mill Camp B.14.d	12/10/1917	12/10/1917
War Diary	Yser Canal	13/10/1917	21/10/1917
War Diary	Landrethun-Les Ardres	22/10/1917	07/11/1917
War Diary	Wolfe Camp B22.d	08/11/1917	13/11/1917
War Diary	Olga Houses	14/11/1917	15/11/1917
War Diary	Double Cotts U.23.d.	16/11/1917	17/11/1917
War Diary	Louis Farm U24.c	18/11/1917	19/11/1917
War Diary	Dragon Camp A.14.b	20/11/1917	25/11/1917
War Diary	Bridge Camp No 1 B14.d	26/11/1917	30/11/1917

Map	Broembeek		
War Diary	Bridge Camp No 1 B.14.d	01/12/1917	01/12/1917
War Diary	Huddlestone Camp C.7.d.1.4	02/12/1917	06/12/1917
War Diary		07/12/1917	07/12/1917
War Diary	Nortkerque	08/12/1917	10/12/1917
War Diary	Bayenghem	11/12/1917	15/12/1917
War Diary	Beaulencourt	16/12/1917	22/12/1917
War Diary	Bertincourt	23/12/1917	23/12/1917
War Diary	Havrincourt Wood K.31.b.61	24/12/1917	25/12/1917
War Diary	K 32.c.7.9	26/12/1917	27/12/1917
War Diary	Flesquieres	28/12/1917	31/12/1917
Miscellaneous	Attached To War Diary December 1919		
Map	Maps		
War Diary	Battn H.Q. K 24.a.90.25	01/01/1918	04/01/1918
War Diary	Battn H.Q. K 24.a.4.4	05/01/1918	07/01/1918
War Diary	Phipps Camp O.6.d 2.2	08/01/1918	10/01/1918
War Diary	H.Q. J 25.d.2.5	11/01/1918	13/01/1918
War Diary	H.Q. K 32.c.7.7	14/01/1918	17/01/1918
War Diary	Batt H.Q. K.15.d.85.40	18/01/1918	21/01/1918
War Diary	Batt HQ London Trench K.21.a.7.7	22/01/1918	24/01/1918
War Diary	H.Q. K 21.a.7.7	25/01/1918	25/01/1918
War Diary	Spoil Heap J 34.c	26/01/1918	31/01/1918
Map	Right Bde Dispositions		
War Diary	Battn H.Q. K.9.c.30.15	01/02/1918	04/02/1918
War Diary	Spoil Map J.35.c	05/02/1918	10/02/1918
War Diary	Phipps Camp O.6.d.2.2	11/02/1918	12/02/1918
War Diary	H.Q. P.1.C	13/02/1918	23/02/1918
War Diary	Bertincourt	24/02/1918	28/02/1918
Operation(al) Order(s)	10th West Yorkshire Regt. Operation Order No. 53	28/02/1917	28/02/1917
Miscellaneous	7th Yorkshire Regiment List of Officers		
Map	Attached to War Diary Feb/18		

WO95/2004

7 Yorks Regt.

Jul 1915 - Feb 1918

[Disbanded]

17 Div - 50 Inf Bde.

17TH DIVISION
50TH INFY BDE

7TH BN THE YORKSHIRE REGT.

JLY 1915 - FEB 1918

DISBANDED

50th Inf.Bde.
17th Div.

Battn. disembarked
Boulogne from
England 14.7.15.

7th BATTN. THE YORKSHIRE REGIMENT.

JULY AND AUGUST

(13.7.15-31.8.15)

1 9 1 5

Feb 1918

Instructions regarding War Diaries and Intelligence Summaries are contained in F. S. Regs., Part II. and the Staff Manual respectively. Title Pages will be prepared in manuscript.

WAR DIARY
or
INTELLIGENCE SUMMARY
(Erase heading not required.)

Army Form C. 2118

7th (Service) Battn YORKSHIRE REGT.

Place	Date	Hour	Summary of Events and Information	Remarks and references to Appendices
FOLKESTONG	13/7/15	10.30pm	Embarked for France – strength 30 officers 937 other ranks.	[initials]
BOULOGNE	14/7/15	3.30am	Disembarked and marched to OSTROVE rest camp and remained there until following morning. Cavalier M.R. MILLIARD of the 6th Regiment of Hussars joined the Battn as interpreter here.	[initials]
REMEILLY–WIRQUIN.	15/7/15	5.30pm	Arrived by train from station PONT de BRIQUES where the Battn was entrained on a train containing the Regimental Transport and machine gun section which had come to France via SOUTHAMPTON and HAVRE. It was discovered that no billets had been allotted to Signallers – machine gunners – transport men and other Head Quarter details and the necessity for sending forward a properly constituted billeting party realised. Time at REMILLY-WIRQUIN occupied in route marching chiefly.	[initials]

1875 Wt. W593/826 1,000,000 4/15 J.B.C. & A. A.D.S.S./Forms/C. 2118.

Instructions regarding War Diaries and Intelligence Summaries are contained in F. S. Regs., Part II. and the Staff Manual respectively. Title Pages will be prepared in manuscript.

WAR DIARY
or
INTELLIGENCE SUMMARY
(Erase heading not required.)

G. H. Q. 3RD ECHELON
31 AUG 1915
INF. SECTION NEW ARMIES

Army Form C. 2118

7th (Service) Battn Yorkshire Regt.

Place	Date	Hour	Summary of Events and Information	Remarks and references to Appendices
ARQUES.	17/7/15	2 pm	Arrived by road and occupied billets. No incident of interest occurred during time spent here.	[initials]
			—— .. ——	
STEENVOORDE	19/7/15	4 pm	Arrived by road after long and trying march. The Battn was inspected by Gen Sir H. Plumer C.B the following day.	[initials]
"	21/7/15		Four company commanders were sent into the trenches occupied by the 3rd Division for two nights.	[initials]
			Time at STEENVOORDE spent in drill – inspections etc. Experiments with gas and smoke helmets were carried out.	[initials]
			—— .. ——	

1875 Wt. W593/826 1,000,000 4/15 J.B.C. & A. A.D.S.S./Forms/C. 2118.

Instructions regarding War Diaries and Intelligence Summaries are contained in F. S. Regs., Part II. and the Staff Manual respectively. Title Pages will be prepared in manuscript.

WAR DIARY
or
INTELLIGENCE SUMMARY
(Erase heading not required.)

Army Form C. 2118

Place	Date	Hour	7th (Serv.) Battn Yorkshire Regt. Summary of Events and Information	Remarks and references to Appendices
LA CLYTTE	23/7/15 To 2/8/15.	1.30am	Arrived by road and occupied huts. Platoons sent into the trenches for instruction throughout the Battn Lieut D. J. WILSON wounded on 23rd whilst conducting a party of N.C.O's to the trenches to be attached to another Battn in the trenches for instruction. 2Lt J. H. F. Clarke wounded on July 23rd in the trenches. 8 N.C.O's and men wounded and two men killed during attachment to other units in the trenches. Bombing sections from each company received instruction from Battns resting from the trenches.	[signature]
VOORMEZEELE	2/8/15		Took over trenches occupied by the 1st Wiltshire Regt on night of 2/3rd August at VOORMEZEELE. One man wounded during the relief	[signature]
"	3/8/15.		Heavily bombarded during the morning. Capt L. E. P. JONES and three men killed and seventeen wounded. Captn Jones buried close to Chateau ROSENTHAL I 26 a 9.5 Map 1/40000	
	4/8/15		Artillery (enemy) less active. Eight men wounded, one killed.	

1875 Wt. W593/826 1,000,000 4/15 J.B.C. & A. A.D.S.S./Forms/C. 2118.

Army Form C. 2118

Instructions regarding War Diaries and Intelligence Summaries are contained in F. S. Regs., Part II. and the Staff Manual respectively. Title Pages will be prepared in manuscript.

WAR DIARY
or
INTELLIGENCE SUMMARY
(Erase heading not required.)

Place	Date	Hour	7th Battn Yorkshire Regt. Summary of Events and Information	Remarks and references to Appendices
VOORMEZEELE	5/8/15		Enemys artillery much less active. One man killed four wounded. Draft of 70 [illegible] men arrived from England. Strength of Battn 26 officers 961 other ranks.	
"	6/8/15		Very quiet. One man wounded.	
"	7/8/15		Very quiet day. Two men wounded.	
"	8/8/15		Very quiet day. two men wounded one killed	
"	9/8/15		Recieved orders to open rapid fire on the enemy at 2.30 am. Similar orders had been given to battns on our right and left. Idea being to divert enemys attention from attack by our troops at HOOGE which was timed to take place at the same time. Enemy shelled our communication trenches and the roads in rear in reply. No casualties.	
"	10/8/15		Quiet day no casualties	
	11/8/15		Quiet day – one man wounded.	
	12/8/15		Quiet day – no casualties	[initials]

1875 Wt. W593/826 1,000,000 4/15 J.B.C. & A. A.D.S.S./Forms/C. 2118.

Instructions regarding War Diaries and Intelligence Summaries are contained in F. S. Regs., Part II. and the Staff Manual respectively. Title Pages will be prepared in manuscript.

WAR DIARY
or
INTELLIGENCE SUMMARY
(Erase heading not required.)

Army Form C. 2118

Place	Date	Hour	7th (Serv) Battn Yorkshire Regt. Summary of Events and Information	Remarks and references to Appendices
VOORMEZEELE (trenches)	13/8/15		Quiet day – two men wounded.	
	14/8/15		Enemys Artillery active. Lieut F.W. CRABTREE killed by sniper. Buried just East of Princess Patricias Cemetery at VOORMEZEELE. Five men wounded. Relieved by 7th Battn Lincoln Regt. Note Time in the trenches occupied in strengthening the parapets and traverses and digging new shelter trenches. Great difficulty was experienced in digging everywhere owing to the number of corpses which had been buried where the trenches were. Very little was seen of the enemy who had very efficient snipers who were favoured by the fact that their trenches were on the crest of a rise in the ground whilst our trenches were at the foot of the rise. They were thus able to cover ground in our rear.	
RENINGHELS	15/8/15		Arrived at a rest camp at RENINGHELS some six miles from the trenches at VOORMEZEELE	
	16/8/15		Half the Battn had baths in the Brewery at RENINGHELS where hot showers were fitted up and a change of underclothing provided.	[signature]

1875 Wt. W593/826 1,000,000 4/15 J.B.C. & A. A.D.S.S./Forms/C. 2118.

Army Form C. 2118

Instructions regarding War Diaries and Intelligence Summaries are contained in F. S. Regs., Part II. and the Staff Manual respectively. Title Pages will be prepared in manuscript.

WAR DIARY
or
INTELLIGENCE SUMMARY
(Erase heading not required.)

Place	Date	Hour	7th Battn Yorkshire Regt. Summary of Events and Information	Remarks and references to Appendices
RENINGHELS	17/8/15		Nothing of importance occurred. Remaining half of Battn had baths and change of clothing.	
"	18/8/15		Nothing of importance occurred.	
	19/8/15		An accident occurred during practice in bomb-throwing. A "pitcher" bomb ~~instant~~ exploded instantaneously in the throwers hand instead of at the end of six seconds. 2Lt T. LARGE, 2Lt G.D. PRESTON and two men wounded, one man killed. A court of enquiry assembled to investigate the matter and found that the bomb had been correctly prepared but that the spark from the lighter went straight ~~[illegible]~~ past the fuse to the detonator causing the bomb to explode instantaneously. Similar cases have occurred elsewhere and the accident was unavoidable.	
	20/8/15		The Battn found two large working parties to assist R.E. in the neighbourhood of VOORMEZEELE.	
	21/8/15		Nothing of importance occurred.	
	22/8/15		Nothing of importance occurred.	[illegible initials]

1875 Wt. W593/826 1,000,000 4/15 J.B.C. & A. A.D.S.S./Forms/C. 2118.

7th YORKSHIRE REGT.

Army Form C. 2118

WAR DIARY
or
~~INTELLIGENCE SUMMARY~~

(Erase heading not required.)

Instructions regarding War Diaries and Intelligence Summaries are contained in F. S. Regs., Part II. and the Staff Manual respectively. Title Pages will be prepared in manuscript.

Place	Date	Hour	Summary of Events and Information	Remarks and references to Appendices
Reninghelst	23/8/15	—	Nothing of importance	
"	24/8/15	—	Nothing of importance	
"	25/8/15	—	Nothing of importance	
"	26/8/15	—	Returned to trenches at VOORMEZEELE and took over the same trenches as we occupied before from 7th LINCOLNS, with the except that three on the extreme left were taken over by the 7th East Yorkshires and our line shortened by that amount. Trenches now occupied by the Battn are. Fire trenches R1, T1, T2, T3, 23B, 23S. Support trenches R5, T7, T7C. One company is now in reserve in dugouts at Headquarters.	

1875 Wt. W593/826 1,000,000 4/15 J.B.C. & A. A.D.S.S./Forms/C. 2118.

Instructions regarding War Diaries and Intelligence Summaries are contained in F. S. Regs., Part II. and the Staff Manual respectively. Title Pages will be prepared in manuscript.

WAR DIARY
or
~~INTELLIGENCE~~ SUMMARY
(Erase heading not required.)

Army Form C. 2118

Place	Date	Hour	Summary of Events and Information	Remarks and references to Appendices
VOORMEZEELE	27/8/15	—	A fairly quiet day – Enemy shelled our fire trenches a little. Four men wounded.	
			——— .. ———	
	28/8/15	—	Quiet day. Enemy sent over an undetonated rifle grenade which landed in the company headquarters dugout occupied by Capt. R.E. Gibbon. Attached to it was found a newspaper entitled "Gazette des Ardennes" or "Journal des pays occupées". In it was, amongst other things, several anti-English articles signed by Belgian Citizens also a list of 2000 recent French casualties. Three men wounded by shell and whizz-bang fire.	
			——— .. ———	
	29/8/15	—	Quiet day. No 12439 Cpl T. Smith Berry accidently shot by comrade, he died soon afterwards. One other man killed. Major Billton 15th Royal Scots Fusiliers arrived from England to be attached for three days for instruction.	

Army Form C. 2118

WAR DIARY
or
~~INTELLIGENCE SUMMARY~~
(Erase heading not required.)

Instructions regarding War Diaries and Intelligence Summaries are contained in F. S. Regs., Part II. and the Staff Manual respectively. Title Pages will be prepared in manuscript.

Place	Date	Hour	Summary of Events and Information	Remarks and references to Appendices
VOORMEZEELE	30/8/15		Quiet day. An enemy mine exploded in front of the 6th Dorsets immediately on our left. No damage was done. Two men wounded.	
"	31/8/15		Nothing of importance. One man wounded.	

1875 Wt. W593/826 1,000,000 4/15 J.B.C. & A. A.D.S.S./Forms/C. 2118.

50th Inf.Bde.
17th Div.

7th BATTN. THE YORKSHIRE REGIMENT.

S E P T E M B E R

1 9 1 5

Instructions regarding War Diaries and Intelligence Summaries are contained in F. S. Regs., Part II. and the Staff Manual respectively. Title Pages will be prepared in manuscript.

Army Form C. 2118

WAR DIARY
or
~~INTELLIGENCE SUMMARY~~
(Erase heading not required.)

Place	Date	Hour	Summary of Events and Information	Remarks and references to Appendices
VOORMEZEELE	30/8/15	—	Quiet day – An enemy mine exploded in front of the 6th Dorsets immediately on our left. No damage was done. Two men wounded.	
"	31/8/15	—	Nothing of importance. One man wounded.	
"	1/9/15		Saps begun to to V shaped ditch which we received orders to dig in front of our trenches. The ditch is intended to be continuous along the whole front and its proportions to be 5ft deep and 9ft wide. This trench when completed will be filled with wire entanglements and the ground behind sloped away in order that the bottom of the ditch may be visible from ~~the~~ our parapets	

1875 Wt. W593/826 1,000,000 4/15 J.B.C. & A. A.D.S.S./Forms/C. 2118.

Army Form C. 2118

Instructions regarding War Diaries and Intelligence Summaries are contained in F. S. Regs., Part II. and the Staff Manual respectively. Title Pages will be prepared in manuscript.

WAR DIARY
or
~~INTELLIGENCE SUMMARY~~
(Erase heading not required.)

Place	Date	Hour	Summary of Events and Information	Remarks and references to Appendices
			In the winter the ditch will fill with water and the whole form a good obstacle.	

9'

30x

5 ft

1875 Wt. W593/826 1,000,000 4/15 J.B.C. & A. A.D.S.S./Forms/C. 2118.

Army Form C. 2118

Instructions regarding War Diaries and Intelligence Summaries are contained in F. S. Regs., Part II. and the Staff Manual respectively. Title Pages will be prepared in manuscript.

WAR DIARY
or
~~INTELLIGENCE SUMMARY~~
(Erase heading not required.)

Place	Date	Hour	Summary of Events and Information	Remarks and references to Appendices
Voormezeele	2/9/15	—	Relieved by 7th Lincoln Regt. One man wounded. Quiet day.	
Reninghelst	3/9/15	—	Returned to Reninghelst Rest Camp.	
"	4/9/15	—	Nothing of importance	
"	5/9/15	—	Nothing of importance.	

1875 Wt. W593/826 1,000,000 4/15 J.B.C. & A. A.D.S.S./Forms/C. 2118.

Army Form C. 2118

Instructions regarding War Diaries and Intelligence Summaries are contained in F. S. Regs., Part II. and the Staff Manual respectively. Title Pages will be prepared in manuscript.

WAR DIARY

or

~~INTELLIGENCE SUMMARY~~

(Erase heading not required.)

Place	Date	Hour	Summary of Events and Information	Remarks and references to Appendices
Reninghelst	6th & 7th Sept	—	Nothing of importance	
			——— " ———	
"	8/9/15		The Battn was inspected by General Sir H. Plumer C.B. at [illegible]	
			——— " ———	
	9th & 10th 9 15		Nothing of importance	
			——— " ———	
Vormezeele	11/9/15		Relieved the 7th LINCOLNS in the same trenches as previously occupied	
			——— " ———	
	12/9/15		Nothing of importance.	

1875 Wt. W593/826 1,000,000 4/15 J.B.C. & A. A.D.S.S./Forms/C. 2118.

Instructions regarding War Diaries and Intelligence Summaries are contained in F. S. Regs., Part II. and the Staff Manual respectively. Title Pages will be prepared in manuscript.

Army Form C. 2118

WAR DIARY
or
~~INTELLIGENCE SUMMARY~~
(Erase heading not required.)

Place	Date	Hour	Summary of Events and Information	Remarks and references to Appendices
VOORMEZEELE	13/9/15	"	Enemy planted red-white and black flag between his lines and ours. ~~[illegible]~~ R.W.S. Croft and two men L/c Greaves and L/Cpl Stewart of C Coy brought it into our lines having cut the wires which attached the flag staff to several bombs. Another bomb was found to be attached to the flag when it was brought into our trenches. This bomb had a bullet hole through it and was considered to be quite harmless. It exploded however in Cpl Greaves hands and killed him.	
	14/9/15		The crater between our lines and the enemy's was reconnoitred by the Scout Officer and the Adjutant and found to be unoccupied and it was discovered that reports stating that enemy had constructed loopholes and other works in it were ~~[illegible]~~ unfounded. Another flag was put up by the enemy between the lines. This flag was not tampered with.	
	15/9/15		Nothing of importance	

1875 Wt. W593/826 1,000,000 4/15 J.B.C. & A. A.D.S.S./Forms/C. 2118.

Instructions regarding War Diaries and Intelligence Summaries are contained in F. S. Regs., Part II. and the Staff Manual respectively. Title Pages will be prepared in manuscript.

WAR DIARY

~~INTELLIGENCE SUMMARY~~

(*Erase heading not required.*)

Army Form C. 2118

Place	Date	Hour	Summary of Events and Information	Remarks and references to Appendices
Voormezeele	16/9/15		Nothing of importance.	
	17/9/15	—	Enemy patrols came to inspect the V shaped ditch, they were driven off by rifle fire. Enemy set fire to long grass in front of some of our trenches with inflammable shells. No damage was done.	
	18/9/15	—	Our artillery shelled parties of Germans felling trees behind their line. These parties were located by Capt Cotton who acted as observer to the Artillery. The Brigadier General inspected the V shaped ditch personally together with the C.O.	
	19/9/15	—	Relieved by 7th Leicesters who had 7 casualties during relief caused by small minenwerfer. One of their Officers was wounded and one of our men who was guiding them into the trenches killed.	

1875 Wt. W593/826 1,000,000 4/15 J.B.C. & A. A.D.S.S./Forms/C. 2118.

Instructions regarding War Diaries and Intelligence Summaries are contained in F. S. Regs., Part II. and the Staff Manual respectively. Title Pages will be prepared in manuscript.

WAR DIARY

or

~~INTELLIGENCE SUMMARY~~

(Erase heading not required.)

Army Form C. 2118

Place	Date	Hour	Summary of Events and Information	Remarks and references to Appendices
RENINGHELST	20/9/15		Arrived in rest billets, and took up quarters in same huts as previously occupied.	
"	21/9/15		Nothing of importance.	
"	22/9/15		CAPT S.B. KAY went sick, and was evacuated to ROUEN the following day, suffering from tonsilitis.	
"	23/9/15		6th DORSETS, 9th NORTHUMBERLAND FUSILIERS (52nd Bde), and 7th YORK REGT, went into 5th Corps reserve till further notice.	
"	24/9/15		Nothing of importance. Bombing instruction carried on as usual. Specimen loophole, disguised by sandbag covering, was built into a parapet.	
"	25/9/15		None of battns. in 5th Corps reserve allowed to leave camp. (At this time the British were attacking at HOOGE and near LA BASSEE & the French in CHAMPAGNE). 2/Lt HR. BELLINGER, from Cadet School, joined for duty.	
"	26/9/15		2/Lts J. DRISCOLL and W. EVERS-SWINDELL, from Cadet School, joined for duty.	
"	27/9/15	7-10.30pm	Relieved 7th LINCOLN REGT. in same trenches as previously occupied East of ST. ELOI; B & A Coys on right & left of front line, C Coy in support, and D Coy in reserve at HQ dugouts. 2/Lt. DRISCOLL remained at RENINGHELST for one weeks Signalling Course at Divisional Headquarters.	
VOORMEZEELE	28/9/15		The enemy appeared to have many less guns, both of large calibre & of the whizzbang variety, on our front than he had during our previous tours of duty in these trenches. Throughout the day & night he threw over a very large number of trench mortar shells & rifle grenades, but only caused two casualties. The greater number of his trench mortars fired	

1875 Wt. W593/826 1,000,000 4/15 J.B.C. & A. A.D.S.S./Forms/C. 2118.

Army Form C. 2118

Instructions regarding War Diaries and Intelligence Summaries are contained in F. S. Regs., Part II. and the Staff Manual respectively. Title Pages will be prepared in manuscript.

WAR DIARY
or
~~INTELLIGENCE SUMMARY~~
(Erase heading not required.)

Place	Date	Hour	Summary of Events and Information	Remarks and references to Appendices
VOORMEZEELE	28/9/15 (cont.)		Towards the left of Tyc. We learned that troops of the 17th Bavarian Regiment (3rd Bavarian division) had been captured by the 1st Army in the fighting south of LA BASSÉE. This made it possible that the troops opposite us had changed, as the 3rd Bavarian Division had recently held the line opposite us between the YPRES-COMINES canal and WYTSCHAETE. Enemy transport was heard, apparently on one of the two roads South of EIKHOF FARM.	
"	29/9/15		The enemy was very quiet during both the day and the night.	
"	30/9/15		Early in the morning a patrol of three went out under 2nd Lt L.G. Hare, with the intention of surprising a German patrol and capturing one or more of its members, in order to ascertain what troops were opposite us. No Germans were seen, either in the open or looking over their parapet. The patrol remained till dawn about 15 yards from the German trenches, and then returned safely. Soon after 6 pm the enemy sent up red rockets, followed by white ones. His artillery at once opened a heavy fire, the front trenches being bombarded with whizzbangs & shrapnel, the supports with whizzbangs and a few crumps. The bombardment was over soon after 7.30 pm. Five casualties were sustained, one man (A Coy) being killed. The enemy's parapet was damaged in several places by our artillery.	

1875 Wt. W593/826 1,000,000 4/15 J.B.C. & A. A.D.S.S./Forms/C. 2118.

50th Inf.Bde.
17th Div.

7th BATTN. THE YORKSHIRE REGIMENT.

O C T O B E R

1 9 1 5

Instructions regarding War Diaries and Intelligence Summaries are contained in F. S. Regs., Part II. and the Staff Manual respectively. Title Pages will be prepared in manuscript.

WAR DIARY
or
~~INTELLIGENCE SUMMARY~~
(Erase heading not required.)

Army Form C. 2118

Place	Date	Hour	7th (Service) Batt. YORKSHIRE REGT. Summary of Events and Information	Remarks and references to Appendices
VOORMEZEELE	1/10/15		Nothing unusual during the day or night.	
"	2/10/15		Many trench mortars fired at SQUARE WOOD during the night. Nothing else unusual.	
"	3/10/15		Quiet day. The telephone in R5 was transferred to 23B. During this tour of duty in the trenches direct lines were laid to the covering artillery from T1 to "D" Battery, 79th BDE. R.F.A., and from 23B to "A" Battery.	
"	4/10/15	6.30–11pm.	Relieved by 6th Battalion SOMERSET LIGHT INFANTRY (43rd Bde., 14th Division) who had been relieved at HOOGE the previous day. No casualties during relief. Strength:	
RENINGHELST to STEENVOORDE	5/10/15		Arrived in hutments usually occupied while resting.	
		6pm	Left for STEENVOORDE by march route, via POPERINGHE and ABEELE. The Battalion went into approximately the same billets as those it occupied 19–21/7/15, in farms between STEENVOORDE and GODEWAERSVELDE.	
STEENVOORDE	6/10/15		Troops resting.	
"	7/10/15		Battalion inspected by C.O. and 2nd/in Command, after which an attack was practised across the open. A party of officers, NCO's, and men spent the afternoon at the Grenade School, TERDEGHEM.	
"	8/10/15		Training of all kinds being carried out. Systematic instruction in Bombing a special point.	

1875 Wt. W593/826 1,000,000 4/15 J.B.C. & A. A.D.S.S./Forms/C. 2118.

Instructions regarding War Diaries and Intelligence Summaries are contained in F. S. Regs., Part II. and the Staff Manual respectively. Title Pages will be prepared in manuscript.

WAR DIARY
or
~~INTELLIGENCE SUMMARY~~
(Erase heading not required.)

Army Form C. 2118

Place	Date	Hour	Summary of Events and Information	Remarks and references to Appendices
STEENVOORDE	9/10/15		Bombing and general training.	
"	10/10/15 to 21/10/15		General training at STEENVOORDE. Squads sent to Bombing School, TERDEGHEM, and party of officers to M.G. School, WISQUES. Attack practised one day by Brigade; Gen. Plumer present.	
POPERINGHE	21/10/15	3-7 pm	Marched via ABEELE and POPERINGHE to hutments about 2 miles East of the latter town. Party of officers went ahead by motorbus to visit trenches of 1st Lincoln Regt.	
HOOGE	22/10/15		Took over trenches of 1st LINCOLN REGT., 3rd DIVISION. Left of line at HOOGE Stables on YPRES-MENIN road (trench C3); right of line in Sanctuary Wood (trench C1). D Coy. on left of line, B. Coy on right; A Coy in support, C Coy in reserve at KRUISSTRAAT.	
"	23/10/15 to 27/10/15		Quiet time in trenches. Weather bad, & trenches very wet; much work necessary to keep them habitable. Enemy very busy improving his trenches and defences; sounds of steam engine heard several times. On 26th Colonel Fife went back to POPERINGHE to command a composite company on a Royal parade, when the King inspected troops from the whole division.	
YPRES	28/10/15		Relieved by 7th East Yorkshire Regt. Two companies went into dugouts and tunnels in the RAMPARTS at YPRES, two to rest billets near the transport lines, near OUDERDOM. One of these was brought up two nights later, and quartered in cellars in the town. Headquarters in the ramparts. Working parties found every night.	
"	28/10/15 29, 30, 31 /10/15			

1875 Wt. W593/826 1,000,000 4/15 J.B.C. & A. A.D.S.S./Forms/C. 2118.

50th Inf.Bde.
17th Div.

7th BATTN. THE YORKSHIRE REGIMENT.

N O V E M B E R

1 9 1 5

Instructions regarding War Diaries and Intelligence Summaries are contained in F. S. Regs., Part II. and the Staff Manual respectively. Title Pages will be prepared in manuscript.

WAR DIARY

or

~~INTELLIGENCE SUMMARY~~

(Erase heading not required.)

Army Form C. 2118

Place	Date	Hour	7th (Service) Bn. Yorkshire Regt. Summary of Events and Information	Remarks and references to Appendices
YPRES	1/11/15		LIEUT C. G. WESTON killed whilst in charge of working party behind trenches at HOOGE.	
"	2/11/15		One officer going on leave every 4 days; other ranks about 10 in each 4 days. Major Cartwright went sick, & was sent to hospital, MONT DES CATS.	
"	3/11/15		Colonel Fife returned from leave.	
HOOGE			Battalion relieved 7th East York. Regt. in trenches.	
"	4, 5 & 6 11/15		Fairly quiet time in trenches; very few casualties. Trenches much in need of revetting & draining.	
BUSSEBOOM	7/11/15		Relieved by 7th East York Regt., and returned to camp (tents) near Busseboom.	
"	8, 9 & 10 11/15		At rest camp, which was very muddy. Physical drill carried on.	
HOOGE	11/11/15		Relieved 7th East York Regt in trenches, which were wetter than ever.	
"	12, 13 & 14 11/15		Nothing unusual during this tour of duty. Much artillery & aeroplane activity, but very few casualties & little damage to trenches.	
"	15/11/15		Attack which we had been told to expect during night 15/16 did not occur. HQ & HQ Signal Office moved to Yeomanry Post during the night, & returned to ZOUAVE WOOD at dawn. Relieved by the 12th MANCHESTER REGT, 52nd Bde, & returned to a camp (huts & tents) near BUSSEBOOM.	
BUSSEBOOM	16th to 23rd 11/15		In rest camp, which was very muddy & uncomfortable. Engaged in refitting, doing a certain amount of physical drill & company drill, & finding large working parties. Some improvements made in a	

1875 Wt. W593/826 1,000,000 4/15 J.B.C. & A. A.D.S.S./Forms/C. 2118.

Army Form C. 2118

Instructions regarding War Diaries and Intelligence Summaries are contained in F. S. Regs., Part II. and the Staff Manual respectively. Title Pages will be prepared in manuscript.

WAR DIARY
or
~~INTELLIGENCE SUMMARY~~

(Erase heading not required.)

7th (S) BATT. YORKSHIRE REGT.

Place	Date	Hour	Summary of Events and Information	Remarks and references to Appendices
BUSSEBOOM	16–23 11/15		defensive work allotted to us.	
YPRES	23/11/15		Took over Ramparts & billets in YPRES from 9th NORTHUMBERLAND FUSILIERS. HQ & C Coy in tunnels of Ramparts, B Coy in cellars near by, A Coy in cellars of Post Office, D Coy in cellars of two houses, Rue de Lille.	
"	23–26 11/15		In Ypres, 1 casualty (shell fire). Finding large carrying & working parties each night.	
HOOGE	27/11/15		Relieved 7th East York Regt. in trenches at HOOGE. Trenches very wet.	
"	28, 29, & 30 11/15		Quiet time in trenches. A good deal of shelling but mostly well behind the lines, towards YPRES. Enemy very quiet in his trenches at night.	

1875 Wt. W593/826 1,000,000 4/15 J.B.C. & A. A.D.S.S./Forms/C. 2118.

50th Inf.Bde.
17th Div.

7th BATTN. THE YORKSHIRE REGIMENT.

D E C E M B E R

1 9 1 5

Instructions regarding War Diaries and Intelligence Summaries are contained in F. S. Regs., Part II. and the Staff Manual respectively. Title Pages will be prepared in manuscript.

WAR DIARY

~~or INTELLIGENCE SUMMARY~~

(Erase heading not required.)

Army Form C. 2118

Place	Date	Hour	Summary of Events and Information	Remarks and references to Appendices
			7th YORKSHIRE REGT.	
HOOGE	1/12/15		Relieved by 12th MANCHESTER REGT, & returned to rest billets near BUSSEBOOM. Quiet relief.	
BUSSEBOOM	2/12/15 to 9/12/15		In rest billets. Carrying on training as far as climate & circumstances would permit. Many large working parties found.	
OUDERDOM	9/12/15		Moved to camp vacated by E. YORK REGT. Camp even muddier than last one.	
"	10/12/15		B. COY., D. COY., & half C. COY. moved to dugouts at KRUISSTRAAT.	
HOOGE	13/12/15		Relieved 7th EAST YORK REGT. in trenches.	
"	14/12/15		Nothing of note.	
"	15, 16 & 17/12/15		Front line trenches vacated each of these three mornings whilst our heavy howitzers bombarded the German front line. German wire along our front thoroughly reconnoitred by Mr. R.G. de Quetteville & Mr. H.K.C. Hare. It was found to be extremely strong, & practically impenetrable. Some K.P. wires were found. The C.O. sniped from a point in the Appendix opposite the German redoubt, & accounted for 2 or 3 Germans.	
"	17/12/15		Relieved by 10th LANCASHIRE FUSILIERS. Normal relief. Returned to usual rest billets.	
BUSSEBOOM	18/12/15		Major Warburton, 14th DURHAM LIGHT INFANTRY, attached to Battn. as 2d in command.	
"	19/12/15	5 am	Germans discharged gas against front of 6th & 49th Divisions, & violently bombarded British lines East & North East of YPRES. Battalion stood to (50th Bde being in Divisional Reserve) during 19th & 20th, but was not called upon to move up, no infantry assault having penetrated our lines.	
"	20/12/15		The trenches, all roads about YPRES & the towns of YPRES, VLAMERTINGHE, & POPERINGHE, were violently shelled, 42 cm. shells falling in VLAMERTINGHE. The effects of the gas were felt in the rest camp (roughly 12,000 yards from where the gas was liberated). Many were made ill, but no one seriously affected.	
YPRES	25/12/15		Moved up to YPRES, occupying billets in Ramparts & in cellars of ruined houses.	

1875 Wt. W593/826 1,000,000 4/15 J.B.C. & A. A.D.S.S./Forms/C. 2118.

Instructions regarding War Diaries and Intelligence Summaries are contained in F. S. Regs., Part II. and the Staff Manual respectively. Title Pages will be prepared in manuscript.

WAR DIARY

or

~~INTELLIGENCE SUMMARY~~

(Erase heading not required.)

Army Form C. 2118

Place	Date	Hour	Summary of Events and Information	Remarks and references to Appendices
YPRES	28/12/15		Quiet day in YPRES. Found 200 men at night for working parties.	
ZILLEBEKE LAKE.	27/12/15		HQ + 3 Coys moved to dugouts in West bank of ZILLEBEKE LAKE adjoining Bde Hq. B Coy moved to KRUISSTRAAT	
TRENCHES	29/12/15		Relieved 7th EAST YORK REGT in Trenches. C3 (HOOGE) now held by battn. on left. Battn in trenches as follows: C Coy in B8 + C1, B Coy in B8 S 4 C1R, A Coy in C1R + RS2, D COY in R7 + RS8. 2/Lt. DRISCOLL affected by gas from gas shells in YPRES, but rejoined same evening.	
"	30 & 31 12/15		Sniping carried on from Appendix with good results. Considerable artillery activity on both sides. Few casualties. Our field guns carried out a short bombardment about midnight, at the close of the old year.	

1875 Wt. W593/826 1,000,000 4/15 J.B.C. & A. A.D.S.S./Forms/C. 2118.

7th Yorkshires
Vol: 5

Jan 1916

17 Div.
50th Bde

Army Form C. 2118

Instructions regarding War Diaries and Intelligence Summaries are contained in F. S. Regs., Part II. and the Staff Manual respectively. Title Pages will be prepared in manuscript.

WAR DIARY

~~or~~

~~INTELLIGENCE SUMMARY~~

(Erase heading not required.)

Place	Date	Hour	9th YORKSHIRE REGT. Summary of Events and Information	Remarks and references to Appendices
HOOGE	1/1/16		Usual artillery activity. Nothing unusual.	
BUSSEBOOM	2/1/16		Relieved by 12th MANCHESTER REGT., & returned to rest camp. Under orders of 52nd Bde.	
"	4/1/16		Transport moved off to GODEWAERSVELDE by road.	
POLINCOVE.	5/1/16		Battalion entrained at QUINTIN siding, POPERINGHE, picked up transport en route, and detrained at AUDRUICQ, halfway between ST. OMER and CALAIS. Rest billets occupied in village of POLINCOVE.	
	Remainder of Month		Month spent in company training, musketry (on a small range near ZOUAFQUES), training reserves of machine gunners &c, route marching, & refitting.	
	18/1/16		Brigade marched past General Plumer, G.O.C. 2nd Army.	
	24/1/16		Brigade route march.	
	31/1/16		Divisional tactical scheme East of FORÊT DE TOURNEHEM.	
			All officers & men now wearing a short length of green braid on each sleeve.	

1875 Wt. W593/826 1,000,000 4/15 J.B.C. & A. A.D.S.S./Forms/C. 2118.

T303
10/3/16

The Officer i/c A.G.'s Dept. BASE.

Herewith War Diary of this unit for the month of February, 1916.

T Huffingtrith [illegible] for Capt. and Adjt.
7th Yorkshire Regt.

10/3/16

17 DW
50 Bde

Instructions regarding War Diaries and Intelligence Summaries are contained in F. S. Regs., Part II. and the Staff Manual respectively. Title Pages will be prepared in manuscript.

WAR DIARY

or

~~INTELLIGENCE SUMMARY~~

(Erase heading not required.)

Army Form C. 2118

Place	Date	Hour	7th YORKSHIRE REGT. Summary of Events and Information	Remarks and references to Appendices
POLINCOVE	1-5/2/16		Last days in rest area. Preparations made for move & for handing over to 3rd Division.	
	6/2/16		Entrained at AUDRUICQ by 8 am, & left for POPERINGHE. Marched from there to a rest camp halfway between RENINGHELST and WESTOUTRE. Orders were at once received to send a	
RENINGHELST.			party of 1 officer & 50 men to relieve a garrison of the 3rd Division in KINGSWAY dugouts along the YPRES-COMINES Canal, & to move to DICKEBUSCH early next day.	
DICKEBUSCH	7/2/16		Relieved London Rifle Brigade in billets at DICKEBUSCH, arriving about 7.30 am.	
"	7-13/2/16		Very quiet time in billets. Parties of officers visited VOORMEZEELE, and the trenches of the T sector which were held by the battalion during the previous summer. CAPT B.E. COTTON in command, C.O. having proceeded on leave from POLINCOVE.	
	14/2/16		Prepared to relieve 12th MANCHESTER REGT in T sector. About 5pm small H.E. and a few shrapnel began to fall in DICKEBUSCH, which the leading Coy was just leaving. CAPT S.B. KAY who had rejoined from England two days earlier, and 2nd LIEUT L.A.D. DAVID were wounded, neither seriously. 2nd LIEUT DAVID rejoined 2 days later. When HQ reached VOORMEZEELE it was found that Major-General Pilcher had stopped the relief owing to the situation on the BLUFF north of the YPRES-COMINES canal, where the Germans after a heavy bombardment & the explosion of mines, had captured about 600 yards of trench held by the 51st Bde, & the first trench North of the Canal (NEW YEAR TRENCH) held by the 52nd Bde. The bombers & machine gunners were already in the trenches & remained there. The signallers were withdrawn, & the whole battalion moved to the G.H.Q. line North of	
G.H.Q. LINE			VOORMEZEELE, and got into touch with the 52nd Bde by wire. Orders were received	

Instructions regarding War Diaries and Intelligence Summaries are contained in F. S. Regs., Part II. and the Staff Manual respectively. Title Pages will be prepared in manuscript.

WAR DIARY
or
~~INTELLIGENCE SUMMARY~~
(Erase heading not required.)

Army Form C. 2118

Place	Date	Hour	Summary of Events and Information	Remarks and references to Appendices
			about 10.30 pm to send 2 Coys to report to 10th LANCASHIRE FUSILIERS. A+D Coys were sent, under the command of CAPT R A YOUNG. The remaining 1½ Coys were detailed to carry bombs to the BLUFF. HQ crowded into the dugouts at the MANCHESTER HQ. One platoon put into V4 as garrison.	
VOORMEZEELE	15/2/16		C Coy. + B Coy less the KINGSWAY detachment spent the night + most of the day in carrying bombs across from VOORMEZEELE to SPOIL BANK, 10 casualties being suffered from shell fire. At night HQ and the portions of B + C Coys in VOORMEZEELE moved into GHQ line again, expecting to be rejoined by A+D Coys, of whom no news could be obtained. This concentration did not take place, +, after 5 hours in driving snow, all returned to VOORMEZEELE.	
VOORMEZEELE	16/2/16		Day spent awaiting news of the 2 Coys on the BLUFF. Capt. Young arrived + brought news that they were holding a strong point (R11) on the BLUFF, and a trench on the left of this. They had not taken part in any actual counter attack. They expected being relieved that night by a battalion of the 76th Bde (3rd Div) which had been brought up from the rest area. This relief took place, + the 2 Coys returned to the rest camp. The C.O. returned this evening, CAPT COTTON having been in command since departure from POLINCOVE.	
RENINGHELST	17/2/16		Returned to Rest Camp in the evening. The total casualties, including the bomb-carrying parties, the bombers who had been at the Bde Grenade School + who took part in the counter-attack by the 6th DORSET REGT (night 15/16), + certain men attached to Tunnelling Coys, who were involved in the original	

1875 Wt. W593/826 1,000,000 4/15 J.B.C. & A. A.D.S.S./Forms/C. 2118.

Instructions regarding War Diaries and Intelligence Summaries are contained in F. S. Regs., Part II. and the Staff Manual respectively. Title Pages will be prepared in manuscript.

WAR DIARY
or
~~INTELLIGENCE SUMMARY~~
(Erase heading not required.)

Army Form C. 2118

Place	Date	Hour	Summary of Events and Information	Remarks and references to Appendices
			German mine explosions, ~~about~~ numbered about 50.	
RENINGHELST	18/19 2/16		At rest camp. Working parties furnished for burying cable from Bdes to Battalions	
VOORMEZEELE	20/2/16		Relieved 12th MANCHESTER REGT in T sector. Quiet relief, complete about 10pm. Trenches much improved by MANCHESTER REGT during their 14 days tour, but still in need of much hard work. Parapets in front line low and thin on the whole. Very little protection or cover afforded in saps to bombing posts. No shelter trenches available in case of heavy bombardment, the new support line (which was dug when the Brigade previously held these trenches in the summer of 1915) in front of the R5-T7 line having been entirely neglected. At the left of our trenches, between 23B + 23, there was a gap of 80 or 90 yards which was not even continuously wired. No continuous trench between R5 + T7. Dispositions: T1, T2, T3, B Coy; 23B, A Coy less 2 platoons; T7, Battalion Bombers; R5, C Coy; HQ dugouts, D Coy less 1 platoon; September Post, 1 platoon D Coy; dugouts + cellars in VOORMEZEELE, 2 platoons A Coy. One company cooker in VOORMEZEELE. Company cooks with their companies in the trenches, owing to arrangements existing for collective cooking.	
"	21/2/16		German snipers active, 2 of our NCOs being killed. Our snipers claim an equal number of the enemy. At night the enemy made two vain attempts to attack our T2 bombing post, + also endeavoured to lure our	

1875 Wt. W593/826 1,000,000 4/15 J.B.C. & A. A.D.S.S./Forms/C. 2118.

Instructions regarding War Diaries and Intelligence Summaries are contained in F. S. Regs., Part II. and the Staff Manual respectively. Title Pages will be prepared in manuscript.

WAR DIARY

or

~~INTELLIGENCE SUMMARY~~

(Erase heading not required.)

Army Form C. 2118

Place	Date	Hour	Summary of Events and Information	Remarks and references to Appendices
			bombers over to their post. Work begun on thickening & raising parapets draining trenches, reclaiming the trench between 23B & 23, wiring the front, working on the disused CT past SHELLEY FARM (the only means of approaching our front line by day being via CELLAR LANE thro' ST. ELOI, & thro' R3 & R1, held by the EAST YORKSHIRE REGT, on our right.	
VIERMEZEELE	22/2/16		Quiet day, artillery being very inactive on our front	
"	23/2/16		A German surrendered after being fired at from the left crater post. He was a young Saxon of the 123rd Regt, & seemed glad to get away from the trenches. This was at about 2 am. He was at once sent down to Bde Hq. Work on front line continued, including erection of a wire shelter against bombs in T2. Very little shelling. Snow and frost greatly hindered work.	
"	24/2/16		Quiet day. D Coy relieved B in front line. Enemy thought to have relieved also.	
"	25/2/16		Very quiet in every way. Trench tramway to R5 in bad order, causing delay with stores &c.	
"	26/2/16		Quiet day. Nearly all artillery activity concentrated on the BLUFF. After we had thrown bombs, the enemy asked 'Are you the Guards?'. The sentry replied "Yes".	
	27 & 28/2/16		Quiet on our front, the BLUFF attracting all attention. B Coy relieved D in front line, night 28/29th.	
	29/2/16		A little more shelling of our trenches. ~~RE~~ Work continued in front & support lines, with RE supervision.	

Copy

17 Ref D.A.G.'s CR No. 410/452 25/4/16

Vol 6

7 Yorks Reg

Instructions regarding War Diaries and Intelligence Summaries are contained in F. S. Regs., Part II. and the Staff Manual respectively. Title Pages will be prepared in manuscript.

WAR DIARY
~~or~~
~~INTELLIGENCE SUMMARY~~
(Erase heading not required.)

Army Form C. 2118

Place	Date	Hour	7th Bn Yorkshire Regt — Summary of Events and Information	Remarks and references to Appendices
POLINCOVE	1-5/2/16		Last days in rest area – Preparations made for move & for handing over to 3rd Division.	
	6/2/16		Entrained at AUDRUICQ by 8 am, & left for POPERINGHE. Marched from there to a rest camp halfway between RENINGHELST and WESTOUTRE. Orders were at once received to send a party of 1 officer and 50 men to relieve a garrison of the 3rd Division in KINGSWAY dugouts along the YPRES-COMINES Canal and to move to DICKEBUSCH early next day.	
DICKEBUSCH	7/2/16		Relieved London Rifle Brigade in billets at DICKEBUSCH arriving about 7-30 am	
	7-13/2/16		Very quiet time in billets. Parties of officers visited VOORMEZEELE, and the trenches of the T sector which were held by the battalion during the previous summer. Capt K E Cotton in command, C.O. having proceeded on leave from POLINCOVE.	
	14/2/16		Prepared to relieve 12th MANCHESTER REGT in T sector – About 5 pm small H.E. and a few shrapnel began to fall in DICKEBUSCH, which the leading Coy was just leaving – CAPT. S.B. KAY and 2nd LT L.A.D. DAVID were wounded neither seriously. 2nd LIEUT DAVID rejoined 2 days later – When H.Q. reached VOORMEZEELE it was found that Major-Gen PILCHER had stopped the relief owing to the situation on the BLUFF north of the YPRES-COMINES canal, where the Germans, after a heavy bombardment and the explosion of mines, had captured about 600 yards of trench held by the 51st Bde, and the first trench North of the Canal (NEW YEAR TRENCH) held by the 52nd Bde. The bombers and machine gunners were already in the trenches & remained there. The signallers were withdrawn & the whole battalion moved to G.H.Q. line North of VOORMEZEELE, and got into touch with the 52nd Bde by wire.	
G.H.Q. Line			Orders were received about 10-30 pm. to send 2 Coys to report to 10th LANCASHIRE FUSILIERS. A & D Coys were sent under the command of CAPT R A YOUNG. The remaining 1½ Companies were detailed to carry bombs to the BLUFF. H.Q. crowded into the	

1875 Wt. W593/826 1,000,000 4/15 J.B.C. & A. A.D.S.S./Forms/C. 2118.

Instructions regarding War Diaries and Intelligence Summaries are contained in F. S. Regs., Part II. and the Staff Manual respectively. Title Pages will be prepared in manuscript.

WAR DIARY

~~or~~

~~INTELLIGENCE SUMMARY~~

~~(Erase heading not required.)~~

Army Form C. 2118

Place	Date	Hour	Summary of Events and Information	Remarks and references to Appendices
			dugouts at the MANCHESTER H.Q – One platoon put into V.4 as garrison	
VOORMEZEELE	15/2/16		C Coy & D Coy less the KINGSWAY detachment spent the night and most of the day in carrying bombs across from VOORMEZEELE to SPOIL BANK, casualties being suffered from shell fire – At night H.Q and the portions of B & C Coys in VOORMEZEELE moved into GHQ line again, expecting to be reformed by A+D Coys, of whom no news could be obtained – This concentration did not take place and after 5 hours in driving snow, all returned to VOORMEZEELE	
VOORMEZEELE	16/2/16		Day spent awaiting news of the 2 Coys on the BLUFF – CAPT YOUNG arrived & brought news that they were holding a strong point (R 11) on the BLUFF and a trench on the left of this – They had not taken part in any actual counter attack – They expected being relieved that night by a battalion of the 76th Bde (3rd DIV) which had been brought up from the rest area – This relief took place, & the 2 Coys returned to the rest camp – The C O returned this evening, CAPT COTTON having been in command since departure from POLINCOVE.	
RENINGHELST	17/2/16		Returned to Rest Camp in the evening – The total casualties including the bomb-carrying parties, the bombers who had been at the Bde Grenade School & who took part in the counter-attack by the 6th DORSET REGT (night 15/16) & certain men attached to Tunnelling Coys, who were involved in the original German mine explosions numbered about 50 –	
RENINGHELST	18+19/2/16		At rest camp – Working parties furnished for burying cable from Bdes to Battns	
VOORMEZEELE	20/2/16		Relieved 12th MANCHESTER REGT in T sector. Quiet relief complete about 10 pm – Trenches much improved by MANCHESTER REGT during their 14 days tour, but still in need	

1875 Wt. W593/826 1,000,000 4/15 J.B.C. & A. A.D.S.S./Forms/C. 2118.

Instructions regarding War Diaries and Intelligence Summaries are contained in F. S. Regs., Part II. and the Staff Manual respectively. Title Pages will be prepared in manuscript.

WAR DIARY

~~or~~

~~INTELLIGENCE SUMMARY~~

~~(Erase heading not required.)~~

Army Form C. 2118

Place	Date	Hour	Summary of Events and Information	Remarks and references to Appendices
			of much hard work – Parapets in front line low and thin on the whole – Very little protection or cover afforded in saps to bombing posts. No shelter trenches available in case of heavy bombardment, the new support line (which was dug when the Brigade previously held these trenches in the summer of 1915) in front of the R5 – T7 line having been entirely neglected. At the left of our trenches, between 23 B & 23, there was a gap of 80 or 90 yards which was not even continously wired – No continuous trench between R5 & T7 –	
			Dispositions: T1, T2, T3, B Coy; 23 B, A Coy, less 2 platoons; T7 Battn bombers; R5, C Coy; HQ dugouts, D Coy, less 1 platoon; September Post, 1 platoon D Coy; dugouts & cellars in VOORMEZEELE 2 platoons A Coy – One company cooker in VOORMEZEELE – Company cooks with their companies in the trenches, owing to arrangements existing for collective cooking –	
VOORMEZEELE	21/2/16		German snipers active, 2 of our NCO's being killed. Our snipers claim an equal number of the enemy – At night the enemy made two vain attempts to attack our T2 bombing post and also endeavoured to lure our bombers over to their post – Work begun on thickening and raising parapets, draining trenches, reclaiming the trench between 23 B and 23, wiring the front, working on the disused C.T. past SHELLEY FARM (the only means of approaching our front line by day being via CELLAR LANE through ST ELOI and through R3 & R1 held by the EAST YORKSHIRE REGT on our right –	
VOORMEZEELE	22/2/16		Quiet day, artillery being very inactive on our front	

1875 Wt. W593/826 1,000,000 4/15 J.B.C. & A. A.D.S.S./Forms/C. 2118.

Instructions regarding War Diaries and Intelligence Summaries are contained in F. S. Regs., Part II. and the Staff Manual respectively. Title Pages will be prepared in manuscript.

WAR DIARY

~~or~~

~~INTELLIGENCE SUMMARY~~

~~(Erase heading not required.)~~

Army Form C. 2118

Place	Date	Hour	Summary of Events and Information	Remarks and references to Appendices
VOORMEZEELE	23/2/16		A German surrendered after being fired at from the left crater post. He was a young Saxon of the 123rd Regt, & seemed glad to get away from the trenches. This was at about 2 am. He was at once sent down to Bde HQ. Work on front line continued, including erection of a wire shelter against bombs in T2. Very little shelling. Snow and frost greatly hindered work.	
"	24/2/16		Quiet day. D Coy relieved B in front line. Enemy thought to have relieved also.	
"	25/2/16		Very quiet in every way. Trench tramway to R5 in bad order, causing delay with stores etc.	
"	26/2/16		Quiet day. Nearly all artillery activity concentrated on the BLUFF. After we had thrown bombs, the enemy asked "Are you the Guards?" The sentry replied "Yes".	
"	27-28/2/16		Quiet on our front, the BLUFF attracting all attention. B Coy relieved D in front line, night 28/29th.	
"	29/2/16		A little more shelling of our trenches. Work continued in front & support lines with RE supervision.	

1875 Wt. W593/826 1,000,000 4/15 J.B.C. & A. A.D.S.S./Forms/C. 2118.

Entraining Programme.

UNIT.	Entraining Station.	Time of departure of train after Zero.	Starting Point.	Hour of starting after Zero.	ROUTE.
10/W/York (1 coy (Transport.	AUDRUICQ.	28	Road junction J.35.d.6.6.	22½.	Nordausques - J.10.c - J.10.a. - BLANC PIGNON - D.15.
10/W/York (less (1coy & (Transport.	"	28	"	24½.	"
Brigade Headquarters	AUDRUICQ	31	Road junction P.5.a.7½.9½.	27¼	"
No:2 Signal Section.	"	31	" " "	25¼	"
50th Bde M.G.Coy.	"	31	Road Junction J.6.b.0.4.	26¾	Polincove - cross roads D.23.a.2.3. - Blanc Bouillon.
Trench Mortar Batys.	"	31	Road junction D.29.d.5.9.	29	Cross roads D.23.a.2.3 - Blanc Bouillon.
7/E/York (1 Coy (Transport.	"	37	Cross roads K.27.a.2½.1½.	31½	Cross roads K.14.a.½.3½ - K.7.Central - road junction ~~XXX~~.K.1.a.3.6 - road junction -J.6.b.0.4. - POLINCOVE - cross roads D.23.a.2.3 - BLANC BOUILLON.
7/E/York (Less 1 Coy & Transport.	"	37	" " "	33½	" " " "
7/Yorkshire (1 Coy & (Transport.	"	40	Road junction P.5.a.7½.9½.	34¼	Nordausques - J.10.c - J.10.a. - Blanc Pignon. - D.15.
7/Yorkshire (Less (1 Coy & (Transport.	"	40	" " "	36¼	" " "
6/Dorset (1 Coy & (Transport.	"	43	Cross roads J.23.a.7.½.	38	Road junction J.16.d - RECQUES - cross roads J.10.c.3.7 - BLANC PIGNON.
6/Dorset (less 1 Coy (& Transport.	"	43	" " "	40	" " "

In case of move to 2nd Army Front, all as above except 6th Dorset, in which case time of departure of train is 34.

Time passing starting point - 1 Company & Transport.......29.

" " " " - 6th Dorset less 1 Coy and transport...................31.

Hour of ZERO will be notified by Brigade to Units.

P.T.O.

Copy No:1 - 10/W/York.
2 - 7/E/York
3 - 7/York.
4 - 6/Dorset.
5 - 50th Bde M.G.Coy.
6 - 50/1 T.M.Bty.
7 - 50/2 T.M.Bty.
8,9,10 - Office Copies.

WAR DIARY.

7th YORKSHIRE REGT.

PLACE	DATE		REMARKS.
VOORMEZEELE	1/3/16	Quiet day in our trenches till evening. From 5 to 5.45 pm our artillery bombarded the BLUFF very heavily, and to some extent the trenches opposite us. From 5.10 to 5.20 the Coys in the front line fired rapid. This provoked a miscellaneous reply from the enemy, who fired whizzbangs, H.E., trench mortars, &c indiscriminately. Casualties about 4, 2 or 3 of whom were suffering from shock. Remainder of evening much quieter than usual.	
"	2/3/16	76th Bde attacked the BLUFF at 4.30 am., and the artillery fired rapid for half an hour. Our trenches and ground behind were shelled but little damage done. Remainder of day quiet on our front, all attention being confined to the BLUFF.	
"	3,4,5/3/16	Quiet days. Work on improvement of trenches continued.	
	6/3/16	Relieved by 12th MANCHESTER REGT. Returned to camp near RENINGHELST.	
RENINGHELST	7-8/3/16	Resting. Small working parties on night of 8th burying cable.	
VOORMEZEELE	9/3/16	Relieved 12th MANCHESTERS in trenches at ST ELOI.	
"	10/3/16	Quiet day	
"	11/3/16	Relieved by 13th KINGS-(LIVERPOOL REGT), 3rd DIVISION.	
RENINGHELST	12/3/16	Resting.	
MOOLENACKER	13/3/16	Marched to MOOLENACKER, near STRAZEELE (between BAILLEUL and HAZEBROUCK). Billets in large farms.	
"	13-21/3/16	In rest area. Coys carrying out training of all kinds. One Battalion route march. HQ and B+C Coys had to change billets on 3rd day owing to a change in the billeting area of the 52nd Bde.	
LA CRECHE.	22/3/16	Marched to LA CRECHE, East of BAILLEUL. Billeted there 1 night.	
ARMENTIÈRES	23/3/16	" " ARMENTIÈRES, and occupied "F" group of billets. HQ at 35 Rue Nationale.	
"	23-30/3/16	In billets, carrying out bombing, platoon training, &c. Officers reconnoitred trenches 78-81, SP "Z" VANCOUVER, and the SUBSIDIARY behind these. These trenches are immediately North of L'EPINETTE, and in front of PONT	

WAR DIARY

9th YORKSHIRE REGT.

PLACE	DATE		REMARKS.
ARMENTIERES	—	BALLOT. Trenches in excellent condition compared with those in the salient, being well revetted, duckboarded, and drained. Front line not held throughout its whole length, but only in certain strong "localities", portions of trench in between being wired.	
"	30/3/16	Relieved 9th NORTHUMBERLAND FUSILIERS in trenches abovementioned. Quiet relief, complete about 9.30 pm. HQ close by PONT BALLOT FARM.	
PONT BALLOT.	31/3/16	Quiet day; enemy using little artillery except whizzbangs. Machine guns extremely active at night. Schemes of work arranged with R.E.	

Instructions regarding War Diaries and Intelligence Summaries are contained in F. S. Regs., Part II. and the Staff Manual respectively. Title Pages will be prepared in manuscript.

WAR DIARY
or
~~INTELLIGENCE SUMMARY~~
(Erase heading not required.)

XVII

Army Form C. 2118.

7 Yorks Reg
Vol 7

Place	Date	Hour	7th YORKSHIRE REGT. Summary of Events and Information	Remarks and references to Appendices
PONT BALLOT	1/4/16		Second day in trenches. Much work carried on in draining, improving parapets and parados, making stops on the flanks of defended localities, wiring undefended localities, and improving the wire in front. Work begun in raising parapet of VANCOUVER support trench, building new cookhouse etc.	
"	2-7/4/16		Fairly quiet time in trenches. Enemy's shelling chiefly by whizzbang guns. Few casualties.	
"	7/4/16		Relieved by 9th NORTHUMBERLAND FUSILIERS. Quiet relief.	
ARMENTIERES	8-15/4/16		In rest billets. Many working parties found both by day and night for work on front and communication trenches. Training carried on as far as possible.	
PONT BALLOT	15/4/16		Relieved 9th N.F. in trenches. Quiet relief.	
"	16-23/4/16		Quiet period in trenches; much work carried on as above. During last day of tour, enemy shelled PONT BALLOT and neighbourhood with high explosive throughout the day; however little damage was done and only one or two casualties were inflicted. A concrete dugout in London Rd, which contained 5 men, received a direct hit. The roof was cracked but the dugout was not blown in.	
"	23/4/16		Relieved by 9th N.F. whose Sergeant-Major was wounded during relief.	
ARMENTIERES	23-30/4/16		In rest billets. One officer & 20 men per Coy. trained in wiring by R.E. and then sent up nightly to wire in front of our own sector.	5 sheets

2449 Wt. W14957/M90 750,000 1/16 J.B.C. & A. Forms/C.2118/12.

Instructions regarding War Diaries and Intelligence Summaries are contained in F. S. Regs., Part II. and the Staff Manual respectively. Title Pages will be prepared in manuscript.

WAR DIARY
or
~~INTELLIGENCE SUMMARY~~

(Erase heading not required.)

Army Form C. 2118.

Place	Date	Hour	Summary of Events and Information	Remarks and references to Appendices
ARMENTIERES	23-30 4/16		Whole battalion inoculated against paratyphoid, and occupied in finding large working parties. Stood to on night of German raid on trenches of West Riding Regt., but had not to leave billets. Extra large working parties were required the following night	

2449 Wt. W14957/M90 750,000 1/16 J.B.C. & A. Forms/C.2118/12.

17

7 York Reg

Vol 9

Army Form C. 2118.

Instructions regarding War Diaries and Intelligence Summaries are contained in F. S. Regs., Part II. and the Staff Manual respectively. Title pages will be prepared in manuscript.

WAR DIARY

or

~~INTELLIGENCE SUMMARY.~~

(*Erase heading not required.*)

Place	Date	Hour	Summary of Events and Information — 7th YORKSHIRE REGT.	Remarks and references to Appendices
PONT BALLOT	1/5/16		Relieved 9th Northumberland Fusiliers in trenches at PONT BALLOT. Quiet relief.	
" "	2,3,4/5/16		Rather more shelling than usual round about the trenches, but little on them. Work continued on construction of localities by day, and on wiring the front by night, with the help of parties from the 9th Northumberland Fusiliers.	
" "	5/5/16		Very quiet day till 6.15 pm, when heavy bombardment of L'EPINETTE began. Right of our trenches somewhat damaged. All quiet by 10 pm. Gas alarms sounded, but there was no gas.	
" "	6/5/16		Quiet day. C.O. + 2 Coy Cmdrs of a N.Z. Battalion arrived for 24 hours' attachment.	
" "	7/5/16		2 more N.Z. Coy Cmdrs arrived for attachment. Col. Fife assumed command of 50th Bde (Brigadier on leave) + Maj. Cotton of 7th Yorkshire Regt.	
" "	8/5/16		Work continued on stops + bays for cross fire on flanks of localities.	
ARMENTIERES	9/5/16		Relieved by 9th Northumberland Fusiliers. Quiet relief. Two Coys went into 52nd Bde reserve at Houplines; remainder of Battn in usual billets, but also in reserve to 52nd Bde.	
" "	10 + 11/5/16		In Armentières, preparing for move to training area.	
ESTAIRES	12/5/16		Marched by night to Estaires, arriving about 2am, 13/5/16	

T2134. Wt. W708—776. 500000. 4/15. Sir J. C. & S.

Instructions regarding War Diaries and Intelligence Summaries are contained in F. S. Regs., Part II. and the Staff Manual respectively. Title pages will be prepared in manuscript.

WAR DIARY

~~or~~

~~INTELLIGENCE SUMMARY~~.

(*Erase heading not required.*)

Army Form C. 2118.

Place	Date	Hour	7th YORKSHIRE REGT. Summary of Events and Information	Remarks and references to Appendices
ESTAIRES	13/5/16		Marched to Morbecque (13 miles).	
MORBECQUE	14/5/16		Marched to Wardrecques (about 8 miles).	
WARDRECQUES	15/5/16		" " Nortleulinghem & Mentque, in Training area (about 15 miles). Col. Fife re-assumed command of Battalion.	
MENTQUE	16/5/16		Resting & cleaning up.	
"	17-20/5/16		Company training.	
"	21-23/5/16		Battalion Training.	
"	24/5/16		Brigade route march & attack (forming part of Corps reserve).	
"	25-29/5/16		Battalion training.	
"	30/5/16		First day of Divisional Training; division (in Corps reserve) attacking.	
"	31/5/16		Parades under Battn arrangements.	

Army Form C. 2118.

Instructions regarding War Diaries and Intelligence Summaries are contained in F. S. Regs., Part II. and the Staff Manual respectively. Title Pages will be prepared in manuscript.

WAR DIARY
or
INTELLIGENCE SUMMARY

(Erase heading not required.)

7 Yorks Regt 50/17 JUNE to JULY Vols 9.10

Place	Date	Hour	Summary of Events and Information	Remarks and references to Appendices
			7th Yorkshire Regt.	
MENTQUE.	1.6.16 To 10.6.16		Training in open warfare continued. Several Divisional Field Days.	
	11.6.16.		Entrained at AUDRICQ for AMIENS. arriving 7.30pm. Marched to BUSSY and billeted for the night.	
	12.6.16	9am	Marched to MORLANCOURT and billeted for the night.	
	13.6.16.	3.30 am	Marched up to the trenches immediately South of FRICOURT and relieved the 20th Manchester Regt of the 7th Division. Trenches in very poor condition chiefly through neglect. Enemy fairly quiet on the whole as regards Artillery.	
	14.6.16 To 20.6.16.		Usual trench routine. Enemy inflicted several casualties with "canisters" which are merely oil drums filled with explosive. A dugout was knocked in and 7 men of D Coy occupying Maple redoubt were killed.	
	20.6.16	7am	Relieved by 6/Dorsets of our own Brigade. and marched to HEILLY where the Battn went under canvas to prepare and rest before future big operations.	

2449 Wt. W14957/M90 750,000 1/16 J.B.C. & A. Forms/C.2118/12.

Instructions regarding War Diaries and Intelligence Summaries are contained in F. S. Regs., Part II. and the Staff Manual respectively. Title Pages will be prepared in manuscript.

WAR DIARY
or
INTELLIGENCE SUMMARY
(Erase heading not required.)

Army Form C. 2118

Place	Date	Hour	7th (S.) Batt'n Yorkshire Regt — Summary of Events and Information	Remarks and references to Appendices
HEILLY	21/6/16		Eight 2nd Lieuts joined the Battalion and were posted to the 4 Coys as follows:– 2 to "A" Coy, 2 to "B" Coy, 2 to "C" Coy + 2 to "D" Coy	
"	21/6/16 to 26/6/16		The Battalion spent these days in route marches & re-fitting + general organisation of machine gun sections and bombing squads.	
"	26/6/16	10.5 PM	Moved to VILLE arriving at 11.45 PM and went into billets.	
VILLE	27/6/16		The day was spent in storing the men's packs and officers' kits. The transport being split up into "A" + "B" Echelon. Only 25 Officers were to be taken into the trenches for the attack which was to have taken place on the morning of 29th. Nine officers were left at VILLE under the command of Capt. Carruthers 7th Yorkshire Regt	
VILLE	27/6/16	9.30 PM	The Battalion moved up to the trenches in front of FRICOURT. The 3 assaulting ~~Bat~~ Coys were placed as follows "A" Coy in the front line trenches on the Right "B" Coy in the Support trenches in "Kingston Avenue" + "C" Coy in the front line trenches on the left. "D" Coy which was to form the Batt'n reserve garrisoned BONTE REDOUBT.	Map MEAULT 62 D NE 2
	28/6/16 to 30/6/16		The day of assault on FRICOURT was postponed for 48 hours. Heavy rain made the trenches almost impassable. The Germans confined their attentions mainly to The CEMETRY held by "A" Coy and heavily shelled + trench mortared the front line at intervals both day + night. Several casualties occurred	

1875 Wt. W593/826 1,000,000 4/15 J.B.C. & A. A.D.S.S./Forms/C. 2118.

50th Inf.Bde.
17th Div.

WAR
DIARY

7th BATTN. THE YORKSHIRE REGIMENT.

J U L Y

1 9 1 6

Attached:

Battn. Operation
Order No. 63.

Instructions regarding War Diaries and Intelligence Summaries are contained in F. S. Regs., Part II. and the Staff Manual respectively. Title Pages will be prepared in manuscript.

WAR DIARY
or
INTELLIGENCE SUMMARY
(Erase heading not required.)

Army Form C. 2118.

7th (S) Batt. Yorkshire Regt.

Place	Date	Hour	Summary of Events and Information	Remarks and references to Appendices
			in consequence 2nd Lt GRIFFITH was wounded and replaced by 2nd Lt WILKINSON from the Reserve Officers at VILLE	
	30/6/16		The Batt. H.Q moved to a dug out at FRICOURT STATION in the evening, formerly occupied by H Q of "C" Coy. Lt Col. R. D'A' FIFE. C.M.G. Commanding the Batt.n	
			A Coy was commanded by Major ~~Kent~~ R.E.D. KENT	
			B Coy " " " Capt L.G. HARE	
			C Coy " " " Capt R.W.S. CROFT	
			D Coy " " " Capt H.L. BARTRUM	
Trenches in front of FRICOURT VILLAGE	30/6/16 to 1/7/16		A heavy artillery bombardment of the whole of the German position was maintained throught the night. The enemy retaliating in a half hearted manner, mainly directing his fire on the front line trenches but doing little damage except to trenches in ~~front of~~ the "CIMETERY"	

2449 Wt. W14957/M90 750,000 1/16 J.B.C. & A. Forms/C.2118/12.

Army Form C. 2118.

Instructions regarding War Diaries and Intelligence Summaries are contained in F. S. Regs., Part II. and the Staff Manual respectively. Title Pages will be prepared in manuscript.

50/17

WAR DIARY
or
~~INTELLIGENCE SUMMARY~~
(Erase heading not required.)

7 Yorks. July 1916

Place	Date	Hour	7th (Service) Battn Yorkshire Regt. 50th Bde — Summary of Events and Information	Remarks and references to Appendices
FRICOURT.	1/7/16		The attached Battn Operation Order No 63 gives the general and detailed orders for the offensive for which the Battn assembled in the trenches opposite FRICOURT VILLAGE on the afternoon of 30th June 1916. The first zero hour was 7.30 am on July 1st when the troops on our left and right attacked, and the 2nd zero hour was at 2.30 pm when the Battalion assaulted. Owing to an unfortunate mistake on the part of the officer commanding A Coy, his company assaulted at 7.45 am. As soon as they began to climb over our parapet terrific machine gun fire was opened by the enemy and the company was almost at once wiped out. The survivors lay in crump holes some 25 yards in front of our wire until after dark. As soon as it was discovered that A Company had assaulted by itself, D Coy (the reserve coy) was brought up into the assembly trenches to take A Coys place.	OO No 63
			At 2pm 1/7/16 our Artillery began the ½ hour preliminary bombardment of FRICOURT VILLAGE. This bombardment was feeble and did little damage to the enemy as the Battalion soon learnt to its cost. At 2.30pm the Battn assaulted and were met by a murderous machine gun and rifle fire. Officers and men were literally mown down and were finally brought to a standstill about half way across to the enemy's trenches.	
			13 officers and over 300 men became casualties in about three minutes. The survivors lay in crump holes until dark with a few exceptions who managed to crawl back. Many magnificent deeds of courage were performed especially in bringing in wounded and in carrying messages under fire.	
	1/7/16 to 2/7/16		The Battn was withdrawn after dark on 1/7/16 and marched some 5 miles behind the line to re-organize at VILLE continuing the march at 4PM 2/7/16 to HEILLY ~~The 51st Bde relieved us and captured FRICOURT VILLAGE on the morning of 2/7/16 without~~	

2449 Wt. W14957/M90 750,000 1/16 J.B.C. & A. Forms/C.2118/12.

Instructions regarding War Diaries and Intelligence Summaries are contained in F. S. Regs., Part II. and the Staff Manual respectively. Title Pages will be prepared in manuscript.

WAR DIARY
or
INTELLIGENCE SUMMARY

(Erase heading not required.)

Army Form C. 2118

Place	Date	Hour	7th (S) Batt Yorkshire Regt — Summary of Events and Information	Remarks and references to Appendices
	1/7/16 to 2/7/16		The Battn was relieved by 6th Batt Dorset Regt which was subsequently relieved the same night by 51st Bgde. This Bgde occupied FRICOURT VILLAGE on the morning of 2/7/16 without a shot being fired, the enemy having evacuated his trenches during the night (about 11.30 PM)	
	2/7/16		The casualties in the Battn amounted to 5 Officers Killed and 10 wounded O.R. 336 Killed and wounded	
HEILLY	2/7/16	6PM.	Arrived from VILLE. The Battn being in Tents in the same place as it occupied at the end of June	
"	3/7/16		A draft of 2 NCOs + 44 men joined the Battn + posted to "A" Coy. Messages received from the G.O.C 50th Bgde + G.O.C XVII Divn congratulating the Battn on its gallantry + devotion to duty on 1st July. The G.O.C XVII Div adding that owing to the self sacrifice of the Batt the Village of FRICOURT was occupied, without a shot being fired, the following day. Moved to billets in VILLE during the afternoon.	
"	4/7/16		Reorganisation of bombing squads and Lewis Gun teams. The men were refitted as far as possible. Bathing parades &c. Capt A.J.W. BARMBY in command of "C" Coy vice Capt R.W.S. CROFT wounded. 2nd Lt L.V.C. HAWKES appointed Adjutant vice Capt. BARMBY	
"	5/7/16	5.30PM	Marched to MEAULTE + went into billets.	
"	6/7/16	8.30PM.	Battn ordered to march in the direction of FRICOURT with the idea of	

1875 Wt. W593/826 1,000,000 4/15 J.B.C. & A. A.D.S.S./Forms/C. 2118.

Instructions regarding War Diaries and Intelligence Summaries are contained in F. S. Regs., Part II. and the Staff Manual respectively. Title Pages will be prepared in manuscript.

WAR DIARY
or
~~INTELLIGENCE SUMMARY~~
(Erase heading not required.)

Army Form C. 2118

Place	Date	Hour	7th (S) Batt Yorkshire Regt — Summary of Events and Information	Remarks and references to Appendices
			forming supports to a further attack on the German position in MAMETZ WOOD the following day. Bivouacked for the night on the BECORDEL – FRICOURT Road	
FRICOURT Wood	7/7/16		Took up a position in FRICOURT WOOD after spending some hours waiting for orders in FRICOURT VILLAGE	
	7/7/16 8/7/16		During the night the Battn moved forward to the advanced trenches to the S.W of MAMETZ WOOD relieving the 6th Batt. Dorset Regt. A + B Coys in the front line. C + D Coys in RAILWAY ALLEY in Support. Battn H.Q in BOTTOM Wood with A Coy. E YORKSHIRE Regt on the left. XXXVIII Div on the Right	Map. MAMETZ WOOD
BOTTOM WOOD	8/7/16	1.22AM	Bombing attack ordered on QUADRANGLE SUPPORT trench at 6 A.M. The 51st Bgde cooperating on the left. Artillery, at the same time, to barrage enemy C.Ts. This attack was subsequently postponed to 7 A.M.	
	8/7/16	7AM	"B" Coy began moving up the C.T. at the hour fixed and advanced about 100 yards. The mud in the trench was over the mens' knees + they soon became very exhausted but continued to move forward up QUADRANGLE ALLEY until held up by machine gun + rifle fire. The 51st Bgde were also held up on the left. This attack failed + the Coy withdrew to its former position in QUADRANGLE TRENCH	

1875 Wt. W593/826 1,000,000 4/15 J.B.C. & A. A.D.S.S./Forms/C. 2118.

Instructions regarding War Diaries and Intelligence Summaries are contained in F. S. Regs., Part II. and the Staff Manual respectively. Title Pages will be prepared in manuscript.

WAR DIARY
or
~~INTELLIGENCE SUMMARY~~
(Erase heading not required.)

Army Form C. 2118

Place	Date	Hour	7th (S) Battn Yorkshire Regt — Summary of Events and Information	Remarks and references to Appendices
Trenches S.W. of MAMETS WOOD			A 2nd attack ordered on QUADRANGLE Support Trench.	
	8/7/16	5.50 P.M.	The orders for this operation were ~~[illegible]~~ issued by the Bgde as follows:- 7th Yorkshire Regt to attack at 5.50 PM with 6th Dorset Regt attacking on the left at a different zero hour. The orders were to rush up to junction of Quadrangle Alley + QUADRANGLE Support + establish necessary stops 30 mins. later, after further Artillery preparation, ~~[illegible]~~ to work N.W. + join hands with 51st Bgde working from PEARL ALLEY. "B" Coy bombers were sent up for this attack + placed under the orders of Lt. H.K.C. HARE commanding "B" Coy	Map MAMETZ WOOD
		7.20 PM	This attack also failed to achieve its object for the same reasons as the 7 AM attack. The mud in the trenches made a rapid advance absolutely impossible, the enemy machine guns enfilading the line of advance the whole way. Both sides of the C.T, having been destroyed by our artillery, gave no protection to the attackers.	
	8/7/16 to 9/7/16	11.50 PM	During the night the Dorset Regt occupied ~~[illegible]~~ "WOOD Trench" on our right without opposition + held it with one Company. Emplacements for Stokes mortar guns constructed in QUADRANGLE ALLEY	

1875 Wt. W593/826 1,000,000 4/15 J.B.C. & A. A.D.S.S./Forms/C. 2118.

Army Form C. 2118.

WAR DIARY
or
~~INTELLIGENCE SUMMARY~~
(Erase heading not required.)

Instructions regarding War Diaries and Intelligence Summaries are contained in F. S. Regs., Part II. and the Staff Manual respectively. Title Pages will be prepared in manuscript.

Place	Date	Hour	7th (S) Batt. Yorkshire Regt Summary of Events and Information	Remarks and references to Appendices
Trenches S.W. of MAMETZ WOOD	9/7/16	12.15 PM.	A third bombing attack on the junction of QUADRANGLE ALLEY + QUADRANGLE Support Trenches, after bombardment lasting 1 hour + 15 mins, failed. The enemy machine guns again holding up the attack from different positions. Stokes guns unable to participate, ground too soft + muddy to allow a suitable emplacements being made. A night surprise attack suggested with artillery support.	
		11.20 PM.	"C" Coy with Capt A.J.W. BARMBY in command ordered to attack once more the junction of QUADRANGLE ALLEY + QUADRANGLE Support. This attack to be with the bayonet over the open and stops were ordered to be formed in QUADRANGLE ALLEY + WOOD Support, bombing parties to work down QUADRANGLE Support + join hands with 51st Bgde working in the opposite direction. Sappers detailed to make strong point at junction if attack succeeded while "C" Coy hold stops. Attack again failed partly ~~at~~ caused by 51st Bgde on the left beginning the assault before "C" Coy + giving the alarm to the enemy in front. Brigade ordered no further attack to be made, Division however ordered another attempt + then countermanded it. Capt BARMBY wounded + Lt. G.D. MACINTYRE missing, believed killed.	

10f

2449 Wt. W14957/M90 750,000 1/16 J.B.C. & A. Forms/C.2118/12.

Army Form C. 2118.

WAR DIARY
or
~~INTELLIGENCE SUMMARY~~

(Erase heading not required.)

Instructions regarding War Diaries and Intelligence Summaries are contained in F. S. Regs., Part II. and the Staff Manual respectively. Title Pages will be prepared in manuscript.

Place	Date	Hour	7th (S) Battn Yorkshire Regt — Summary of Events and Information	Remarks and references to Appendices
Trenches SW of MAMETZ WOOD.	10/7/16		XXXVIII Div on our right attacked MAMETZ WOOD. Objective line running E + W just S of where WOOD SUPPORT joins Wood	
		4.15 AM.	~~Battn~~ 50th Bgde ordered to cooperate about 6 AM + push up QUADRANGLE ALLEY + the railways + get a footing in WOOD SUPPORT.	
			The objective of XXXVIII Div. altered to "secure all of MAMETZ WOOD"	
			The Battn did not move during the day but materially assisted the attack on MAMETZ Wood by directing Lewis + Machine gun fire on strong points held by the enemy especially at a point where WOOD SUPPORT trench joins MAMETZ WOOD. The Germans eventually retired from Quadrangle ALLEY + WOOD Support trenches, the Battn Lewis Guns + Machine Guns attached to the Battn doing great execution	
		4.24 P.M.	The East Yorkshire Regt. did not succeed in their attack on WOOD Support Trench.	
	11/7/16	1 AM.	The Bgde was relieved by 21st Divn. The Battn handed over to 8th Battn Lincolnshire Regt. Before doing so "B" Coy sent patrol to ~~the~~ QUADRANGLE Support, WOOD Support + Northern part of QUADRANGLE ALLEY + found them all unoccupied by the enemy. Two wounded men of NORTHUMBERLAND Fusls found in a dug out	

2449 Wt. W14957/M90 750,000 1/16 J.B.C. & A. Forms/C.2118/12.

Army Form C. 2118.

Instructions regarding War Diaries and Intelligence Summaries are contained in F. S. Regs., Part II. and the Staff Manual respectively. Title Pages will be prepared in manuscript.

WAR DIARY
or
~~INTELLIGENCE SUMMARY~~

(Erase heading not required.)

7th (S) Batt. Yorkshire Regt

Place	Date	Hour	Summary of Events and Information	Remarks and references to Appendices
	11/7/16		+ 3 wounded Germans. One of these was brought in.	
GROVE TOWN SIDING.			Battn marched from the trenches and entrained at noon for SALEUX subsequently being conveyed partly by lorries to MOLLIENS-VIDAMES where it arrived about 10.30 PM. + went into billets.	
			The losses of the Battn since the 2nd July amounted to 2 Officers wounded and 104 OR Killed, wounded + missing	
			The entraining strength at GROVE TOWN was. 349 all ranks excluding transport which went by road.	
MOLLIENS VIDAMES	12/7/16		Resting	
	13/7/16		Refitting, training &c.	
			Total casualties since the beginning of operations as at present ascertained Officers: Killed 6, Wounded 12 NCOs + Men: Killed 73, Wounded 322, Missing (believed killed) 44	
	14/7/16		Battn Strength 26 Officers and 525 NCOs + men. These figures include all men attached to Bde + Div H.Q, Trench Mortar Batteries, M.G. Coys + ~~transport &c.~~ Fighting Strength 19 Officers. O.R. 412	

Wt. W5951/M95 750,000 1/16 J.B.C. & A. Forms/C.2118/12.

Instructions regarding War Diaries and Intelligence Summaries are contained in F. S. Regs., Part II. and the Staff Manual respectively. Title Pages will be prepared in manuscript.

WAR DIARY

or

~~INTELLIGENCE SUMMARY~~

(Erase heading not required.)

Army Form C. 2118

7th (S) Battn Yorkshire Regt

Place	Date	Hour	Summary of Events and Information	Remarks and references to Appendices
MOLLIENS-VIDAMES	15/7/16	6.15AM	~~Batt~~ 50th Bgde marched to BELLANCOURT + went into billets. The Battn at BELLANCOURT. The billeting party under 2nd Lt. WALTON left at 2.30 A.M. Draft 1 N.C.O. + 14 O.R. Posted as follows 1 Cpl A Coy, 3 O.R. to "B" Coy; 1 Private to "C" Coy	
BELLANCOURT	16/7/16		R.C. parade at the Church at 9.30 AM.. Coys held kit inspections &c.	
	17/7/16		Coys were inspected by C.O at 10.15 AM in battle kit. A Court of Inquiry was held at 2 PM to inquire into the injuries sustained by No 10591 Corp MITCHELL. H. of "B" Coy.	
	18/7/16		Draft 10 Privates posted to "B" Coy, 1 Sgt to "B" Coy.	
	19/7/16		Draft 5 Officers posted as follows. Lt H.P. GREGORY to "D" Coy; 2nd Lts R.T. RUDGE and C.J. EYRE. to "B" Coy; 2nd Lts B. ROUSE + G.D. STANSFIELD to C Coy.	
	20/7/16		Draft 2 NCO's and 63 MEN. posted as follows 1 Cpl + 14 men to "B" Coy; 1 Sgt and 24 men to "C" Coy; 25 men to "D" Coy.	
	18/7/16 to 22/7/16		Battn re-organising and training bombers, Lewis gun teams &c. Battn route march on 21/7/16.	
	21/7/16		All officers cobs + wheeled transport except 2 cookers 2 G.S + 1 limber waggon left by road for BRUCAMPS + will continue march, to unknown destination, the following day.	

1875 Wt. W593/826 1,000,000 4/15 J.B.C. & A. A.D.S.S./Forms/C. 2118.

Instructions regarding War Diaries and Intelligence Summaries are contained in F. S. Regs., Part II. and the Staff Manual respectively. Title Pages will be prepared in manuscript.

WAR DIARY
or
INTELLIGENCE SUMMARY
(Erase heading not required.)

Army Form C. 2118

7th (S) Battn Yorkshire Regt.

Place	Date	Hour	Summary of Events and Information	Remarks and references to Appendices
BELLANCOURT	22/7/16.	5.30PM.	The Bgde marched to CONDE arriving about 10 PM and went into billets. The distance was about 11 miles.	
CONDE	23/7/16.		The Bgde remained all day with orders to be ready to move at any time. L/Cpl. Hamilton was accidentally drowned + was buried in the cemetery there.	
	23/7/16 to 24/7/16		Half the Bgde including the Battn marched about 10 PM, a distance of 2½ miles to HANGEST Station. There was a long delay before entraining. Train left about 6 AM for MERICOURT.-L'ABBÉ. 2 Cookers 2 G.S + 1 limber waggon came by road leaving CONDE during the morning of 23rd	
MERICOURT	24/7/16		Arrived about 10 A.M. + marched to a camp near DERNANCOURT where the whole Bgde bivouacked. The Battn was allotted 3 tents only. All transport arrived during the day ~~with~~ also the remainder of the Bgde.	
near DERNANCOURT	25/7/16 to 27/7/16.		The usual Coy training continued. Special instruction in attack from trenches, crawling forward while artillery barrage is still on enemy front line &c. Lewis Gun teams + bombers under their respective commanders. Number of bombers reduced to 8 per Coy + 32 Battn bombers.	

1875 Wt. W593/826 1,000,000 4/15 J.B.C. & A. A.D.S.S./Forms/C. 2118.

Instructions regarding War Diaries and Intelligence Summaries are contained in F. S. Regs., Part II. and the Staff Manual respectively. Title Pages will be prepared in manuscript.

WAR DIARY
or
INTELLIGENCE SUMMARY
(Erase heading not required.)

Army Form C. 2118

7th (S) Battn Yorkshire Regt

Place	Date	Hour	Summary of Events and Information	Remarks and references to Appendices
near DERNANCOURT	27/7/16	6PM.	Ceremonial parade of the 50th 51st + 52nd Bgdes with trench mortar + machine gun Coys. and Field Ambulances. G.O.C. XVII Div Major Genl. Robertson C.B. distributed the ribbon of the Military Medal which had been awarded to N.C.Os + men for gallantry in the field during the recent operations. The Battn was awarded 15 medals out of 35 awarded to the Bgde. The following NCO's + men have been decorated. No. 14124 Pte Ramsay. J.T. — No 13007 Pte Sutherland. J. — No 16108 Pte Kenning. W. " 11310 " Andrews. F. — " 12385 " Patchett. G. — " 11701 " Cruikshanks. T. " 16067 " Larke. H.G. — " 18036 " Tucker. S. — " 21089 " Forrester. C. " 11165 " Devaney. P — " 8236 L/Cpl Gatehouse. S. — " 12334 " Oxberry. G.W. " 18798 " Marwood. J. — " 12376 Pte Tiernan. P. — " 12474 " Gell. J.T. Since the awards, 1 man has been killed + 5 wounded. During the evening 1 man was killed + 1 wounded accidentally, detonating bombs.	
"	28/7/16 to 31/7/16		Companies continued training under Coy commanders. A draft of 2 Officers arrived + joined the Battn on 28th Lt. H.A. WILKINSON posted to "C" Coy, 2nd Lt B. J. HOUSE posted to A Coy; Rejoined 2nd Lt A.C. GOODALL. Ration strength of Battn 31/7/16 – 31. Officers, 611 O.R.	

1875 Wt. W593/826 1,000,000 4/15 J.B.C. & A. A.D.S.S./Forms/C. 2118.

BATTALION OPERATION ORDER NO. 63.

War Diary.

7th Yorkshire Regiment Operation Order No 63

Ref. 1/20,000 Map

MONTAUBAN.

Note – In these orders zero is the hour of assault.
June 29th 1916 is the day of assault.

1. Scheme of attack. In conjunction with the French who are operating from MARICOURT Southwards, the 4th Army will attack on the 29th June with the line MONTAUBAN – South side of MAMETZ WOOD – POZIERES and northwards as objective.
The 17th Corps is attacking with 2 Divisions in the line. The 7th Division on right and the 21st Division on left. The 17th Division is in Corps Reserve.
The 7th Division will attack northwards with line S25 b5.3 to WILLOW AVENUE at X29 b5.6 as objective.
The 21st Division will attack towards East with line X29 b5.6 through QUADRANGLE as objective.
These attacks leave triangle FRICOURT – FRICOURT WOOD untouched to be dealt with in 2nd stage of attack.
The 50th Infty Brigade will be attached to the 21st Division and will cover the right flank of the 21st Division by occupying the North corner of FRICOURT village in the 1st stage of attack with 1 Battalion.
In 2nd stage of attack the Brigade will clear FRICOURT village and FRICOURT WOOD in conjunction with the 22nd Infty Brigade of the 7th Division.
A 2nd zero hour for this assault will be ordered.

Objectives 1st Stage. In the 1st stage objectives of the 50th Brigade are as follows –

1. To clear front system of German trenches and that part of FRICOURT between boundries
   - on South F3 a.5.3 – F3 b5.3
   - on North X27 c3.2 – X27 d.0.4
   - a East LONELY COPSE (inclusive) – SUNKEN ROAD – WELL LANE – and trench running S.W. from point 534.1.
2. Occupy position in neighbourhood of RED COTTAGE to protect right flank of 21st Division in SUNKEN ROAD.

The above operations will protect right flank of 63rd Brigade 21st Division and 20th Brigade 7th Division will at the same time form a defensive flank facing N.W. on line

N.E. corner of MAMETZ – ORCHARD ALLEY – its junction with APPLE ALLEY – APPLE ALLEY to our front line trenches

Objectives 2nd Stage In the 2nd stage of the attack for which a separate Zero hour will be ordered when objectives of 1st stage have been attained the objectives of the 50th Infty Brigade are as follows—

50th Bde 1st objective — Clear up the eastern edge of FRICOURT VILLAGE from WELL LANE to COTTAGE TRENCH. COTTAGE TRENCH to WILLOW AVENUE joining there with 22nd Brigade.

2nd objective — Clear FRICOURT WOOD as far as WILLOW TRENCH and trench running N. NE to X28c8.0.

22nd Bde 1st objective — The 20th Manchester Regt and 1st Royal Welsh Fusiliers of the 22nd Infty Bde will clear ROSE TRENCH from its junction with ORCHARD ALLEY

2nd objective. Clear WILLOW AVENUE as far as BUNNY WOOD

2. **Preliminary Moves** The 7/Yorkshire Regt will march from HEILLY to VILLE on June 26th and from VILLE to trenches on June 27th

Assembly in trenches — The Battn will assemble within limits of following boundaries.

North ROYAL AVENUE (incl)
South RONDEL AVENUE (incl)
West SURREY road and KINGSTON (incl)

The main "up" lines are—
1. Royal Avenue
2. Kingston – Sussex Street
3. South Avenue – Tyneside – Rondel via Sussex Street

The main "down" line is
Willow Avenue.

Until the moment of assault front trenches will be held as follows—

Right of each company in front line will be marked by a sentry group and 1 Lewis gun per coy will be posted at suitable spots. These guns will prevent enemy repairing his wire on night 28/29 by firing except between 1am and 3am when patrols of 22nd Bde will be out. Bombers whose duty it will be to throw Smoke bombs will be posted at intervals along the front line. The remainder of assaulting companies will be distributed in depth as far as possible and in dugouts. A lookout man to be stationed at entrance to each dugout.

On the night of 27/28 D company will be in BONTE REDOUBT and Battn Head Quarters at F 8 a 5.3.

On night 28/29 D company will move forward to KINGSTON Road and Battn: Head Quarters to the [illegible]

3.
Preparation of wire

All wire in front of front line trenches, close support and reserve trenches will be cut on the night 28/29, the night before the assault. Care must be taken that the fact of wire having been cut is not visible to the enemy.

4.
Dress & equipment

"Battle Kit" will be worn and tools, grenades and sandbags will be carried as detailed and practised in training area

5.
Gas Helmets

Gas Helmets will be worn rolled up on the head.

6
Ammunition

The 100 rounds S.A.A. hitherto carried in haversacks will be carried slung over shoulders in cotton Bandoliers

7
ARTILLERY BARRAGES

After 1st stage of attack on June 29th by the 7th and 21st Divisions, intense Artillery Barrage will be opened on FRICOURT village and Wood lasting for 30 mins. This will cease at Zero time when assault will take place. During the last 5 mins our heavy Artillery will cease fire to enable assaulting

line to creep forward as near as possible to the German trenches.
At zero time barrage will lift to line RED COTTAGE – ROSE COTTAGE – COTTAGE TRENCH – and at 15 mins after zero barrage will again lift on to FRICOURT WOOD 120 yards from and parallel to road running from ROSE COTTAGE towards RED COTTAGE.
The last mentioned barrage will continue until 1 hour and 45 mins after zero

8. Details for Assault.

The assault on FRICOURT will be carried out by the Battalion as follows

A Coy On the right will assault from WING CORNER Trench (inclusive) to the SALIENT South of road leading into Western side of FRICOURT

B Coy Will assault from left of A Coy to WICKET CORNER (inclusive)

C Coy. Will assault from left of B Coy to German TAMBOUR on contour 80 (inclusive)

D Coy. Will be in Battn. Reserve.

Companies will assault in 3 lines.

9. Bombing Detachments

Sufficient bombing detachments to deal with flanks on lines of company advances will be detailed, prior to the assault, in front lines. Two detachments of Battn. Bombers in addition will be attached to C Company. The remainder of the Battn. Bombers will accompany Head Quarters.

10. Lewis Guns.

Will accompany the 2nd line of each coy

11. Wire Cutters.

As many men as possible in assaulting companies will carry wire cutters or wire breakers.

(8)

12 Method of Assault

As soon as the 30 mins bombardment of [illegible] begins assaulting companies will move forward from [illegible] and will line up ready to cross over parapets [illegible] 30 mins i.e. 10 mins before zero. [illegible] parapet and lie down 5 mins before zero they will creep forward as near as possible to enemy wire. Exactly at zero A Company will assault [illegible] CORNER. As soon as A Company reaches German trench B Company will assault and as soon as B Company reaches WICKET CORNER C Company will assault. A Company will at once send a patrol with bombers towards SUNKEN ROAD Trench to gain touch with the 22nd Brigade. This patrol will keep in touch with 22nd Brigade and will advance along WILLOW AVENUE as far as COTTAGE TRENCH [illegible] C Company will warn this patrol that they must expect to meet 22nd Brigade, and that until 15 mins after the assault our Artillery barrage will be on COTTAGE Trench. C Company will detach a patrol with bombers to gain touch with the 10th West Yorkshire Regt on our left.

(b) The fronts of the objectives allotted to companies are as follows —

A Coy. WILLOW AVENUE (incl) to ROSE COTTAGE (incl)

B Coy. ROSE COTTAGE (excl) to [illegible] (incl)

C Coy. [illegible] (excl) to right of West York. R in WELL LANE

The left boundary of C Company during advance will be N.W. corner of German Tambour — junction of HARE LANE and RED TRENCH — Right of West York. R. in WELL LANE.

(c) All dugouts and cellars encountered during the advance will be bombed. While any party is inside a dugout or cellar one man will remain at entrance to prevent another party throwing in a bomb.

(d) All prisoners taken will be handed over at once to coy 3rd line.

hands of prisoners in proportion of 5 % will conduct them to our original front line trenches where they will hand them over to the East Yorkshire Regt and will then rejoin their own Company.

13
Consolidation of 1st objective

The line of the 1st objective will be immediately consolidated and [illegible] Guns placed in position. While this is being done Companies will reorganize and front line will be thinned. During consolidation Battn bombing detachments will block SUNSHINE ALLEY and [illegible] trench and Battn Scouts will cover the front.
Bombers and Scouts must be warned that Artillery barrage on FRICOURT WOOD to within 100x of new line will continue until 1.45 after Zero.

2nd objective.

At 1.45 after Zero the Battn with West York. R on left will continue the advance through FRICOURT WOOD.
C Coy will not form part of front line in the 2nd advance but will follow B Coy in half Coy columns.
Right boundary of the Battn advance will be SUNSHINE ALLEY and the left boundary will be the clearing running N.E. through FRICOURT WOOD.
On reaching the N end of WILLOW trench the right of A Coy will halt. The remainder of A & B Coys front line will move forward until they reach the track leading N.NE from WILLOW Trench. At each end of this track the R.E of the 21st Division will make Strong Points and A Coy will consolidate WILLOW Trench. Companies must be warned that the 63rd Brigade are constructing another strong point in front of them at N.E. corner of FRICOURT WOOD.

14.
Reserve Company.

15 mins before Zero time D Coy [illegible] again to move from KINGSTON Road into front line trenches hitherto held by A & B Coys. This Coy will not advance further until ordered and will then do so by platoons in fours as circumstances may require.

15. **Vermorel Sprayers** The 3rd line of assaulting coys will carry Vermorel Sprayers from front trenches. These must be previously filled with solution.

16. **Carriers** 3 Carriers will be detailed for each Lewis Gun. 8 men per coy will be required to carry bombs under the Batt. Bombing officer. 8 men are to be told off to carry for each platoon bombing detachment.

17. **Reports** Prior to the assault reports to Batt. Head Quarters at the Railway Station. After the assault orderlies with reports will follow road leading from the Church to S.W. Corner of FRICOURT and thence, if necessary, to the Station.
O.C. Coys and platoons must bear in mind the importance of reporting the situation in writing at every stage. Reports should be in duplicate and sent by separate orderlies.

18. **General Instructions** All ranks whilst stationed in BONTE REDOUBT are to be warned that they must on no account look over the parapet.
Instructions concerning details in connection with the advance are issued herewith.

[illegible]
Capt & Adjt
7th Batt. Yorkshire Regiment.

No. 1 Copy to A Coy
" 2 " " B Coy
" 3 " " C Coy
" 4 " " D Coy
" 5 " " L.G.O.
" 6 " " B.B.O.
" 7 " " H.Q. 50th Bde
" 8 " " Q.M.
" 9 " " T.O.
" 10 }
" 11 } retained.
" 12 }

Instructions in Connection with forthcoming Operations.

Medical Arrangements.

The 53rd Field Ambulance will be attached to the 50th Bde.

Aid Posts are established (1) at Kings Cross

(2) On Willow Avenue at F 8 a 5.6.

Advanced dressing Stations are at :-

(1) foot of WILLOW AVENUE F 7.6. central

(2) at F. 2. c 3.7.

APPENDIX B

The following points require special attention prior to & during the Advance.

(1) Prior to the Advance every precaution will be taken to ensure the men

(a) Arriving as fresh as possible in their assembly trenches.

(b) Having plenty to eat & drink prior to the occupation of positions of Assault.

(c) That every man has his full ration with him & that his water bottle is full.

(2) During the Advance it is necessary to have the leading lines close up to the Artillery Barrage, so that positions may be occupied the moment the Barrage lifts.

To ensure this, in the first instance, the leading two lines must leave their trenches before the bombardment ceases, and advance as far as possible towards the German lines.

(3) All advance must be made above ground & only those people should enter trenches who have been told off to :-

(a) Block & clear trenches.

(b) Consolidate & hold trenches.

APPENDIX B. (contd)

(4) Although the Advance must be made <u>in the boldest possible manner</u>, troops cannot be expected to capture trenches covered by uncut wire & occupied by the enemy.

When uncut wire is encountered & no openings can be seen, the following procedure will take place:-

(a) Leading troops to at once take up a fire position & push Wire Cutters forward to cut the Wire.

As soon as a passage is made, troops will at once press forward.

(b) If Wire cannot be cut owing to enemy's fire, patrols must at once be pushed out to the flank to ascertain where openings exist & rear troops must at once take advantage of these to pass through & turn the enemy's flank.

(c) If no openings exist word must at once be passed back & openings made with the aid of Stokes Guns & the Artillery.

(NOTE)

In all Cases where Artillery fire is asked for, exact information must be sent as to the Spot where it is required.

(5) When a portion of the line is held up, troops on the flanks must avoid being drawn into the fight — They must push straight through to their ultimate objective & leave those isolated detachments to be dealt with later on.

APPENDIX B (continued)

(6) As each objective is reached, the leading troops must press forward & seize and consolidate themselves in position which will cover the consolidation of the main position.

(7) Probably the best method of consolidating a trench is for a portion of the Infantry to take up a fire behind the enemy's parapet whilst the remainder ~~to~~ make firing niches in the enemy's parados.

No time should be lost in forming niches for the Lewis Guns who will then be in a position to cover the remainder of the Consolidation.

(8) Strong points are being constructed by the Engineers & the Pioneer Battalion. These parties are not to be interfered with by Infantry Commanders except for urgent tactical reasons. As soon as these works are ready for occupation they will come under the Officers in Command of the area where they are situated & will be garrisoned by Lewis guns until handed over. They will, ~~if~~ in case of attack, be held by the working party and any Infantry in the neighbourhood.

Lewis Guns of Pioneer Battalion must be placed in position to defend these localities as soon as possible.

(9) It must be impressed upon all ranks that once a position has been reached, it must be held at all costs, till reinforcements can arrive. There will be masses of troops in rear who will be pressing forward.

APPENDIX B (continued)

(10) Commanders must ensure that once an ~~the~~ objective has been reached, all troops not required for consolidation are at once to reorganise for attack.

The Senior Officer on the spot must immediately take Command of all troops in the neighbourhood whether belonging to his Regiment or not.

APPENDIX D

Accessories to the Attack

GAS Attack.

(1) A Gas attack will be delivered along the front as follows –

(a) If wind is favourable on night – V/W

(b) If wind is not favourable on night V/W attack will be on night W/X

(c) If wind is not favourable on night W/X attack will be made on night X/Y

Brigade H.Q will be informed by Divisional H.Q. by 7a.m. on V day (and if necessary on following days) if gas is to be discharged.

(2) On Z day, if wind is favourable, whiffs of gas from cylinders available will be turned on at 15 minutes before Zero on the position of our line between our right & the TAMBOUR.

(3) During Gas Attacks the front trenches must be cleared of men as far as ~~the~~ situation permits

(4) Gas Helmets must be worn

(5) No discharge of Gas will be made if there is likely to be any danger to our own men.

APPENDIX E.

(5) All men in the front line trenches will be warned to keep well under cover during the preliminary bombardment as splinters from heavy howitzers blow back considerably.

(6) In the event of any round from our own heavy artillery falling short in our own trenches, information will be sent at once to G.O.C. Heavy Artillery stating accurately

(a) The exact place where the round fell
(b) The exact time at which round fell.

APPENDIX G

Communication with Contact Aeroplanes

(1) On Z day flares will be lit by Infantry as follows.

(a) On reaching the first Objective
(b) On reaching the Second Objective
(c) During the third phase on reaching the East edge of FRICOURT VILLAGE and ROSE TRENCH (F.4.c 3560 – F.4.a.0602)
(d) All along the line of the most forward infantry at the following hours

9 A.M.
1 P.M
5 P.M
9 P.M.

(2)
(a) 3 Aeroplanes will be detailed for Contact Work. Type Moran Parasol. Special marking – a broad black band under left hand plane. One contact Aeroplane at a time will be in the Air.

APPENDIX H.

DISCIPLINE

1 (a) So many unfortunate incidents have arisen through the unauthorised passing down of the word RETIRE, that the use of this word is absolutely forbidden in the 21st Division. All ranks are to distinctly understand that if such an order is given it is either a device of the enemy or given by some unauthorised person who has lost his head.

In any case this order is never to be obeyed

(b) If it is ever necessary to withdraw temporarily a flank for some tactical reason, the order will invariably be in writing & will state definitely the troops referred to, & the exact place to which they are to retire. Any officer, N.C.O. or man who orders a withdrawal without having received a written & signed order will be liable to be tried by Court Martial.

(2) Many incidents have occurred in this war of men searching for souvenirs instead of instantly consolidating a position gained, & in consequence being found unready to meet the enemy's counter-attack. It is therefore to be distinctly understood that any officer, N.C.O., or man found in possession of any such souvenirs will be tried by Court Martial.

APPENDIX H

DISCIPLINE

(2) (continued)

Divisional arrangements will be made to have souvenirs collected & distributed to those units who have taken part.

(3) In order to save waste, whenever iron rations are used, the greatest care must be taken that only sufficient tins are opened to feed the number of men present at the time.

This should work out at one tin to three men.

(4) All ranks must be impressed with the necessity of having full water bottles before the Advance & of economising every drop of water during the advance. It is always hard to say in an advance when more water will be available.

On ~~[illegible]~~ reaching an objective a party should at once be told off to collect water & Ammunition from all dead men & casualties who are being taken to the rear.

(5) From date of this order no papers, orders & maps of our trenches will be carried by officers and O.R in the trenches or, later on, by those taking part in the attack.

The G.O.C. wishes to impress on Brigadiers the importance of All Ranks knowing the above orders thoroughly the directs that the necessary arrangements shall be made to ensure that these orders are known to all ranks.

[signature]
Captn. & Adjt.
7th Battn. Yorkshire Regt.

1/5000
Fricourt.
König Trench
König Support
Red Lane
Red Trench
Red Cottage
Lonely Trench
Lonely Support
Well Lane
Hosky Trench
Sunshine Alley
Hare Lane
Rose Cottage
Rabbit Lane
German Tambour
Green Trench
Wicket Corner
Station
Fricourt Trench
Rose Alley
Cooper Trench
Rose Trench
Wing Corner
Cemetery
Thorn Lane
Papen Trench
Orchard Alley
Rectangle Sup.
The Rectangle

50th Brigade.
17th Division.

1/7th BATTALION

THE YORKSHIRE REGIMENT

AUGUST 1 9 1 6

10.Y.
7th Yorks.

Vol 11

7th YORKSHIRE Regt

August 1916.

Army Form C. 2118

Instructions regarding War Diaries and Intelligence Summaries are contained in F. S. Regs., Part II. and the Staff Manual respectively. Title Pages will be prepared in manuscript.

WAR DIARY

or

~~INTELLIGENCE SUMMARY~~

(Erase heading not required.)

7/YORKSHIRE REGT.

Place	Date	Hour	7th (S) Battn. Yorkshire Regt. Summary of Events and Information	Remarks and references to Appendices
near BERNANCOURT	1/8/16		Battn. continued training	
"	2/8/16	6.15 AM	Battn. marched with the remainder of the Bgd. to BELLEVUE Farm + bivouacked. Draft 1 Cpl + 42 men posted as follows A Coy 6: B. Coy 10; C Coy 11: D. Coy 16	
BELLEVUE FARM	3/8/16.		Practice attack by Battn. on trenches near BECOURT WOOD. Draft of 1 Officer and 115 O.R. posted as follows Capt S.B. KAY to command "C" Coy. "A" Coy. 29: "B" Coy 29: "C" Coy 29: "D" Coy 28	
"	4/8/16		Draft 1 Cpl posted to "B" Coy. Capt KAY transfd. to "B" Coy. to replace Lt. H.K.C HARE evacuated sick.	
"	"	8. PM	Battn. moved to "POMMIERS REDOUBT" between MONTAUBAN and MAMETZ + went into Divisional Reserve. Front line LONGUEVAL + DELVILLE WOOD held by 2 Battns. of 51st + 52nd Bgds. with 2 Battns. of each of these Bgds in Support. The Bgd. depot formed near BELLEVUE FARM. Transport + 8 Officers remained there.	
POMMIERS REDOUBT	5/8/16 to 9/8/16.		Uneventful. Training continued. Draft 6/8/16 1 Cpl posted to A Coy	
	9/8/16.		Relieved West Yorkshire Regt in old German ~~front~~ 2nd line between DELVILLE WOOD and HIGH WOOD.	

1875 Wt. W593/826 1,000,000 4/15 J.B.C. & A. A.D.S.S./Forms/C. 2118.

Instructions regarding War Diaries and Intelligence Summaries are contained in F. S. Regs., Part II. and the Staff Manual respectively. Title Pages will be prepared in manuscript.

WAR DIARY
or
~~INTELLIGENCE SUMMARY~~
(Erase heading not required.)

Army Form C. 2118

7th (S) Batt. Yorkshire Regt.

Place	Date	Hour	Summary of Events and Information	Remarks and references to Appendices
	10/8/16		Working party of 300 digging communication trench	
	11/8/16		Continued digging and consolidating. Draft 92 OR. posted as follows:- 26 to A Coy, 26 to B Coy, 20 to C Coy, 20 to D Coy. Lt. G.W. NELSON posted to "D" Coy.	
	12/8/16		Relieved by 7th Batt. Rifle Brigade at 6 A.M. Battn. returned to BELLEVUE FARM Camp. Casualties from 4/8/ to 12/8/16 6 Killed + 11 wounded.	
BELLEVUE FARM.	13/8/16	6 AM.	Marched back to old camp near DERNANCOURT.	
DERNAN-COURT	14/8/16		Training	
"	15/8/16	2 AM	Entrained at MERICOURT Station. Transport by road. Arrived at CANDAS and marched to HEUZECOURT arriving 1 PM.	
HEUZECOURT	16/8/16	2-30PM	Marched to BONNIERES arriving 7-30 PM.	
BONNIERES	17/8/16	9 AM	Marched with Brigade to DOULLENS arriving 1.30 PM.	
DOULLENS	18/8/16	3.AM.	Marched to BAYENCOURT arriving 8.30 AM.	

1875 Wt. W593/826 1,000,000 4/15 J.B.C. & A. A.D.S.S./Forms/C. 2118.

Army Form C. 2118

WAR DIARY
or
~~INTELLIGENCE~~ SUMMARY
(Erase heading not required.)

Instructions regarding War Diaries and Intelligence Summaries are contained in F. S. Regs., Part II. and the Staff Manual respectively. Title Pages will be prepared in manuscript.

Place	Date	Hour	7th S. Batt. Yorkshire Regt. — Summary of Events and Information	Remarks and references to Appendices
BAYENCOURT	18/8/16		The C.O. and Coy Commanders inspected the trenches in front of HÉBUTERNE and made arrangements for relieving 1st Batt. 13th London Regt. tomorrow. The Coy Commanders stayed the night in the trenches.	
"	19/8/16	4PM	Relieved the 1st Kensington Batt. 13th London Regiment at HEBUTERNE. Relief completed 4P.M. Trenches very good but require revetting, draining &c before the winter.	
Trenches HEBUTERNE	20/8/16		Usual trench routine. Very quiet by day + night. A few shells into the village during the day + a certain amount of machine gun fire at night. Working parties by day improving trenches and by night wiring in front of advanced posts support + front lines	
"	21/8/16		Two machine gun emplacements located + a few of the enemy seen behind their lines. Enemy working parties active at night + an enemy patrol seen. Aeroplanes crossing enemy lines were greeted with heavy M. Gun fire. 2nd Lt. H.R. WATT very slightly wounded. 2 men wounded, one of these died 24th. Usual working parties in the trenches and wiring carried on at night. Quiet night.	
"	22/8/16		Enemy appear to be doing a considerable amount of work on his trenches. Our trenches received rather more attention than usual from enemy artillery. No damage done. Repairing + improving trenches. Some deep dugouts have been begun. There is, at present, very little accomodation for the men in the sector occupied by the Battn.	
"	23/8/16		An enemy working party shelled. The Germans are doing a good deal of work on their wire + front trenches at night. Less enemy M. Gun fire than usual. Our snipers claim one hit. A few trench mortar shells fired at our	

1875 Wt. W593/826 1,000,000 4/15 J.B.C. & A. A.D.S.S./Forms/C. 2118.

Instructions regarding War Diaries and Intelligence Summaries are contained in F. S. Regs., Part II. and the Staff Manual respectively. Title Pages will be prepared in manuscript.

WAR DIARY
or
~~INTELLIGENCE SUMMARY~~
(Erase heading not required.)

Army Form C. 2118

7th (S) Batt. Yorkshire Regt

Place	Date	Hour	Summary of Events and Information	Remarks and references to Appendices
Trenches. HEBUTERNE	23/8/16		unoccupied front line during the day. A few whizzbangs fell in HEBUTERNE ~~last~~ at night without doing any damage. An enemy patrol retired on seeing one of ours.	
"	24/8/16		A few ·77mm + 4·2" shells fell ~~during~~ the day + did no damage whatever. Work continues on enemy trenches but less movement of the enemy was seen behind their lines. Work continued on our trenches under RE supervision. A machine gun post formerly held only at night is in future to be occupied by day as well. Work begun on making approach to this post passable by day.	
"	25/8/16		Our support was again shelled this morning. No damage. A good deal of movement seen behind enemy's front line + he appears to be doing a lot of work on his trenches.	
"	"	3·30PM	The Battn was relieved by 7th East York Regt ~~6th Batt Dorset Regt~~ + went into Bgde Reserve at SAILLY AU BOIS. A platoon, made up from men from each Coy remained in The Keep, HEBUTERNE to be used for the construction of deep dug outs. This platoon will be detached from the Battn except when the Battn is in Divnl Reserve. Offrs + Men are accomodated in billets + cellars in the village of SAILLY-AU-BOIS	
SAILLY-AU-BOIS	26/8/16		About ½ the Battn is employed during the day on working parties + the remainder by night	

1875 Wt. W593/826 1,000,000 4/15 J.B.C. & A. A.D.S.S./Forms/C. 2118.

Army Form C. 2118

Instructions regarding War Diaries and Intelligence Summaries are contained in F. S. Regs., Part II. and the Staff Manual respectively. Title Pages will be prepared in manuscript.

WAR DIARY
or
~~INTELLIGENCE SUMMARY~~
(Erase heading not required.)

7th (S) Battn Yorkshire Regt.

Place	Date	Hour	Summary of Events and Information	Remarks and references to Appendices
SAILLY-AU-BOIS	27.8.16 to 30.8.16		The whole Battn employed on working parties in the trenches under RE supervision. C.O. went on leave 29/8/16	
			Draft of 2 Officers :- 2nd Lt. D.M. ROBERTSON posted to A. Coy: 2nd Lt. G.H. MURPHY posted to B Coy. 29.8.16.	
"	31.8.16		Relieved 7th East Yorkshire Regt in the trenches at HEBUTERNE. Relief completed at 7.25 P.M	

1875 Wt. W593/826 1,000,000 4/15 J.B.C. & A. A.D.S.S./Forms/C. 2118.

Confidential

Vol 12

50/17 11.Y. 7 sheets

7th Yorks Regt

Sept 1916.

Instructions regarding War Diaries and Intelligence Summaries are contained in F. S. Regs., Part II. and the Staff Manual respectively. Title Pages will be prepared in manuscript.

WAR DIARY
or
~~INTELLIGENCE SUMMARY~~

(Erase heading not required.)

Army Form C. 2118.

Place	Date	Hour	Summary of Events and Information — 7th (S) Battn Yorkshire Regt	Remarks and references to Appendices
Trenches. HEBUTERNE	1/9/16.		Quiet night. Two heavy trench mortars were located & shelled. Patrols encountered none of the enemy. Usual trench routine. A great deal of work is being carried on re-claiming trenches, draining & making deep dug outs &c. Hostile artillery inactive.	Trench Map France. Sheet 57D N.E. Edition 2. C. 1/20,000.
	2/9/16. to 3/9/16.		Quiet in the trenches. A few shells fell in HEBUTERNE on 2/9/16 during the afternoon 3 of these left a strong smell of sulphur for over 12 hours in the craters formed. At night machine gun fired directed on our front line 2 or 3 times during the night 2nd–3rd. Enemy working parties are seen every day chiefly on their rear lines and behind the trenches. Our patrols have seen no movements of the enemy outside ~~their~~ his trenches	Trench Map HEBUTERNE attached.
	4/9/16.		Usual trench routine & working parties, 2 men wounded in the afternoon by shell fire	
		8.30 P.M.	A discharge of gas on our right by 99th Infantry Bgde from K23.a.5.7. to K17.a.5.2 had little or no effect on the enemy on our front. Our artillery fired for 3/4 hour ~~[illegible]~~ The reply by the enemy was slow & mainly directed ~~[illegible]~~ on our trenches between the front & support lines.	
	5/9/16.		Lt. Col Fife returned from leave & took over the command of the Battn.	
		8.30 PM	The brigade on ~~[illegible]~~ the left (62nd Brigade) discharged gas. The wind carrying the gas accross our front but not over the trenches held by the Battn. Our artillery supported & fired on enemy support & communication trenches. The enemy replied in a half hearted manner on our front line and old disused trenches further forward. No damage done & no casualties. All quiet before 10 P.M. ~~The Gas was discharged by 52nd Bgde on our left~~.	

2449 Wt. W14957/M90 750,000 1/16 J.B.C. & A. Forms/C.2118/12.

Instructions regarding War Diaries and Intelligence Summaries are contained in F. S. Regs., Part II. and the Staff Manual respectively. Title Pages will be prepared in manuscript.

WAR DIARY
or
INTELLIGENCE SUMMARY
(Erase heading not required.)

Army Form C. 2118.

Place	Date	Hour	Summary of Events and Information	Remarks and references to Appendices
Trenches HEBUTERNE	6/9/16.		The Battⁿ was relieved by 7th E. Yorkshire Regt. Relief completed by 7.30 P.M. Battⁿ marched to BAYENCOURT + went into billets. The Battⁿ is now in Divisional Reserve. During the tour of the trenches 2 men were wounded by a shell whilst carrying up tea to the Right front Coy.	
BAYENCOURT.	7/9/16.		~~Battⁿ~~ Usual routine on coming out of the trenches, baths, Kit inspections &c. "C" Coy moved to huts close to the village.	
"	8/9/16.		G.O.C. 17th Division inspected the Battⁿ by platoons in their billets.	
"	9th + 10th		Battⁿ employed at night removing gas cylinders from the trenches.	
"	10/9/		Regimental Canteen opened. Three men wounded by bomb accident at Bgde bombing school.	
"	11/9/16.		A new rifle range completed + used by the Battⁿ at J. 10. a. 0. 6.	
"	8/9/16 to 11/9/16.		Usual Battⁿ training under Coy. arrangements. Route marches, platoon + Coy drill, physical training, rifle exercises, instruction in making barbed wire entanglements &c. Signallers, bombers, + Lewis gunners under their respective commanders.	
"	11/9/16.	noon	Battⁿ becomes Bgd. Reserve + not Divisional Reserve.	

2449 Wt. W14957/M90 750,000 1/16 J.B.C. & A. Forms/C.2118/12.

Instructions regarding War Diaries and Intelligence Summaries are contained in F. S. Regs., Part II. and the Staff Manual respectively. Title Pages will be prepared in manuscript.

WAR DIARY
or
INTELLIGENCE SUMMARY
(Erase heading not required.)

Army Form C. 2118.

Place	Date	Hour	Summary of Events and Information	Remarks and references to Appendices
HEBUTERNE	12/9/16	Afternoon	Battn. relieved 7/E. York Regt. in front of HEBUTERNE. Quiet relief.	
"	12–16 9/16		Work in trenches consisted of preparation of old trenches used on July 1st for use again as assembly trenches, in preparation for forthcoming attack. The new work was not seriously hindered by shell or trench mortar fire though German artillery showed increasing activity in reply to our concentration of guns. Casualties 1 killed and 6 wounded. Patrols which went out each night found enemy very unenterprising.	
SAILLY-AU-BOIS	16/9/16		Relieved by 7/Lincoln Regt., 51st Bde, and marched to Sailly au Bois.	
HALLOY.	17/9/16		Marched to Halloy, taking over a camp of canvas huts which afforded little shelter from two days' heavy rain which fell.	
"	17–20 9/16		At Halloy training carried out as far as possible. C.O. & Coy cmdrs. visited trenches modelled on enemy trenches S of Gommecourt.	
	21/9/16		All plans changed; division going into 3rd Army Training area. Marched	
OCCOCHES.			to OCCOCHES	
MAIZICOURT	22/9/16		Marched to MAIZICOURT. Col. Fife in command of Bde; Major R.E. Cotton commanding Bn.	
DRUCAT	23/9/16		" " DRUCAT, 3 miles N of ABBEVILLE, and billeted there, together with Bde Hq.	
	24/9/16		Began training of all kinds. Weather very favourable.	
	25–end of month		Training continued. Bn attended lecture on bayonet fighting by Major	

2449 Wt. W14957/M90 750,000 1/16 J.B.C. & A. Forms/C.2118/12.

Campbell, 3rd Army instructor. Gen Allenby, G.O.C. 3rd Army,

Instructions regarding War Diaries and Intelligence Summaries are contained in F. S. Regs., Part II. and the Staff Manual respectively. Title Pages will be prepared in manuscript.

WAR DIARY
or
INTELLIGENCE SUMMARY
(Erase heading not required.)

Army Form C. 2118.

Place	Date	Hour	Summary of Events and Information	Remarks and references to Appendices
DRUCAT	28/7/16		visited Bn. during training hours.	
"	29/30 9/16.		Training continued under Coy commanders. Bombers, signallers + Lewis Gun detatchments under their respective commanders. Ration strength. 36 Officers 805 other ranks. On 14th a draft of 127 men joined the Battn + the following day 9 O.R.	

2449 Wt. W14957/M90 750,000 1/16 J.B.C. & A. Forms/C.2118/12.

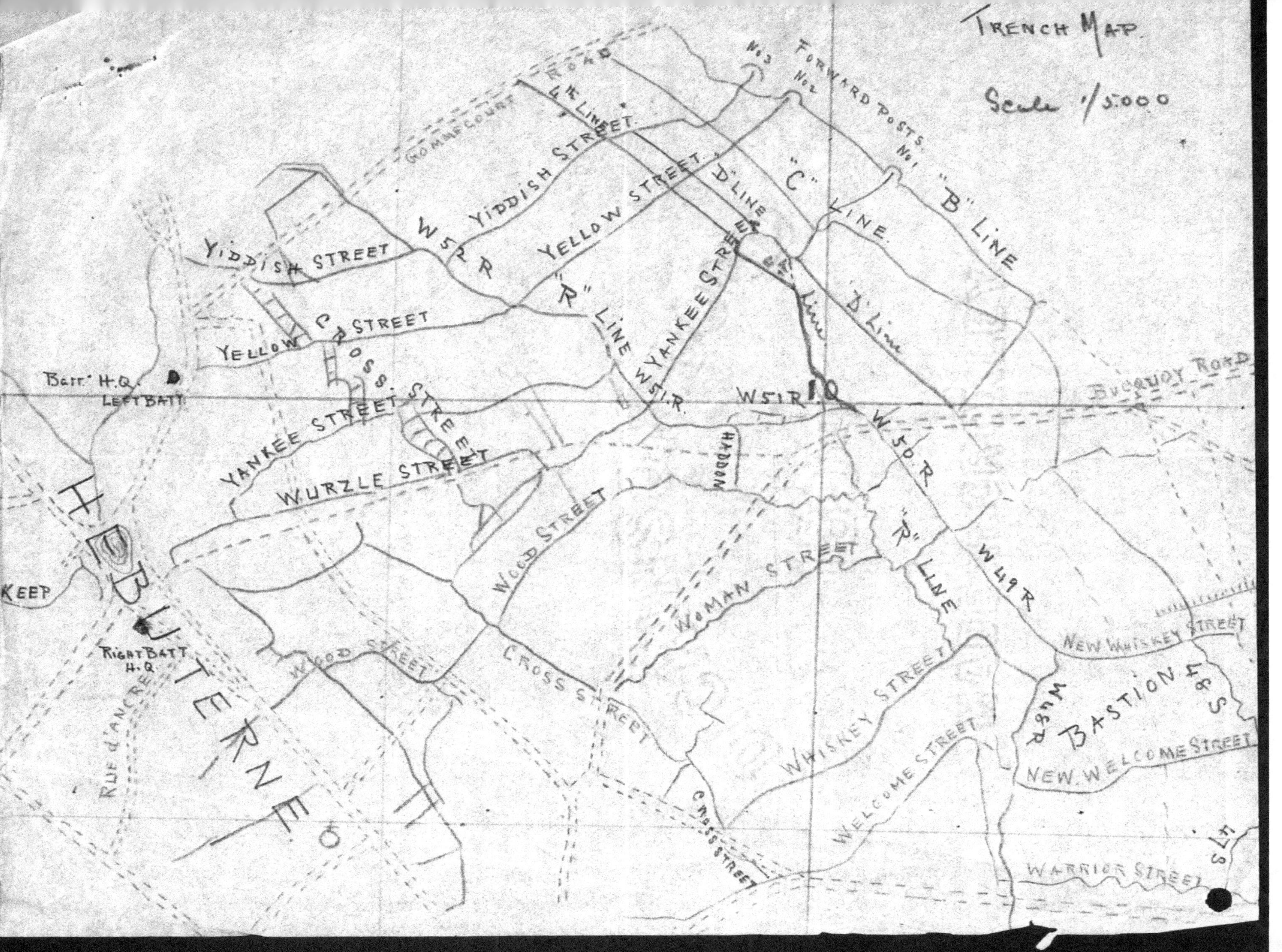
TRENCH MAP
Scale 1/5000
FORWARD POSTS
No 3
No 2
No 1
"B" LINE
"C" LINE
"D" LINE
'D' Line
4th LINE
ROAD
GOMMECOURT
YIDDISH STREET
YELLOW STREET
W52R
"R" LINE
YANKEE STREET
W51R
W51R
W50R
W49R
W48R
HADDON
YIDDISH STREET
YELLOW STREET
CROSS STREET
YANKEE STREET
WURZLE STREET
WOOD STREET
WOMAN STREET
"R" LINE
BUCQUOY ROAD
NEW WHISKEY STREET
BASTION 48 S
NEW WELCOME STREET
WHISKEY STREET
WELCOME STREET
CROSS STREET
CROSS STREET
WOOD STREET
WARRIOR STREET
47 S
Batt. H.Q.
LEFT BATT.
KEEP
HEBUTERNE
RIGHT BATT H.Q.
RUE d'ANCRE

50/17 12.4.

WAR DIARY

OF

7TH YORK REGT

FOR

OCTOBER 1916.

Army Form C. 2118.

Instructions regarding War Diaries and Intelligence Summaries are contained in F. S. Regs., Part II. and the Staff Manual respectively. Title Pages will be prepared in manuscript.

WAR DIARY
or
~~INTELLIGENCE SUMMARY~~
(Erase heading not required.)

Place	Date	Hour	7th (S) Batt. Yorkshire Regt. Summary of Events and Information	Remarks and references to Appendices
DRUCAT. 1/10/16 ~~1/9/16~~ to 4/10/16.			Training continued under Coy Commanders. Special instruction in bayonet fighting. Two more Lewis Guns allotted to Battn making 2 per Coy + 2 Battn Guns.	
~~5/9/16~~ DRUCAT.	5/10/16.		Battn training under Commanding Officer.	
"	6/10/16	9.45AM	Marched to MAISON-PONTHIEU arrived 1.45PM. Went into billets	
MAISON-PONTHIEU	7/10/16	8.15AM	Marched to BARLY arrived 1PM. Went into billets	
BARLY	8/10/16 to 10/10/16	8.30AM	Battn parade 9/9/16. Marched to HALLOY, arrived 1PM. Went into billets, 1 Coy in huts.	
HALLOY	11/10/16.	8.40AM	Marched to SOUASTRE, arrived 1PM Went into billets	
SOUASTRE	12/10/16.		Coy parades in the morning. Battn parade in afternoon, practice attack on trenches.	
	13/10/16.		Training under Coy commanders. Practice in making wire entanglements &c	

2449 Wt. W14957/M90 750,000 1/16 J.B.C. & A. Forms/C.2118/12.

Army Form C. 2118.

Instructions regarding War Diaries and Intelligence Summaries are contained in F. S. Regs., Part II. and the Staff Manual respectively. Title Pages will be prepared in manuscript.

WAR DIARY
or
~~INTELLIGENCE SUMMARY~~

(Erase heading not required.)

Place	Date	Hour	7th (S) Battn Yorkshire Regt. Summary of Events and Information	Remarks and references to Appendices
SOUASTRE	14/10/16		Battn moved to SAILLY-AU-BOIS and went into bivouacks.	
SAILLY-AU-BOIS	14/10/16 to 17/10/16		Battn employed on work under RE, laying water pipes, carrying parties &c. in preparation for expected advance on German position in front of HEBUTERNE.	
"	17/10/16	1.45 PM	Battn less 2 Coys took over trenches, in the afternoon, from 5th Battn Cameronians in HEBUTERNE. The remaining 2 Companies remain in SAILLY-AU-BOIS in billets. under MAJOR R.E. COTTON.	
Trenches HEBUTERNE	18/10/16.		Battn less 2 Coys relieved by 5th Batt. Gloucestershire Regt + returned to SAILLY-AU-BOIS + joined the rest of the Battn in billets. No casualties. In the intended attack the 50th Bgde were allotted about 500 yds of front 10th W. Yorkshire on Right, 6th Dorset Regt on left were to have assaulted in 4 lines. 7th Battn Yorkshire Regt in support in the trenches with 7th E. Yorkshire Regt in Bgde Reserve. This attack was subsequently cancelled.	
SAILLY-AU-BOIS	19/10/16.		Battn marched to HALLOY arriving about 4.30 P.M. + went into billets	
HALLOY	20/10/16.		Battn marched with Bgde to TALMAS. arriving 2.30 PM. + went into billets	

2449 Wt. W14957/M90 750,000 1/16 J.B.C. & A. Forms/C.2118/12.

Army Form C. 2118.

Instructions regarding War Diaries and Intelligence Summaries are contained in F. S. Regs., Part II. and the Staff Manual respectively. Title Pages will be prepared in manuscript.

WAR DIARY
or
~~INTELLIGENCE SUMMARY~~
(Erase heading not required.)

Place	Date	Hour	Summary of Events and Information — 7th (S) Batt. Yorkshire Regt	Remarks and references to Appendices
TALMAS	21/10/16		50th Bgde Group marched to LAHOUSSOYE. Arriving about 2.30 PM. Batt. went into billets.	
LAHOUSSOYE	22/10/16		Bgde marched to MEAULTE arriving 2.30 PM. Batt. in billets.	
MEAULTE	23/10/16.		Batt. resting	
MEAULTE	24/10/16 to 26/10/16.		} Batt. continued training	
"	27/10/16	6.40 AM	Brigade Group marched to MANSEL CAMP (F.11.d) The Batt. accomodated in tents.	MAP 62 D. N.E.
MANSEL CAMP	28/10/16		Fatigue parties collecting timber from old German trenches and improving camp, making chalk paths &c. A German bomb thrower + large wooden trench mortar salvaged by the Batt. + sent to Ordnance to be re-claimed for Batt. after the war.	
MANSEL CAMP	29/10/16		Improving the camp + collecting timber. Heavy rain.	

2449 Wt. W14957/M90 750,000 1/16 J.B.C. & A. Forms/C.2118/12.

Instructions regarding War Diaries and Intelligence Summaries are contained in F. S. Regs., Part II. and the Staff Manual respectively. Title Pages will be prepared in manuscript.

WAR DIARY
or
~~INTELLIGENCE SUMMARY~~
(Erase heading not required.)

Army Form C. 2118

Place	Date	Hour	7th (S) Battn Yorkshire Regt. Summary of Events and Information	Remarks and references to Appendices
MANSEL CAMP.	30/10/16		Coy Commanders reconnoitring ground + roads in direction of LONGUEVAL	
MANSEL CAMP	31/10/16	8.30AM	Battn moved to "B" Camp situated about point S.23.d 4.4 between BURNAFAY WOOD + TRÔNES WOOD + went into bivouacks. The weather continued unsettled and the transport was, in consequence, difficult to move Ration strength 30 Officers 728 O.R	MAP Sheet 57c S.W Edition 4 A

marsh

13.4.

17 sheets

Vol 14

7th Yorkshire R.

Nov 16

HEADQUARTERS
17th DIVISION.

No. A/104.

Date

D. A. G.

B A S E.

Will you please attach the enclosed Operation Order to the War Diary of the 7th Yorkshire Regiment, which was forwarded to you on 5/12/16 under My No. A/104.

for Brigadier-General.

8/12/16. Commanding 17th Division.

RECEIVED:

A. H. Wilkie Capt

9.12.16.

FOR D.A.G.,
G.H.Q., 3RD ECHELON.

Instructions regarding War Diaries and Intelligence Summaries are contained in F. S. Regs., Part II. and the Staff Manual respectively. Title Pages will be prepared in manuscript.

WAR DIARY
or
~~INTELLIGENCE SUMMARY~~

(Erase heading not required.)

Army Form C. 2118

Place	Date	Hour	7th (S) Batt. Yorkshire Regt. Summary of Events and Information	Remarks and references to Appendices
'B' Camp S23.d.4.4	1/11/16		Preparations for taking over front line trenches between GUEUDECOURT and LESBŒUFS. Reconnoitring parties from all 4 Coys went up to Battn. headquarters of 6th Batt. Dorsetshire Regt at N34c1.9, 500 yds NW of LESBOEUFS.	Map Sheet 57c S.W. Edition 4.A
"	2/11/16.	5PM	Battn. less 1 Coy ('D') relieved 6th Batt Dorsetshire Regt in the front line trenches. 1 Coy. (A) in front line, 2 Coys (B+C) in support. 'D' Coy remaining in 'B' Camp at Battn. reserve. Trench strength 16 Officers 366 OR. A sapping platoon of 1 Officer + 51 OR remained out of the trenches to make mine dugouts. 2 Officers + 50 O.R moved to 'A' Camp close to 'B' Camp + formed a carrying party for R.E. stores &c. The state of the ground after the recent wet weather makes all transport extremely difficult. Rations, water, &c have to be carried on pack animals. 50th Bgd. depot camp formed on MONTAUBAN - CARNOY Road where all officers + men left out of the trenches or not otherwise employed remain while Battn. is in the line. Relief completed at 2.45 am, 3/11/16.	
N34c1.9	3/11/16		Battalion holding ZENITH + SPRING trenches in N28d, with 7/Lincoln on left in ZENITH, and 7/E. YORK on right - A Coy; B Coy in Spectrum + Shin Alley C Coy in Shin Alley. HQ with that of 7/E. York in the Sunken Rd N34c1.9. Shelling normal + promiscuous during morning, largely round the Sunken Road. Bombardment became intense by 2pm, and about	Maps A + B. attached

1875 Wt. W593/826 1,000,000 4/15 J.B.C. & A. A.D.S.S./Forms/C. 2118.

WAR DIARY

or

~~INTELLIGENCE SUMMARY~~

(Erase heading not required.)

Army Form C. 2118

Instructions regarding War Diaries and Intelligence Summaries are contained in F. S. Regs., Part II. and the Staff Manual respectively. Title Pages will be prepared in manuscript.

Place	Date	Hour	7th (S) Battn Yorkshire Regt. Summary of Events and Information	Remarks and references to Appendices
N34c1.9	3/11/16		4 pm A Coy reported having seen 4 lines of enemy advancing against battalion on left. He thought first line had got in, but had helped to wipe out the other three by rifle + Lewis gun fire. Shortly afterwards the 7/Lincolns delivered an attack against 80 yds of ZENITH still held by enemy. 2/Lt H.R. WATT, Battalion Bombing Officer, and a few York. bombers took part in this attack, which was quite successful, + resulted in the capture of some forty prisoners. 2/Lt. WATT slightly wounded in cheek by German bomb. During night B Coy relieved a Coy. of 7/Lincoln on left of A Coy in ZENITH + SPRING, with 2 platoons in SPRING + 1 in ZENITH (B Coy only 3 platoons at this time). D Coy. came up at night from Trones Wood camp, relieving B., with 1 platoon in SPECTRUM and 3 in ROSE trench, between Bn Hq and GUEUDECOURT.	
"	4/11/16		No change in dispositions. Enemy very nervous during day, putting down heavy barrages on ZENITH and on ground behind. Orders received at night for an attack by a "battle patrol" of 40 men to be made following morning on FINCH trench, N29c, in conjunction with ~~heavy~~ 7/E. York on right; attacks on a large scale being made further to the right + left. Crump-holes between lines were to be cleared of enemy snipers during night. Two officers' patrols of B Coy investigated the crump-holes, but found them unoccupied.	

1875 Wt. W593/826 1,000,000 4/15 J.B.C. & A. A.D.S.S./Forms/C. 2118.

Instructions regarding War Diaries and Intelligence Summaries are contained in F. S. Regs., Part II. and the Staff Manual respectively. Title Pages will be prepared in manuscript.

WAR DIARY

or

~~INTELLIGENCE SUMMARY~~

(Erase heading not required.)

Army Form C. 2118

Place	Date	Hour	7th (S) Batt Yorkshire Regt — Summary of Events and Information	Remarks and references to Appendices
N34c1·9	5/11/16	11·10am	A Coy's battle patrol attacked in two lines. Enemy were seen in force running from their trench, but, seeing how small our assaulting party was, they halted and opened fire on them. CAPT. L.W. GOLDSMITH was severely wounded (& died later in the day), and 2/Lt S.J. HOUSE was also hit. With both officers knocked out the attack did not reach the objective, or the few men who did reach it fell into the hands of greatly superior numbers of the enemy. D Coy sent up 2 platoons at dusk either to occupy ZENITH if the morning attack had succeeded, or to repeat the attempt if it had failed. It was finally ascertained about 5.45 pm that the objective was not in our hands. D Coy's	Bde & Batt Orders attached.
		10 pm	2 platoons attacked at 10 pm, crawling forward from ZENITH. They were soon detected by the enemy and rifle fire was opened on them. 2/Lt A.C. GOODALL was killed, and Lt. H.P. GREGORY wounded. The attack did not attain its objective. Orders were received at 9.50 pm that the attack was not to take place unless the trench on our right was in the hands of 7/E. York, who had attacked in the morning. It was then too late to stop the attack which came under fire chiefly from its right flank. During the day 2/Lt C.J. EYRE had been wounded by a bullet in the hand, and during the shelling of our trenches CAPT. S.B. KAY was wounded and 2/Lt R.T. RUDGE killed, B Coy being thus left with	

1875 Wt. W593/826 1,000,000 4/15 J.B.C. & A. A.D.S.S./Forms/C. 2118.

Instructions regarding War Diaries and Intelligence Summaries are contained in F. S. Regs., Part II. and the Staff Manual respectively. Title Pages will be prepared in manuscript.

WAR DIARY
or
~~INTELLIGENCE SUMMARY~~
(Erase heading not required.)

Army Form C. 2118

Place	Date	Hour	7th (S) Battn Yorkshire Regt — Summary of Events and Information	Remarks and references to Appendices
N34c1.9	5/11/16		one officer, 2/Lt H. COLLINS. The remaining platoon of D Coy in ROSE Trench went up to SPECTRUM during the evening. C Coy was constantly engaged in carrying rations, ammunition, and bombs to the front line.	
"	6/11/16		The quietest day of the tour in the trenches. Battalion was relieved at night by 6/Dorset Regt. and returned to "F" camp near Montauban. Casualties: Officers. Killed 3. Wounded 5. Other Ranks. Killed 27. Wounded 70. Missing 10. The condition of the trenches, which in many places were from 3' to 4' deep in water and mud, and the lack of any shelter whatever caused much sickness in the nature of trench feet amongst the men.	
"	7/11/16	3.PM	Battn moved to "H" camp on the MONTAUBAN–CARNOY Road & went into huts. 2nd Lt Huffington took over the command of "B" Coy.	TRENCH MAP
"H" Camp	8/11/16 to 9/11/16		Battn resting. The Brigadier General informed the Battn that in spite of the attacks by A & D Coys on 5th not succeeding, the object of the higher command was attained which was to prevent the whole of the enemy artillery fire being concentrated on other parts of the front.	Sheet 57c S.W.
"	10/11/16	10 AM.	Battn marched to "C" Camp (S23.B) & halted for dinner.	Edition 4A.
"C" Camp	10/11/16	3.30PM	Battn moved from "C" camp and relieved the 6th Battn Dorsetshire Regt in the line, taking over the same trenches held on 2.11.16 with the exception that	Maps A & B attached

Instructions regarding War Diaries and Intelligence Summaries are contained in F. S. Regs., Part II. and the Staff Manual respectively. Title Pages will be prepared in manuscript.

WAR DIARY
or
~~INTELLIGENCE SUMMARY~~
(Erase heading not required.)

Army Form C. 2118

Place	Date	Hour	7th (S) Batt. Yorkshire Regt. Summary of Events and Information	Remarks and references to Appendices
Trenches N34c.1.9	10/11/16		one Coy held "Cow trench" in the support line instead of "~~Shin Alley~~ Rose Trench". Relief complete by 8 PM. Strength in trenches 336 all ranks. Major R.E. Cotton in command. The trenches were held as follows. A Coy 2 platoons in SHIN ALLEY, 2 platoons in GUSTY Trench. "B" Coy Cow Trench. "C" Coy + "D" Coy 2 platoons each in ZENITH + 2 platoons each in SPRING Trench.	
			One prisoner captured on night 10th–11th	
	11/11/16 to. 13/11/16		One prisoner captured on night 11th–12th. A great deal of digging was done by the Battn during it's tour in the trenches. New CTs dug + the front line trenches were kept fairly dry. The enemy snipers were easily dominated by our men and the enemy artillery, though active at times, did no very great damage + caused few casualties. The weather was fine.	
			On night 12th–13th D + B Coys were relieved by 3rd Batt. Coldstream Guards	
	14th/11/16		+ on the night of 13th–14th the remainder of the Battn was relieved by Irish Guards. D + B Coys on relief marched to "C" Camp + moved to MANSEL CAMP the following day. The remainder of the Batt, on relief, marched to "F" Camp near MONTAUBAN	
	14/11/16	5PM	Battn less 2 Coys marched to MANSEL CAMP F 11.D.	MAP 62D N.E
			The total casualties during the Battn's tour in the trenches amounted to OR. 6 Killed, 15 wounded, 1 missing. Very few cases of trench feet.	

Instructions regarding War Diaries and Intelligence Summaries are contained in F. S. Regs., Part II. and the Staff Manual respectively. Title Pages will be prepared in manuscript.

WAR DIARY

or

~~INTELLIGENCE SUMMARY~~

(Erase heading not required.)

Army Form C. 2118

Place	Date	Hour	7th (S) Battn Yorkshire Regt. Summary of Events and Information	Remarks and references to Appendices
MANSEL CAMP	15/11/16	8 AM.	Battn ~~marched~~ to MEAULTE + went into billets.	
"	16/11/16	8.45 AM	Battn entrained at EDGEHILL STATION + proceeded to HANGEST. + marched to MOLLIENS-VIDAMES + went into billets. Draft received 5 O.R.	
MOLLIENS-VIDAMES	17/11/16		Resting	
	18/11/16		Draft. 39 O.R	
"	19/11/16		Church parades. Construction of rifle range begun.	
"	20/11/16 to 30/11/16		Battn in training, under Coy commanders, ~~and~~ Lewis Gun + bombing Officers. Usual Platoon + Coy drill, musketry &c &c. Draft of 4 O R received on 20th + 1 Officer, Capt J. R. STONE, + 5 O R on 24th	
"	30/11/16		Ration strength 16 Officers 622 N.C.O's + men Battn effective strength 26 " 754 " "	

1875 Wt. W593/826 1,000,000 4/15 J.B.C. & A. A.D.S.S./Forms/C. 2118.

H/14.

7 E York
7 York
MG Company.
Ref. 00112

4·11·16

① Zero will be at 11-10 am tomorrow, November 5th.
② Flares will be lit at Zero + 2 hours and at 3 30pm
③ A watch is forwarded herewith to set watches by.
④ The attack will be preceded by a bombardment of Heavy Arty. - At Zero an intense barrage will be placed on the front of the Div. from N 35 a 3 3 to N29c1 8. This barrage will at once start creeping back at rate of 25 yds. a minute to the main LE TRANSLOY line - a standing barrage will be maintained on the CEMETRY CIRCLE and on the portions of trench in N 29 a & c. - A barrage will also be put on MOONRAY and SUNRAY.

Before Zero the Div. Arty. will search the area around ORION while a 6" battery will fire on the road junctions in N 35a and b.

Acknowledge.

Note. Battalions will inform STOKES under their orders.

(sgd) H. J. Simson, Captain,
Bde Maj. 50th Bde.

7 pm.

on the objectives.

6. OC 50th M.G. Company will get in touch with OC 7/8 York and 9/ York at once and will arrange drill for covering Machine Gun fire to keep down fire of enemy snipers and Machine Guns.

7. 4 Guns of 50th T.M. Battery move into the trenches tonight and 2 guns are at the disposal of each Battalion Commander.

8. Shell holes between our front line and the objectives will be cleared of enemy snipers and MG guns by patrol tonight.

9. Should these attacks fail by day, fresh attacks will be made at night.

10. The front trenches on the whole Brigade front will be cleared as far as possible before ZERO to avoid casualties from enemy barrage by distributing garrison more in depth.

11. The objectives when reached will be held as lightly as possible by day.

Every effort will be made during the night following the attack to link ORION to the piece of trench about N 29 c 3.0 (WINTER) and thence to the trench about N 29 c 0.5 SPRING connecting with ZENITH.

The 19th Brigade are arranging to connect up the SUNKEN road to the right of 7/8 York about N35a central.

12. Assaulting troops are to be warned that they may have difficulty in recognising the objectives as trenches on reaching them and should know before hand what distance they have to go.

13. Bde Hqrs will remain at S 24 b central.

Acknowledge. (sgd) H.J. Simson, Capt.
Bde Maj. 50th Bde.

Issued at 5.30 pm thro sigs.

to	7/8 York	10/W York	For information
	7/ York	6/ Dorset	
	MGCo	17/ Div	
	TMBy	19 Bde	
		Centre Group	

SECRET.

50th Infantry Brigade Operation Order. No. 112.

Ref. Trench map and Sheet 57C SW. 1/10000.

4-11-16

① The 7/E. York will attack and occupy ORION and the gun pits near it form their present front line with their left on SUNKEN ROAD about N35 a 1.9.

At the same time 7/York will attack the trench N35 a 3.9 to N29 C 1 1 to be known in future as WINTER shown on attached aeroplane photo (issued to O.C. 7/E York and 7/York only)

② These attacks are to be in the nature of battle patrols and are limited to 60 or 70 men in the case of 7/E York and 30 or 40 men in the case of 7/York.

③ Zero hour will be notified later.

④ On the right the 19th Bde will co-operate by bombing up SUNKEN ROAD at N35 b. 19 to N35 a 5.5 joining there with 7/E. York. There will be no attack on the immediate left, but attacks on a large scale will take place further on the right and left.

⑤ Artillery barrage has been fixed so as to make it safe for assaulting troops to leave our front line at ZERO and move straight

7 Yorkshire Regt 17 Appx 6 Vol

OPERATION ORDER 81

by

Lieut. Col. R. D' A. FIFE

Commdg. 7th Y O R K Regt.

---

1. Ref. Bde Operation Order No. 112, copy issued herewith.

2. THE SHELL HOLES between our front line and objective will be cleared tonight by bombing patrols furnished by O.C. "B" Coy., who will call upon O.C. "A" Coy for additional patrols if necessary.

The men of these patrols must be warned that only shell holes between our line and objective are to be cleared, and that no further advance is to be made by them tonight.

3. THE ATTACK will be carried out by a battle patrol of "A" Coy. with two bombing squads: total strength including bombers, 2 Officers, 40 O R.

4. ATTACK will be made in two lines - A bombing squad will be on each flank of the first line.

5. DIRECTION The advance will be by the right. An Officer and one N.C.O. will be responsible for direction and for obtaining touch with the left of EAST YORK after the objective is reached.

6. O.C. "A" and "B" Coys. will endeavour to cover the advance by means of Lewis and M.G. fire which should not be opened unless the enemy first open fire.

7. THE POSITION WILL BE CONSOLIDATED as quickly as possible after capture, for which purpose every man in the second line will carry a shovel.

8. AFTER CAPTURE The line may be thinned by withdrawing some of the assaulting troops whose place will then be taken by one or more Lewis Guns.

9. O.C. "A" Coy will call upon O.C. "B" Coy for bomb carriers to replace bombs used in theassault.

10. O.C. "A" Coy. will arrange the immediate despatch of progress reports to Battn. H.Q. by relays of Orderlies. All reports to be sent in duplicate. 8 Orderlies will be supplied by Battn. H.Q. for this purpose.

11. ACKNOWLEDGE.

(signed) L.V.C. Hawkes,

Lieut. Adjt.,
7th Yprk R.

ROSE
WINDY
THISTLE
SHINY ALLEY
3 3
3 4
WINDMILL LANE
COW TRENCH
N
TRENCH MAP
B

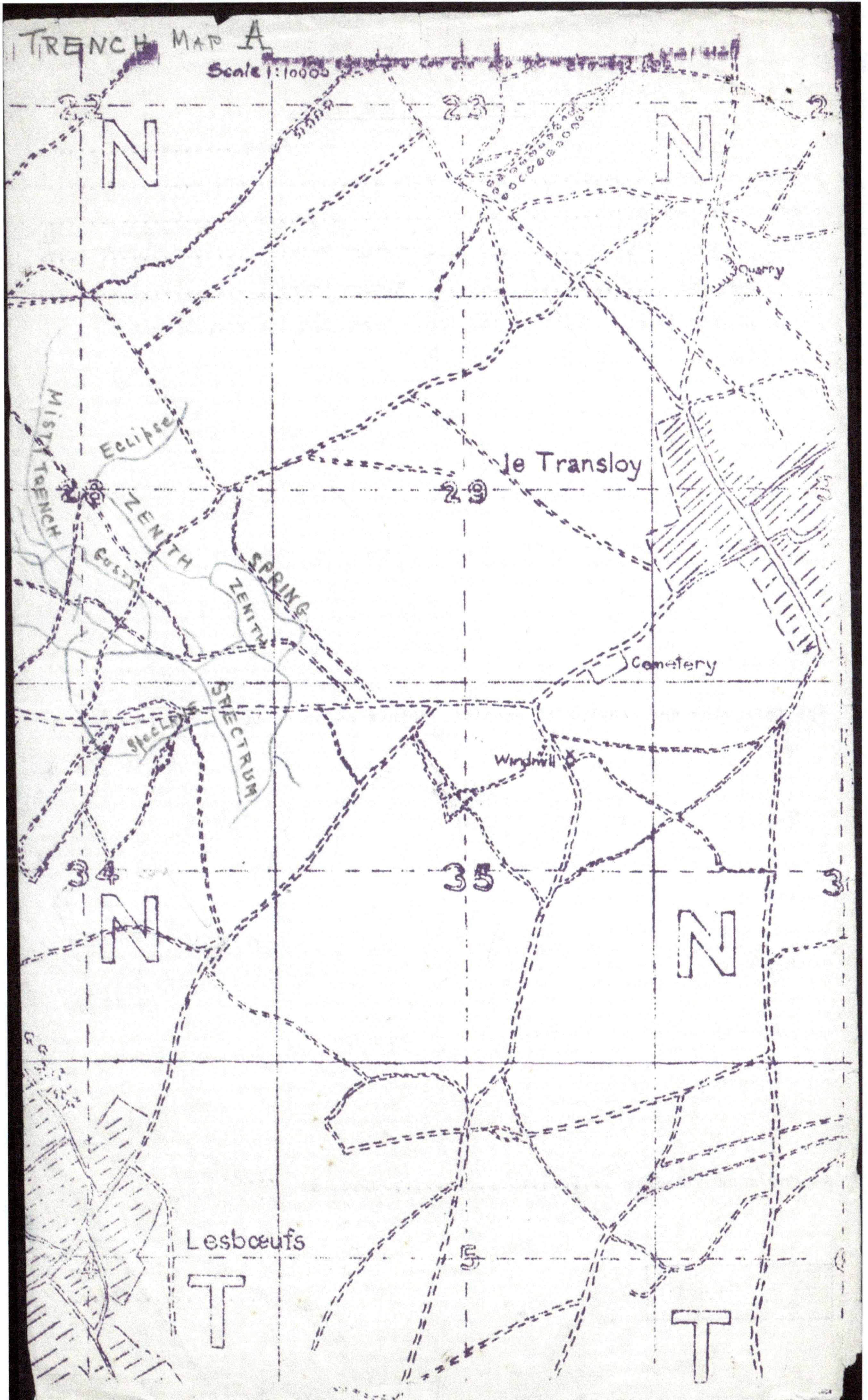
TRENCH MAP A
Scale 1:10000
N
N
le Transloy
Quarry
MISTY TRENCH
Eclipse
ZENITH
SPRING
ZENITH
Cemetery
SPECTRUM
Windmill
34
35
N
N
Lesbœufs
5
T
T

PATROL REPORT.

Date ....

Patrol Leader .... Coy. .... Bn. ....

Strength of patrol : ....

Departure point : .... Return Point: ....

Departure hour : .... Return hour: ....

The following is an account of the route taken and the work done :

The following are answers to specific points referred to in orders given me:

(a)

(b)

(c)

(d)

(e)

(f)

Report despatched by .... at ..... a.m.
..... p.m.

Draw a sketch on the reverse of this sheet.

Sgd....................

Confidential

Headquarters,
50 Brigade

I forward herewith War Diary from 1/7/16 to 30/11/16.
Please acknowledge receipt.

[signature] Major/Adjt
for Lieut: Col.
Commdg. 7th Yorkshire Regt.

1 DEC 1916

H.Q.
50th Brigade.

SERVICE BATTN. ... SHIRE REGT.
No. 1/3010
Date 3-1-17

7

Herewith War Diary
for December.
Please acknowledge receipt.

Ronald E. [illegible] Major
for O.C. 7th Yorks R.

3/1/17

Vol 15

14.Y.
3444 9 sheets
8B

WAR DIARY FOR
THE MONTH
OF
DECEMBER 1916
FOR
4TH YORKSHIRE REGIMENT

Instructions regarding War Diaries and Intelligence Summaries are contained in F. S. Regs., Part II. and the Staff Manual respectively. Title Pages will be prepared in manuscript.

WAR DIARY
or
~~INTELLIGENCE SUMMARY~~
(Erase heading not required.)

Army Form C. 2118

Place	Date	Hour	7th (S) Battn Yorkshire Regt — Summary of Events and Information	Remarks and references to Appendices
MOLLIENS-VIDAMES	1/12/16 to 8/12/16		Battn training continued under Coy commanders &c. Commanding Officer proceeded on leave to England on 3/12/16. Major RE GOTTON commanding during his absence. Drafts 1st Dec 8 OR. 3rd Dec 8 O.R	
	3/12/16		Brigadier Genl C. YATMAN D.S.O. took over the command of 50th Bgde from Bgd Genl W. GLASGOW	
	6/12/16		Genl YATMAN inspected the Battn	
	7/12/16		Transport inspected by G.O.C 50th Bgde.	
	9/12/16 to 10/12/16		Coys + specialists training under their respective Commanders. Draft 4 O.R. 10/12/16.	
	11/12/16		Battn parade practice Artillery formation &c. Draft 36 O.R	
	12/12/16 13/12/16		Coy training musketry &c.	
	14/12/16	6AM	Marched to HANGEST + entrained for MERICOURT arrived 1PM. EDGEHILL. Lt. Col R D'A. Fife C.M.G. returned from leave + took over command of the Battn. Brigade in Corps reserve	
MERICOURT L'ABBÉ	15/12/16		Coys continued training	

1875 Wt. W593/826 1,000,000 4/15 J.B.C. & A. A.D.S.S./Forms/C. 2118.

Map of trenches noted in margin will be forwarded in 2 or 3 days time. Unobtainable at present

Ronald E. Fulton.
Major.
7th Batt Yorkshire Regt
3/1/17.

Instructions regarding War Diaries and Intelligence Summaries are contained in F. S. Regs., Part II. and the Staff Manual respectively. Title Pages will be prepared in manuscript.

WAR DIARY
or
~~INTELLIGENCE SUMMARY~~

(Erase heading not required.)

Army Form C. 2118

7th (S) Battn Yorkshire Regt.

Place	Date	Hour	Summary of Events and Information	Remarks and references to Appendices
MERICOURT L'ABBÉ	16/12/16		Battn route march	
"	17/12/16		Church parades. Draft 2 Officer. 2nd Lts. F.R. MILX HOLLAND + J.B. CUTTS.	
"	18/12/16		Parades + ~~fatigue~~ working parties.	
"	19/12/16		Lecture to Officers at Div H.Q. Subject "Initiative"	
"	20/12/16		} Training continued under Coy arrangements.	
"	21/12/16		} Draft of 1 Officer 2nd Lt ROUSE and 122 OR joined the Battn on 20th	
"	22/12/16	10.50AM	Battn marched to VILLE + went into billets	
VILLE	23/12/16		Preparations for moving up to front trenches near LES BOEUFS	
"	24/12/16	11AM	Battn marched to No XXII CARNOY CAMP between CARNOY + MONTAUBAN + went into huts.	
CARNOY CAMP	25/12/16	2PM.	The Battn marched to GUILLEMONT CAMP Strength 14 Officers + 402 OR. the remainder joined the Bgde depôt camp No XXII. MAJOR R E COTTON in command of 50th Bgde Depôt camps. Battn in Divl Reserve	344d
GUILLEMONT	26/12/16		Battn marched to trenches near LES BOEUFS. Relieving 8th Battn ~~South~~ ~~Staffordshire~~ DORSETSHIRE Regt. Relief completed 8.50PM Distribution of Coys as follows Trench map A. Coy 3 platoons in ZENITH Trench 1 Platoon OZONE AVENUE. B Coy in	

1875 Wt. W593/826 1,000,000 4/15 J.B.C. & A. A.D.S.S./Forms/C. 2118.

Instructions regarding War Diaries and Intelligence Summaries are contained in F. S. Regs., Part II. and the Staff Manual respectively. Title Pages will be prepared in manuscript.

WAR DIARY
or
INTELLIGENCE SUMMARY
(Erase heading not required.)

Army Form C. 2118

7th (S) Batt Yorkshire Regt

Place	Date	Hour	Summary of Events and Information	Remarks and references to Appendices
			Summer Support and SUMMER Trench. C Coy in FALL Trench & AUTUMN Trench	
			D Coy in Support. 3 platoons in COW Trench, 1 platoon in THISTLE Trench, AUSTRALIAN Corps on left. 7th East Yorkshire Regt on Right.	
Trenches LES BOEUFS	27/12/16 28/12/16		During the Battn's tour in the trenches the 2 left Coys wired thinly the whole front, and worked hard at improving the trenches. The weather was wet most of the time with a hard frost on night of 27th. Rear Coy employed carrying water and R.E. stores.	
	28/12/16		The Battn was relieved by 8th S. Staffordshire Regt. Relief completed by 8 P.M. Casualties O.R. 2 Killed, 1 died of wounds, 8 wounded. 1 wounded & returned to duty. Battn returned to CARNOY Camp No XXII	
			Sgt. Orde "B" Coy wounded on a working party from Depôt camp. Draft of 4 OR. Details left out of the trenches supplied Divnl fatigues daily & drilled under Battn Instructors.	
CARNOY Camp XXII	29/12/16		Battn resting. Baths afternoon.	345d
"	30/12/16		ditto + ~~baths~~ ~~later working party of 250 laying pipe line~~	
"	31/12/16		~~near~~ Working party of 250 to GUINCHY. Battn moved to GUILLEMONT leaving 184 all ranks at camp XXII. CARNOY.	

1875 Wt. W593/826 1,000,000 4/15 J.B.C. & A. A.D.S.S./Forms/C. 2118.

Instructions regarding War Diaries and Intelligence Summaries are contained in F. S. Regs., Part II. and the Staff Manual respectively. Title Pages will be prepared in manuscript.

WAR DIARY
or
~~INTELLIGENCE SUMMARY~~
(Erase heading not required.)

Army Form C. 2118

7th (S) Battn Yorkshire Regt.

Place	Date	Hour	Summary of Events and Information	Remarks and references to Appendices
GUILLE-MONT.	31/12/16		Ration strength 18 Officers 739 O.R. Strength of Battn 27 " 948 " Lt H R Watt awarded Military Cross for distinguished conduct in the field 26/12/16. Military Medals awarded to Cpl. McGregor A. Pte Saunders F. R., Corpl Noble H. Corpl. Thorpe. W. Corpl Mitchell H. 26/12/16	

346d

1875 Wt. W593/826 1,000,000 4/15 J.B.C. & A. A.D.S.S./Forms/C. 2118.

For War Diary 7th Yorks Regt.

347d
213

N
W — E
German Line
German Line
German Line
3 5 a c b d
N
ZENITH
SPECTRUM Supp.
SUMMER Support.
OZONE AV.
AUTUMN Support.
FALL TRENCH
BENNETT TRENCH
Winter RESERVE
DEWDROP
RAINY Tr. RESERVE
SNOW RESERVE
FROSTY RESERVE
T
5 a b c d
3.4
Windy Tr
AVENUS
Windy
Thistle Trench
BURNABY
FOGGY
21ST
SHAMROCK
MID LANE
Batt H.Q.
CORPS BOUNDRY
LES BOEUFS
FLUFF
Brigade Boundry
Batt H.Q.
COW TRENCH
Scale 1/10,000.

15.Y.

WAR DIARY

FOR

JANUARY

OF

7TH YORKSHIRE

REGIMENT.

Vol 16

5.25 d

8B

1917

17/8

Instructions regarding War Diaries and Intelligence Summaries are contained in F. S. Regs., Part II. and the Staff Manual respectively. Title Pages will be prepared in manuscript.

WAR DIARY
or
~~INTELLIGENCE SUMMARY~~
(Erase heading not required.)

Army Form C. 2118.

Place	Date	Hour	7th (S) Battn. Yorkshire Regt. Summary of Events and Information	Remarks and references to Appendices
GUILLEMONT.	1/1/17		Battn. remained in ~~Div~~ Brigade Reserve. Training & cleaning the camp. Capt L. G. HARE awarded the Military Cross. & Lt Col R D'A Fife CMG & Capt. A.K.W. BARMBY mentioned in Despatches.	
"	2/1/17		Battn. relieved 12th Battn. Manchester Regt. Relief completed by 8.50 P.M. The disposition of the Divisional front changed. The Australian Corps having taken over the left Battn. front of the left Brigade group on the night of ~~3~~ 1st Jan the Yorkshire Regt took over "Lincoln" & "Bennett" trenches & become Right Battn. of Left Bgde Group. with 7th Lincolns on ~~the~~ right & 7th E. Yorkshire on ~~the~~ left. One Coy (A) in the front line. 2 half Coys of B & D Coys in support. "C" Coy in reserve. The remaining platoons of B & D Coys in a large dugout.	
Trenches near LES BOEUFS	3/1/17.		Weather continued wet. Impossible to go round the front line during daylight owing to the state of the C.Ts. Overland route of boards almost as far as the front line. Lt. A. James killed by a German sniper at 1.30 P.M. During the night working parties were wiring the Battn. front & improving the trenches generally.	
"	4/1/17		Battn. relieved by 8th Battn. South Staffordshire Regt. Relief completed 7.10 PM & the Battn. returned to CARNOY. Camp XXII. Casualties 1 Officer killed 1 man accidentally wounded.	526d
CARNOY Camp No XXII.	5/1/17		Battn. resting. Usual fatigues & working parties found by details that have not been in the trenches	

2449 Wt. W14957/M90 750,000 1/16 J.B.C. & A. Forms/C.2118/12.

Army Form C. 2118.

WAR DIARY
or
INTELLIGENCE SUMMARY
(Erase heading not required.)

Instructions regarding War Diaries and Intelligence Summaries are contained in F. S. Regs., Part II. and the Staff Manual respectively. Title Pages will be prepared in manuscript.

7th (S) Batt Yorkshire Regt.

Place	Date	Hour	Summary of Events and Information	Remarks and references to Appendices
Carnoy Camp 22	6/1/17		Parades under Coy arrangement + baths for the whole Battn. Draft 1 Officer 2nd Lt. V.W. PURCELL.	
"	7/1/17		Battn. moved back to GUILLEMONT + went into Bgde Reserve. 135 OR remaining in detail camp for training + furnishing Div. + Corps working parties. A C + D Coys in GUILLEMONT, B Coy in the FLERS line.	
GUILLEMONT	8/1/17	4 P.M.	The Battn was relieved by 7th Batt. Border Regt and marched to the front line trenches + took over ~~from~~ as follows: 2½ Coys relieved 9th Northumberland Fusls. 1½ Coys relieved 6th Dorset Regt. The Battn. disposed as follows:- front line "D" Coy in "MERCIER" Trench on the right, ½ Coy "C" "Lincoln" Trench, ½ C Coy Thunder Trench with A Coy in "Antelope" Trench (the last 2 trenches in the Support line). "B" Coy "Bovril" trench in Reserve. Relief completed 7.50 p.m.	Trench Map [illegible]
Trenches near LES BOEUFS	9/1/17		One prisoner belonging to 125th Regt was captured about 7.30 P.M. A hostile patrol approached MERCIER Trench + was dispersed. 3 of the enemy were killed. A draft of 3 Officers. 2/Lt Jolly, 2/Lt MAY and 2/Lt Bacon joined the Battn.	
"	10/1/17		The Battn improved the trenches and wiring parties were out in front on both nights. Relieved 8 PM by 8th S Staffordshire Regt. The Battn returned to CARNOY Camp. There were no casualties	

5272

Army Form C. 2118.

WAR DIARY

or

~~INTELLIGENCE SUMMARY~~

(Erase heading not required.)

Instructions regarding War Diaries and Intelligence Summaries are contained in F. S. Regs., Part II. and the Staff Manual respectively. Title Pages will be prepared in manuscript.

7th (S) Battn Yorkshire Regt

Place	Date	Hour	Summary of Events and Information	Remarks and references to Appendices
CARNOY Camp No 22.			Battn in Divn Reserve	
	11/1/17		Resting + cleaning up.	
	12/1/17			
"	13/1/17	11.30 AM	Battn marched to MEAULTE + went into billets	
MEAULTE	14/1/17	9.30 AM	" " " LA NEUVILLE + " " "	
LANEUVILLE	15/1/17		Resting	
"	16/1/17	11 AM	Battn moved to CORBIE and went into billets. The Divn in Corps Reserve	
CORBIE	17/1/17		MAJOR MAIRIS re-joined the Battn. Battn training begun under Coy arrangements. Specialists under their respective commanders.	
"	18/1/17 to 19/1/17		Training continued. Several men went to courses in Musketry, L Gun etc. H.Q. Coy formed under the Adjt. consisting of Battn Bombers, Signallers, Snipers, 2 Lewis Gun teams, orderlies, Orderly Room staff, H.Q. Servants, Police, Instructors, QM Stores + Transport.	
"	20/1/17		Battn parade under C.O. Exercising in artillery formation, extensions etc. Draft of 3 officers. 2/Lt DOWNS, 2/Lt THACKER, 2/Lt BLACK.	
"	21/1/17		Church parades	528d

2449 Wt. W14957/M90 750,000 1/16 J.B.C. & A. Forms/C.2118/12.

Instructions regarding War Diaries and Intelligence Summaries are contained in F. S. Regs., Part II. and the Staff Manual respectively. Title Pages will be prepared in manuscript.

Army Form C. 2118.

WAR DIARY
or
~~INTELLIGENCE SUMMARY~~
(Erase heading not required.)

Place	Date	Hour	7th (S) Batt Yorkshire Regt Summary of Events and Information	Remarks and references to Appendices
CORBIE.	22/1/17		Battn. inspected by the Brigadier Genl. + Royal Humane Society's certificate presented to B.S.M. ADOLFO for gallantry in attempting to save L/c pl HAMILTON from drowning at GONDE on 23 July /16. Lt. Col R. D'A. Fife, CMG went for a commanding Officers conference. MAJOR MAIRIS D.S.O taking command of the Battn. during his absence.	
"	23/1/17 & 24/1/17		Battn. practiced in attacks on trenches. Capt. R.W.S. Croft re-joined the Battn.	
"	25/1/17.	8.45AM	The Battn. conveyed in lorries to ~~FREGICOURT~~ BRONFAY where the details not proceeding to trenches were left under Major MAIRIS D.S.O. The Battn. marched to FREGICOURT + arrived about 7.30 P.M. The 2nd-in-command + Coy Commanders preceded the Battn. and reconnoitred the trenches to be taken over tomorrow	
FREGICOURT.	26/1/17.	5.45PM	Battn. under Major R.E. COTTON marched to the trenches and relieved 10th Battn. Rifle Brigade in the SAILLY-SAILLISEL sector. The sector taken over being the Left of the Right Bgde Group of the Divn. Relief completed 8.30 P.M. "B" Coy on the Right, "C" Coy on the left in the front line. "D" Coy Support line. A Coy holding Strong Points in rear.	Trench Map No 2.
SAILLY-SAILLISEL	27/1/17.		Exact distribution of Coys as follows. "B" Coy 9 ~~[illegible]~~ forward posts + 1 platoon in BEAN Trench with 10th Batt. K.R.R on their right. "C" Coy 3 forward posts with remainder of Coy in CROW Support Trench. "D" Coy 3 platoons in CROW Support	

2449 Wt. W14957/M90 750,000 1/16 J.B.C. & A. Forms/C.2118/12.

Instructions regarding War Diaries and Intelligence Summaries are contained in F. S. Regs., Part II. and the Staff Manual respectively. Title Pages will be prepared in manuscript.

WAR DIARY
or
INTELLIGENCE SUMMARY

(Erase heading not required.)

Army Form C. 2118.

Place	Date	Hour	7th (S) Batt. Yorkshire Regt Summary of Events and Information	Remarks and references to Appendices
Trenches SAILLY–SAILLISEL	27/1/17	contd	+ 1 platoon in SOUTH COPSE S. Point. A. Coy. 3 platoons in CHATEAU Strong Point. 2 platoons CUSHY Strong point. Batt H. Q. at Chateau.	
			There was an attack some distance on our left at 5.30 AM. but the enemy very slightly shelled the area occupied by the Batt.	
"	28/1/17		In the afternoon one shell damaged parapet in Crow Support + another blew up a few Stokes mortar shells. Patrols out during the nights of 26th + 27th but saw nothing of the enemy. The advanced posts are well wired in front + owing to the hard frosts easy to approach at night on duck board tracks. Improvement of trenches carried out.	
			The Battn. was relieved 8.5 PM by 10th Batt. W. York Regt. The 7th E. York Regt relieved the K.R.R on the right on the night of 27th/28th + the 8th S. Staffordshire Regt relieved the 7th Border Regt on the left the same night.	
			Casualties 1 man slightly wounded. Battn. returned to cellars + dug outs in COMBLES in Bgde Reserve. 1 Coy in HAIE Wood + 1 Coy CEMETRY	
COMBLES.	29/1/17		Working parties	
"	30/1/17		Battn. again moved up to the line + relieved 10th Batt. W. York Regt in the SAILLY-SAILLISEL sector Relief completed 8.45 P.M. A + D Coys front line C Coy support. B Coy Strong points.	
Trenches. SAILLY SAILLISEL	31/1/17		Quiet night. Germans damaged CANE ALLEY with one shell in the morning + the duck board track in several places near S. line.	

2449 Wt. W14957/M9c 750,000 1/16 J.B.C. & A. Forms/C.2118/12.

Army Form C. 2118.

Instructions regarding War Diaries and Intelligence Summaries are contained in F. S. Regs., Part II. and the Staff Manual respectively. Title Pages will be prepared in manuscript.

WAR DIARY

or

~~INTELLIGENCE SUMMARY~~

(Erase heading not required.)

Place	Date	Hour	7th (S) Batt. Yorkshire Regt Summary of Events and Information	Remarks and references to Appendices
Trenches SAILLY – SAILLISEL	31/1/17		A trench mortar dropped ~~two~~ shells near Coy HQ in CAME ALLEY & killed one man & wounded 2. While patrolling the German wire at night one man was killed. The body was recovered. Total casualties 2 Killed + 2 wounded	
				Officers	O.R.
			Ration strength	22	627
			Effective strength	33	937

2449 Wt. W14957/M90 750,000 1/16 J.B.C. & A. Forms/C.2118/12.

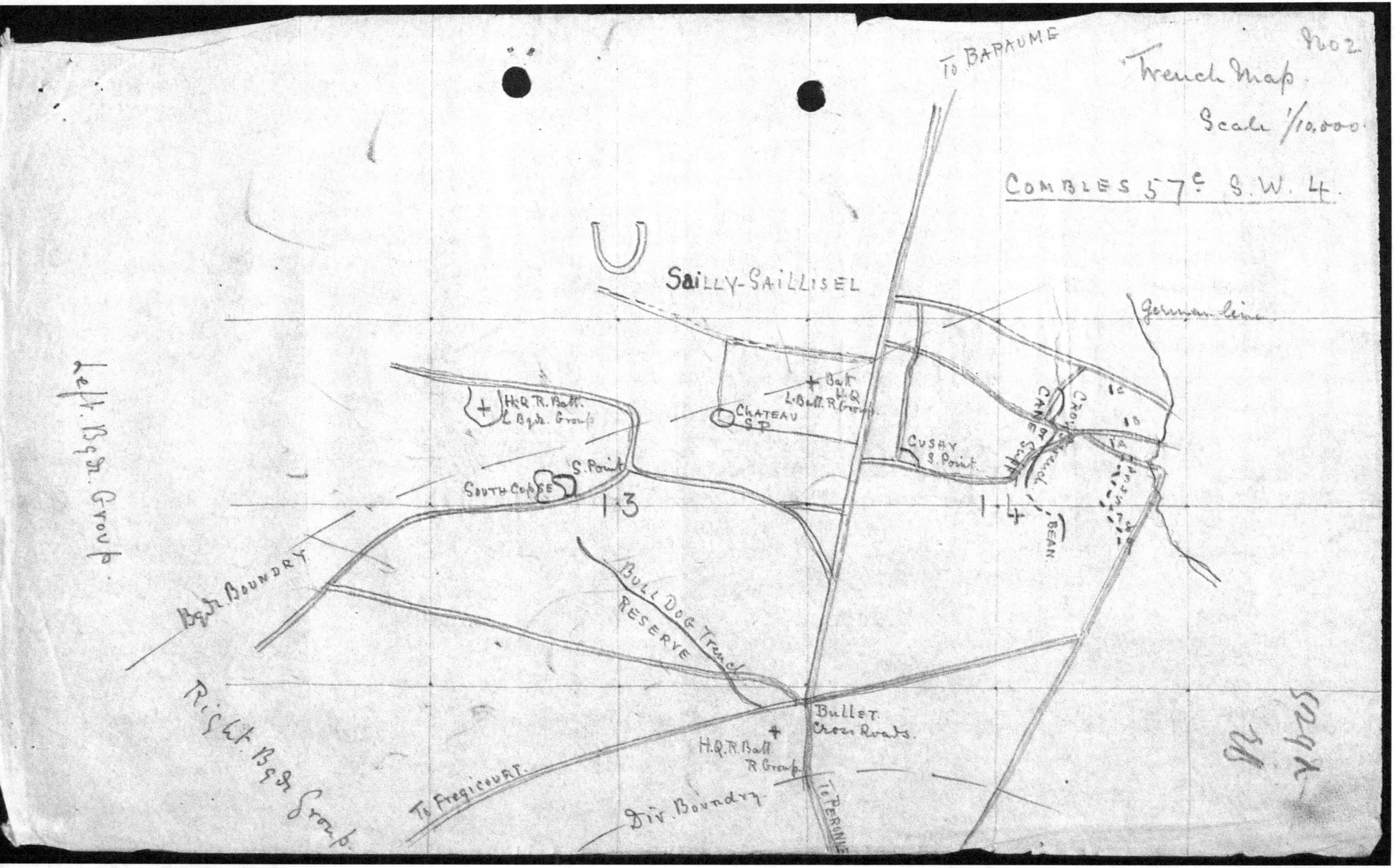

No 2

"Trench Map"

Scale 1/10,000

COMBLES 57c S.W. 4.

To BAPAUME

SAILLY-SAILLISEL

German line

+ Batt. H.Q. L. Batt. R. Group

CHATEAU S.P.

+ H.Q. R. Batt. L. Bgde. Group

S. Point

SOUTH COPSE

1.3

CUSHY S. Point

CANE or SUPP

CROW Trench

1C

1B

1A

1.4

BEAN.

BULL DOG Trench

RESERVE

Bgde. BOUNDRY

Left. Bgde. Group

Bullet Cross Roads.

+ H.Q. R. Batt. R. Group.

To PERONNE

To Fregicourt.

Div. Boundry

Right Bgde. Group

5291

EB

50/17

16 ½ [illegible]

Vol 17

War Diary

for

February 1914

4th Bn. Yorkshire Regiment

Army Form C. 2118.

Instructions regarding War Diaries and Intelligence Summaries are contained in F. S. Regs., Part II. and the Staff Manual respectively. Title Pages will be prepared in manuscript.

WAR DIARY
or
~~INTELLIGENCE SUMMARY~~
(Erase heading not required.)

Place	Date	Hour	7th (S) Battn. Yorkshire Regt. Summary of Events and Information	Remarks and references to Appendices
Trenches SAILLY-SAILLISEL	1/2/17		Battn. relieved by 12th Battn. MANCHESTER Regt. Relief completed at 8.45 P.M. Battn. went back by train from GUILLEMONT to BRONFAY FARM Camp. Casualties during the 48 hours in the trenches 4 OR Killed and 4 O.R. Wounded.	
BRONFAY Camp	2/2/17		Col. Fife C.M.G. having returned from Commanding Officers Conference resumed command of the Battn. Battn. resting.	
"	3/2/17 and	}	Practice attack from trenches in contemplation of operations to take place on 8th	
"	4/2/17	}		
"	5/2/17		Capt H.K.C. Hare re-joined the Battn. The Battn. moved to COMBLES. HQ + 2	
		2.15 PM	Coys in COMBLES. 1 Coy HAIE.WOOD, 1 Coy CEMETERY.	
COMBLES	6/2/17		Preparations for going into the trenches, fitting ~~of~~ equipment, practice with rifle grenades &c.	
"	7/2/17		Battn. marched to the trenches and took over the same sector held by it on 1 Feb. Relieved 12th Battn. MANCHESTER Regt. Relief completed by 9.30 P.M. In accordance with 52nd Bgde Operation orders and Battn. Operation orders dated 5th + 6th respectively. The Battn., during the night, took up their positions as specified in these orders + made all final arrangements. The Right of the line on the	Copies of 52nd Bgde Op. Orders + Battn. O.O.

Instructions regarding War Diaries and Intelligence Summaries are contained in F. S. Regs., Part II. and the Staff Manual respectively. Title Pages will be prepared in manuscript.

WAR DIARY
or
~~INTELLIGENCE SUMMARY~~

(Erase heading not required.)

Army Form C. 2118.

Place	Date	Hour	7th (S) Battn Yorkshire Regt. Summary of Events and Information	Remarks and references to Appendices
	7/2/17 (Contd)		Battn was held by 7th East Yorkshire Regt + on the left by 9th Battn Northumberland Fusrs. 2 Coys of 12th Battn Manchester Regt were attached to the Battn. One Coy in BEAN Support + 1 Coy in Strong points CUSHY, CHATEAU + SOUTH COPSE	Trench Maps Nos 1 + 2 + 3.
Trenches SAILLY-SAILLISEL	8/2/17.	7.30AM	At ZERO hour A + B Coys assaulted the German position on a front of 2 platoons each in 2 lines. A Coy on the right commanded by Capt. W.D. WILKINSON. B Coy on left commanded by Capt. T HUFFINGTON. The attack was a complete success. The Artillery barrage was very effective but many casualties were caused by some of the 18 pounders firing short + caused losses in "C" Coy that was carrying bombs, S.A.A. + consolidating material. The "stops" on the R + L were made within a few minutes of the assaulting Coys reaching their objective in the German trench. The enemy were taken completely by surprise + between 70 + 80 prisoners were taken including 2 Officers. The Officers and men behaved with great gallantry and, in spite of a temporary loss of some 40 yards of trench on the extreme right owing to shortage of bombs caused by the casualties in "C" Coy, the whole of the objective was occupied and consolidated within a few hours. The enemy delivered 2 counter attacks on the left + 3 on the right. They were all repulsed with heavy losses	

Army Form C. 2118.

Instructions regarding War Diaries and Intelligence Summaries are contained in F. S. Regs., Part II. and the Staff Manual respectively. Title Pages will be prepared in manuscript.

WAR DIARY

or

~~INTELLIGENCE SUMMARY~~

(Erase heading not required.)

7th (S) Batt. Yorkshire Regt.

Place	Date	Hour	Summary of Events and Information	Remarks and references to Appendices
	8/2/17 Contd.		The hostile artillery barrage was put down on the support line within a few minutes of the assault & maintained throught the day. It increased in intensity during the evening & was responsible for a considerable number of casualties. The 1st Aid post at the CHATEAU containing many wounded was completely wrecked by one 4.2 shell.	
			2 Coys of 12th Batt. Manchester Regt came up after dark. One occupied our old front line of posts & the other South Copse & Chateau Strong point. A party from 93rd F. Coy RE with a sapping platoon of E. York Regt wired the whole of the front of the captured trench, which was named GREEN HOWARDS Trench, during the night.	
			Pte Cummings, " Sowerby, L/Cpl Stephenson } Awarded Military Medals for Bravery in the Field.	
	9/2/17.		The enemy made no further counter attacks and the Batt. was relieved by 10th Batt. West Yorkshire Regt. Relief completed by 11. P.M. returned to BRONFAY.	
			Casualties. **Killed.** Officers: Capt. T. Huffington. NCOs & Men: 68. **Wounded.** Officers: 2/Lt Collett *, " Jolly *, " Purcell, " Griffith *, " Black. NCOs & Men: 118. **Missing** O.R.: 4	
			* Since died of wounds.	

2449 Wt. W14957/M90 750,000 1/16 J.B.C. & A. Forms/C.2118/12.

Instructions regarding War Diaries and Intelligence Summaries are contained in F. S. Regs., Part II. and the Staff Manual respectively. Title Pages will be prepared in manuscript.

WAR DIARY
or
INTELLIGENCE SUMMARY
(Erase heading not required.)

Army Form C. 2118.

Place	Date	Hour	7 (S) Battn Yorkshire Regt. Summary of Events and Information	Remarks and references to Appendices
BRONFAY Camp.	10/2/17		Messages of congratulation recd from the Commander-in-Chief, Army, Corps Division + Bgde H.Q. for the success of the Battn on 8th inst. Battn resting.	
	11/2/17.		Church parades.	
	12/2/17.		Battn refitting + re-organising	
	13/2/17.	3 PM.	Battn moved up to the trenches at SAILLY-SAILLISEL. and relieved the 12th Batt. Manchester Regt. Relief completed by. 12 midnight. Distribution as follows. C + D Coys in "GREEN HOWARDS Trench. "C" Coy on the Right. A Coy in 3 left posts in old front line. B Coy in CANE ALLEY Draft. 8 O.R. Battn H.Q. owing to heavy shelling moved to HEBULE. Quarry.	
Trenches Sailly. Saillisel	14/2/17		In the early hours of the morning on returning from the front line the Commanding Officer Lt.Col R D'a Fife was wounded in the left arm by a shell + Capt. HARPER the M.O. killed. Capt. BARTRUM taking temporary command.	
		9.30 PM.	Lt. Col. G.B. MAIRIS D.S.O. took over the command of the Battn. The hostile shelling was heavy throught the night.	

2449 Wt. W14957/M90 750,000 1/16 J.B.C. & A. Forms/C.2118/12.

Instructions regarding War Diaries and Intelligence Summaries are contained in F. S. Regs., Part II. and the Staff Manual respectively. Title Pages will be prepared in manuscript.

Army Form C. 2118.

WAR DIARY

or

~~INTELLIGENCE SUMMARY~~

(Erase heading not required.)

Place	Date	Hour	7th (S) Battn Yorkshire Regt. Summary of Events and Information	Remarks and references to Appendices
Trenches SAILLY-SAILLISEL	15/2/17		A German counter attack delivered about 5 PM was repulsed with loss. German shelling continued throughout the day becoming intense in the neighbourhood of the Battn H.Q., Cane Alley + SAILLY during the afternoon. Battn relieved by 10th Batt. W. York Regt. Relief completed by 2 AM. + returned to COMBLES. Draft 85 O.R.	
COMBLES	16/2/17	7 PM.	Battn moved in motor busses to BRONFAY.	
BRONFAY	17/2/17	}	Battn resting	
	18/2/17	}.	Church parades on 18th Draft of 37 O.R.	
"	19/2/17	11 AM.	Battn marched to MEAULTE + went into billets.	
MEAULTE	20/2/17 to 28/2/17.		The Lewis Gun teams 4 per Coy + bombers 32 per Coy made up to strength + the training under Coy Commanders + Specialist Officers continued as far as possible. The strength of Coys for training being much reduced owing to Corps working parties. 24/2/17. 9. O.R.	
	26/2/17		The following awards have been made to the Battn for gallantry in the field during the operations on 8th inst. D.S.O. Capt. W.D. Wilkinson M.C. M.C. Coy S.M. Keetley H. D.C.M. L/Cpl. Marsden F.	

2449 Wt. W14957/M90 750,000 1/16 J.B.C. & A. Forms/C.2118/12.

Army Form C. 2118.

WAR DIARY
or
~~INTELLIGENCE~~ SUMMARY

(Erase heading not required.)

Instructions regarding War Diaries and Intelligence Summaries are contained in F. S. Regs., Part II. and the Staff Manual respectively. Title Pages will be prepared in manuscript.

7th (S) Battn Yorkshire Regt

Place	Date	Hour	Summary of Events and Information	Remarks and references to Appendices
MEAULT.	19/2/17		Ration Strength. Officers 22, O.R 584 — Effective Strength. Officers 32, O.R. 774	
"	22/2/17		Draft. 2nd Lt. F.A. FOLEY	
"	27/2/17		" " H.C. RADLEY	

2449 Wt. W14957/M90 750,000 1/16 J.B.C. & A. Forms/C.2118/12.

Diary

SECRET.   Copy.No.

52ND.ORDER No.136.   Feb. 5th.1917.

Ref.. Trench Map Scale 1/10,000

1. The 52nd Infantry Brigade Group will attack and capture the German front line trench opposite the left subsector from U.14.B.85.25 to U 15.C.05.70, approximately a frontage of 300 yards, early on the morning of the 8th Feb.1917, with a view to improving our position and securing observation. The captured trench will be consolidated and one post on each flank will be formed to connect up eventually with our present line.

2. The enemy troops believed to be holding this line are the 12th.Bavarian R.I.R., of the 5th.Bavarian Reserve Division.

Enemy strong points exist at:-

U. 15.C. 15.25. and U.14.B.92.20.

Hostile Machine Guns are suspected at:-

U.15.C.15.25.	U.14.b.92.20.
U.15.c.27.52.	U.14.d.9.8.
U.15.c.11.68.	U.14.b.95.55.

A cellar is suspected at approximately U.15.4.0.

3. Battalions on the flanks will not make any attack but will support the attack of this Brigade with Lewis Gun fire, rifle fire and rifle grenades.

4. The attack will be carried out by the 7th.Yorkshire Regt. who will occupy the left subsector on the night of the 7/8th February preparatory to the attack.

5. For the purpose of this operation the right Battn. (7th.East Yorkshire Regt.) will give up posts ~~No. 13.~~ and 17 to the 7th Yorkshires.

One Company of the 12th.Manchester Regt. will occupy the Bean Support trench as a local Reserve, also one Coy of the same Regiment will occupy the strong points CUGNY - CHATEAU and SOUTH COPSE on the night 7/8th February and both Companies will come under direct orders of the O.C. 7th Yorkshire Regt.

6. The Battalion on the right flank (7th East Yorkshire Regiment) will be responsible for establishing communication between the right post in the captured trench and the left post in the right subsector by dusk and one Lewis gun and 3 bombers will be detailed to forma post about midway between them. Communication on the left flank will be linked up by the Company of the 7th. Yorkshire Regt. occupying posts "A" and "B".

7. At an hour zero to plus one the Artillery barrage will be put down 50 yards in front of the enemy's line; from plus one to plus three it will be 25 yards in front, from plus three to plus four, on the enemy's front line. At plus four the barrage will be lifted 50 yards and will gradually creep back to the final position for the standing barrage.

At zero, that is, the commencement of the barrage, the Infantry, who previous to this will have been formed up in our trenches will advance as close up to our barrage as possible.

To assist in the attack a smoke barrage will be placed on both flanks to screen the advance.

8. The 50th. and 52nd. Machine Gun Companies (less two guns) will support the attack with indirect fire to cover all approaches to the enemy's line, Two guns of the 52nd. M.G.Co., will advance with the assaulting troops into the German trench and will there improvise emplace-ments as quickly as possible.

Four guns from each of the 3rd. Guards Brigade Sector and North Copse Sector will also assist with cross fire.

Arrangments have been made for two stokes guns to cooperate in the assault by opening a hurricane bombardment on both flanks of the objective.

9. Every man of the attacking wave will carry 170 rounds of S.A.A., 2 mills bombs and 4 sandbags, 25% of the men will also carry a pick or a shovel (half picks half shovels).

10. S.O.S. Rockets must be taken forward with the carrying party and placed in readiness, also flares to be lit at intervals of 50 yards in the captured trench at 8 a.m. and 9.30 a.m. for observation by a contact aeroplane.

11. Blocking parties will be specially told off to establish blocks on each flank, and in the case of the left flank, it will be necessary to establish a bombing post about 15 yards to the left of the objective and to seize a second German sap running out of the main trench about 20 yards to the left of the objective. A track or trench also runs back from the German trench about U.14.B.90.15 which must be blocked.

12. One Section of the 93rd. Field Coy. R.E. will be held in readiness to move forward at dusk to help in the consolidation work, if called upon.

13. A Reserve Dump of S.A.A. grenades, very lights, S.O.S. rockets, rations and water &c. have been made at the CHATEAU DUMP (U.15.B.5.3.)

14. Troops taking part in the attack will not carry with them any maps or papers, containing information of any value to the enemy. Special maps will however be supplied to all Officers taking part in the assault.

15. An Officer from Bds.Headquarters will synchronise watches at Battn H.Qrs. at 8 p.m. February 7th.

16. An Artillery Liaison Officer will be attached to the Headquarters of the 7th.Yorkshire Regt. and will report at least one hour before zero to the Battn.Hd.Qrs.

17. The Bde. Signalling Officer will arrange to provide 8 pigeons to the assaulting Battalion.

18. A Situation report will be forwarded by the assaulting Battn.half hour after zero and every hour onwards till 12 noon, after which reports should be sent as the situation demands. An Officer representing the Bde. will be stationed at MOUCHOIR COPSE.

M. F. Morgan
Captain,
Brigade Major,
Right Group, Centre Division.

Issued at 3-30 p.m.

ACKNOWLEDGE.

Copies Nos.			
1 to 3	Staff.	16.	50th Trench Mortar Betty
4	War Diary,	17.	93rd.Field Co R.E.
5	File.	18.	17th.Division G
6.	10th.West Yorks Regt.	19.	17th.Division Q.
7.	7th.East Yorks Regt.	20.	C.R.E.17th.Divn.
8.	7th.Yorks Regt.	21.	A.D.M.S. 17th. Division.
9.	6th.Dorset Regt.	22.	50th.Infantry Bde.
10.	10th.Lancashire Fus.	23.	51st. " "
11.	12th.Manchester Regt.	24.	3rd. Guards Bde.
12.	50th.M.G.Co.	25.	52nd. Bde.Signal
13.	51st.M.G.Co.	26.	Right Group R.A.
14.	52nd.M.G.Co	27.	
15.	3rd.Guards M.G.Co.	28.	

TRENCH MAP
SECRET No 14
PROVISIONAL
20th Divn Topo Sect
11
12
Morval
17
18
13
14
15
23
24
19
20
21
8
9
GREEN HOWARD TRENCH

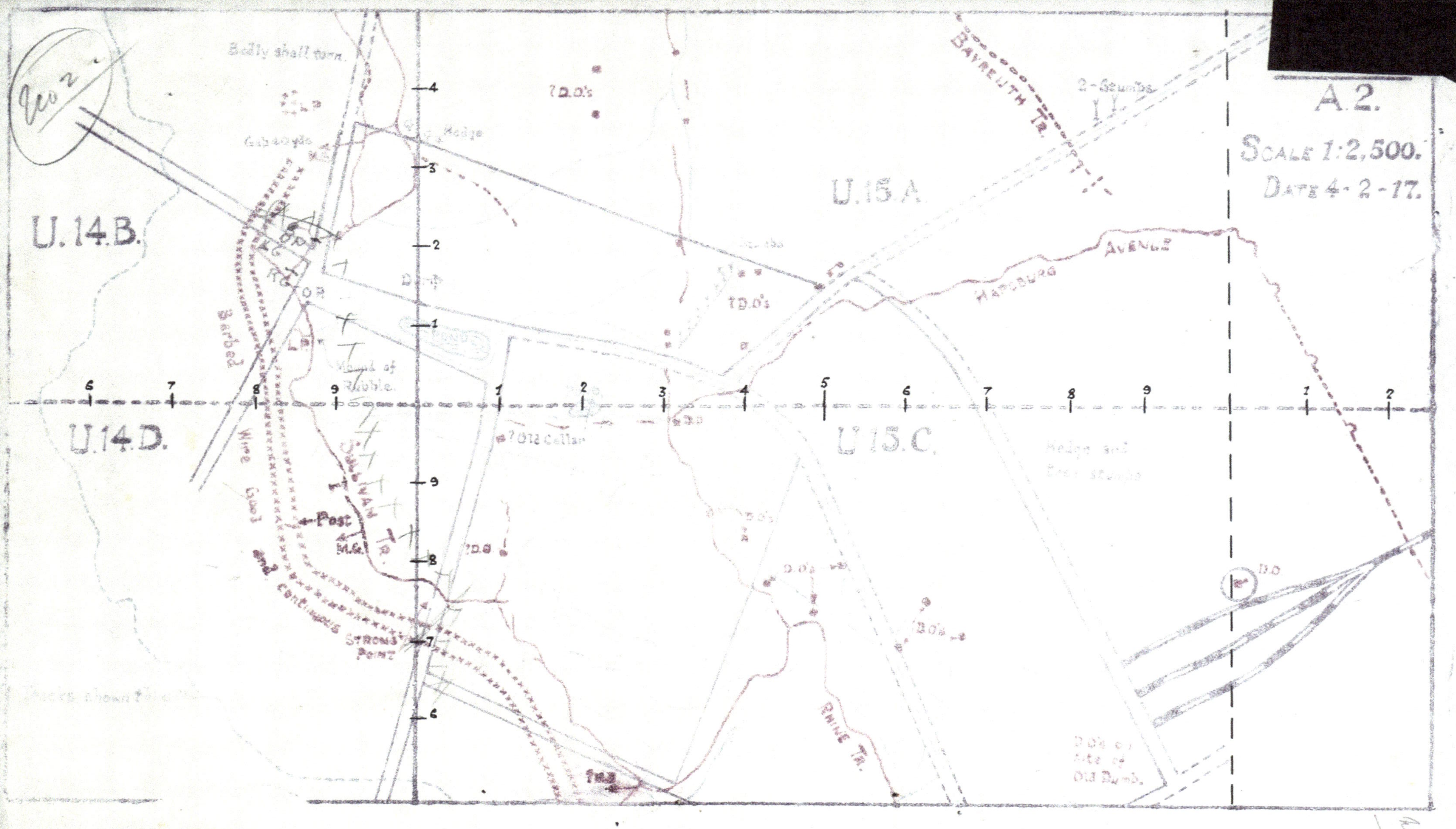

A.2.
SCALE 1:2,500.
DATE 4-2-17.
U.14.B.
U.14.D.
U.15.A.
U.15.C.
BAYREUTH TR.
HAMBURG AVENUE
RHINE TR.
SULLIVAN TR.
Badly shell torn.
7 D.O's
2-Stumbs.
T.D.O's
Mound of Rubble.
? Old Cellar
Hedge and Tree stumps
Barbed Wire Good and continuous
STRONG POINT
Post
M.G.
D.O's
D.O's on site of Old Dump.

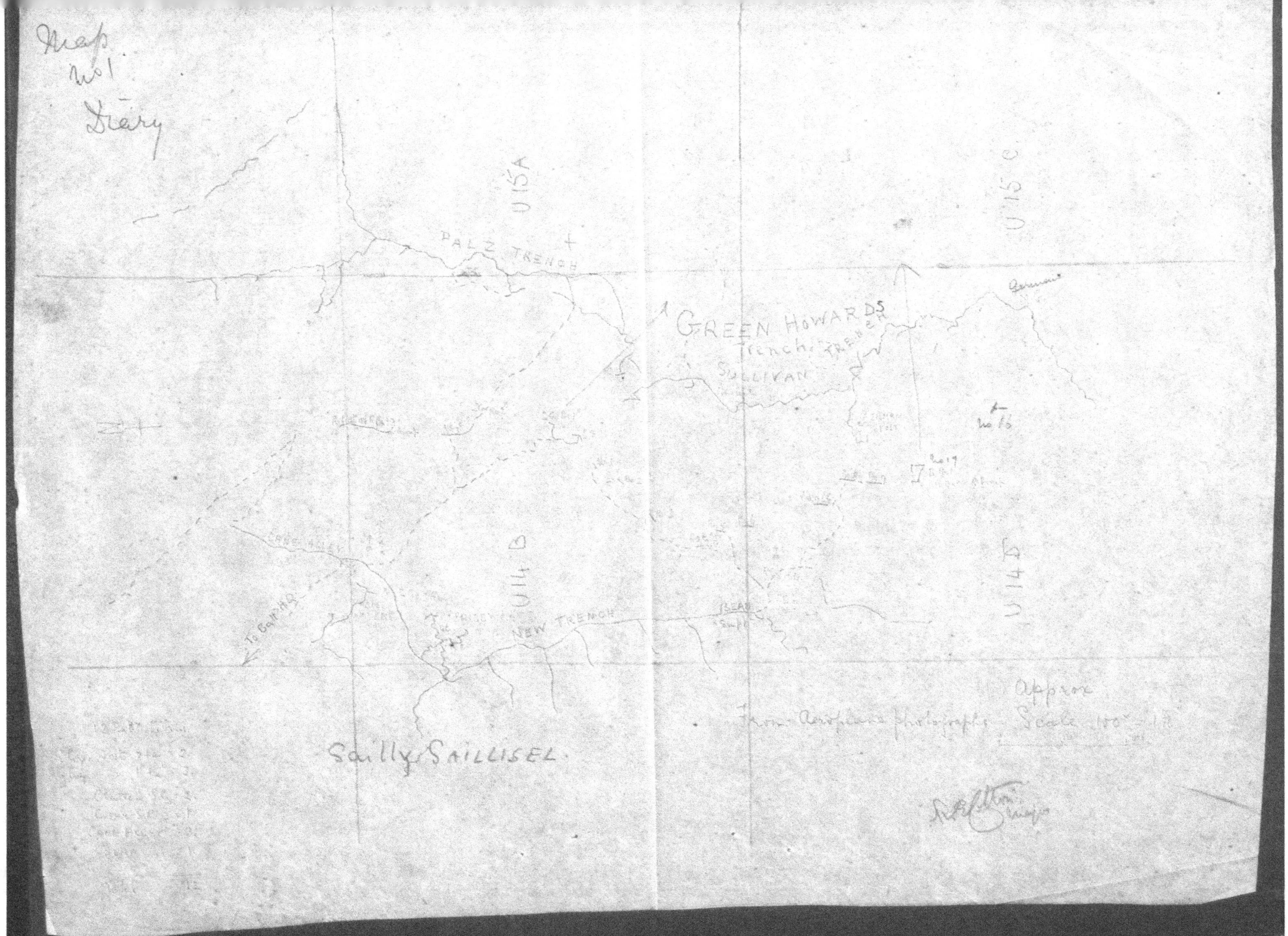

Map No 1

Diary

U15A

PALZ TRENCH

U15 C

GREEN HOWARDS

Trench

SULLIVAN

U14 B

NEW TRENCH

U14 D

To Bn HQ

Sailly SAILLISEL

From Aeroplane photographs

Approx Scale

Copy No. 60

SECRET. War diary

OPERATION ORDER

by

Lieut. Col. R. D'A. FIFE. C.M.G.

Commanding 7th Battalion Yorkshire Regiment.

No. 8. ---------- 6-2-17

GENERAL PLAN OF OPERATION.

1. On Febry. 8th the enemy's front line trench between U 14 b 8.525 and U 15 c 05.70 will be assaulted and consolidated as part of our front line system. The assault will be assisted by an intense bombardment which will begin at zero hour, the advance of the assaulting troops being covered by a creeping barrage.

Stokes guns will co-operate and covering fire, both direct and indirect, will be provided by Vickers guns.

After assault, and during consolidation an artillery barrage will be maintained round the area.

ASSEMBLY BEFORE ASSAULT.

2. During the night of 7th - 8th Febry. the Battalion will be disposed as follows:-

A. Coy. in Posts 17 to 6 inclusive.

B. Coy. in Posts 5 to 1 inclusive.

C. Coy. in BRAN SUPPORT and NEW SUPPORT.

D. Coy., less the garrisons of Posts A. and B. in CANE ALLEY.

Two squads of Battalion Bombers will be attached to A. Coy. and two squads to B. Coy.

All consolidating material will be placed immediately in front of the parapet of C. Coys. trenches during the night and each man will stand to at the usual time opposite to the material which he is to carry.

DISPOSITIONS FOR ASSAULT.

3. The assault will be carried out in two lines by A. and B. Coys. each on a front of two Platoons, with two Platoons in the second line. The formation of each line will be that laid down in orders recently circulated.

The second line will follow the first at a distance of 40 yards.

A third line consisting of the whole of C. Coy. less Lewis Gunners, will follow the second line at a distance of 50 to 60 yards.

This line will act as carriers of consolidating material, bombs, and ammunition, the men wearing battle kit with slung rifles.

BATTALION RESERVE. D. Coy. less the garrisons of posts A. and B. will be in Battalion Reserve.

One Company of the 12th Manchester Regt. will occupy the BEAN SUPPORT trench as a local reserve, also one Company of the same Regt., will occupy the strong points CUSHY-CHATEAU and SOUTH COPSE on the night 7/8th Febry. and both Coys. will be under direct orders of the O.C. 7th Yorkshire Regt.

THE ASSAULT. 4. The signal for the assault will be the commencement of an intense bombardment by 17 batteries of 18 pounders, forming a barrage on " No Man's Land" and the enemy's trenches.

The moment the bombardment begins, the three lines will leave their trenches.

The two assaulting lines will deploy at 3 paces interval with the Right on No. 17 Post and the Left on No. 1 Post, the first line advancing 5 paces before deploying, to enable the second line to deploy clear of the Posts.

The third line will advance as soon as possible after the men have picked up their loads, the right flank stepping short, to enable the left to close up into alignment.

The advance of each line will be by the right.

For one minute after zero, the barrage will be 50 yds. in front of the enemy's trench.

At the end of one minute the barrage will lift to 25 yds. in front of the enemy's trench.

At the end of THREE minutes, the barrage will lift into the enemy's trench.

At the end of FOUR mins. the barrage will lift to 75 yds. behind the enemy's trench and from this point will continue to creep gradually back on to the enemy's SUPPORT trenches.

The deployment of assaulting lines should occupy one minute.

After this the two lines will advance and will not halt unless compelled to wait for the barrage to lift. In this case all ranks will kneel down, but will not on any account lie down, and the advance will be continued as soon as the barrage permits.

The rate of advance will be very slow, and dressing of lines must be preserved.

The last 25 yards of the advance will be made in double time as soon as the barrage lifts off the enemy's trench.

The moment at which the Artillery opens fire will be noted by Officers and N.C.O.s in order that they may know when to expect lifts in the barrage.

As soon as the first barrage lifts, the enemy sap opposite No. 9 post will be rushed and a Lewis Gun established in it to keep down enemy's fire from the right flank.

The three Lewis guns in posts A. and B. will be similarly employed to keep down the enemy's fire from the

THE ASSAULT contd. left flank.

CONSOLIDATION 5. Immediately on reaching the enemy's position O.C. A. Coy. will take steps to secure his right flank - This will be done by blocking the trench beyond his right flank with barbed wire knife rests and wire, the work to begin at the point farthest from his flank and to be continued towards his flank.

The length of trench blocked should be not less than 50 yards.

A Battalion bombing squad and a squad of rifle grenadiers will then hold this flank, on which a Lewis Gun will also be posted.

Immediately on reaching the enemy's position, O.C. B. Coy. will take steps to secure his left flank. This will be done by establishing a bombing post in the end of the northern of the two enemy saps which run out from the enemy's line at U 14 b 8.2.

The trench will then be blocked with barbed wire from the point where the northern sap joins it, for 50 yards, passing the point where the southern sap joins it, and a post of rifle grenadiers will be established at the southern or inner end of the block.

A Lewis gun will be placed at the end of the southern sap and another Lewis gun half way between the left flank and U 14 b 9.1 where a communication trench appears to run back from enemy's trench. This communication trench will also be blocked with barbed wire to a distance of 50 yards from the captured trench, and a bombing post established behind the block.

The wire carrying parties, except those detailed for the special duty of blocking the flanks, will put out a continuous line/ of knife rests and French barbed wire along the whole of the new front, at a distance of 50 yards from the trench and round both flanks.

These parties will then return to our original front line of posts, which they will garrison until further orders.

The senior Officer in the front line will use his discretion as to retaining the remainder of the carrying parties for consolidation and defence against counter attack.

For reversing the captured trench, fire steps will be improvised by means of empty boxes and planks brought forward by the carrying parties.

EQUIPMENT & DRESS. 6. Every man of the attacking waves will carry 170 rounds of S.A.A. 2 Mills grenades, and 2 sandbags. 25% of the men will carry a pick or a shovel (three picks to 1 shovel) These men will be in the second line.

Dress: Battle kit with jerkins.
All men will wear sandbags over their boots.
Greatcoats will not be worn.

EQUIPMENT AND DRESS contd

Officers will be dressed and equipped like the men and will carry rifles.

COMMUNICATION.

7. The Battalion Signallers will establish communication by a chain of visual signalling posts from the captured trench according to special orders issued to them.

Pigeons will also be provided.

Reports if required to be sent by messenger, will be sent in duplicate by separate messengers to Battalion H.Q. at The CHATEAU.

Situation reports from the front line will be forwarded ½ hour after zero and every hour afterwards up to 12 noon.

S.O.S. rockets will be taken forward by the carrying parties and placed in readiness, flares will be lighted in the captured trench at 8am and 9/30am for observation by contact aeroplanes.

MAPS AND DOCUMENTS.

8. Special maps will be supplied to all Officers taking part in the assault. No other maps or papers containing information of value to the enemy will be carried by any Officer or man.

RATIONS & RUM.

9. The assaulting and carrying troops will be provided with hot food at 6am under Battalion and Company arrangements.

A ration of rum will be issued to all troops taking part in the attack.

The issue of rum must be completed a clear 15 mins. before zero hour.

[signature] Capt.
Adjt. 7th Yorkshire Regt.

Issued to:-

No. 1 A. Coy.
2 B. Coy.
3 C. Coy.
4 D. Coy.
5 B.B.O.
6. Signal Sgt.
7 C.O.
8 Office copy.
9 Adjt.
✓10 War diary.
11 17th Divn. (for information)
12 52nd Brigade (for information)
13 12th Manchesters.
14 do.
15 do.

No 10

APPENDIX 'A'

ARTILLERY BARRAGE.

(Reference para:6, 17th Div: Operation Order No.109)

1. The arrangements for the Artillery Creeping Barrage are :-

<u>Zero to 0.1.</u> Standing Barrage is put down on enemy's front Line - U.15.c.25.55 to U.14.b.95.35.

Moving Barrage put down 50 yards in front of above line.

<u>0.1 to 0.3.</u> Standing Barrage remains on enemy's front Line.

Moving Barrage moves back to within 25 yards of enemy's front line.

<u>0.3 to 0.4</u> Standing Barrage on enemy's Front Line.

Moving Barrage on enemy's Front Line.

<u>0.4 to 0.6.</u> Both Barrages lift off enemy's Front Line to a line 75 yards beyond it. Thence it moves on 50 yards every two minutes until it reaches the Support Line, where it will remain as long as required.

2. The signal for the troops to leave the trenches will be the putting down of the barrage, when they will advance forward as close under the barrage as possible: if necessary halting and kneeling but NOT lying down.

<u>NOTE.</u> Barrages are not marked on the map 'W'.

SECRET. Copy No 10

FURTHER INSTRUCTIONS

No. A/8/2

1. SIGNALS - Two signallers will go forward with each assaulting Company and will as far as possible accompany the Company Commander until arriving in the enemy's trench: They will then make every effort to get into touch with two Signal Stations established in our old front line at posts to be chosen by Signal Sergt.

These posts will pass messages back to a station established in NEW SUPPORT at about U 14 b 22 who will be in telephonic communication with Battalion H.Q. etc. This station will be known as NEW STATION.

O.C. D. Coy will be in NEW SUPPORT and if required can encode messages which require it.

The greatest care must be taken as to what messages are sent in clear.

Effort will be made to run wires to our new front line by day and this will certainly be done as soon as dark.

Pigeons: Four per Company will go forward with 2nd line and will be used if necessary for communication: Each signaller will carry one pigeon book.

2. PRISONERS - Prisoners will be taken back by C. Coy. to BEAN SUPPORT and then handed over to the Provost Sergt. who will arrange for their disposal. If necessary he will call on O.C. D. Coy. for additional escort, but an escort of 10% is the maximum that should be used.

3. TELESCOPIC RIFLES AND SNIPING APPARATUS - These will not be taken forward in the assault.

D. Coy. will retain their rifles and all snipers will parade at Battn. H.Q. at 9am tomorrow for distribution of rifles and sights by the Adjutant. Snipers of B. and A. Coys will immediately make use of any opportunities they may have on arrival in the enemy's lines.

4. Attention is called to "Instructions for training of Divisions for offensive" para XXX111.

All B.A.B. codes will be sent to Orderly Room by 8pm tonight.

5 Acknowledge

[signature]

Capt.

6th Feb. 1917. Adjt. 7th Yorkshire Regt.

Issued to:-

No. 1 to A. Coy.
2 B.
3 C.
4 D.
5 C.O.
6 Adjt.
7 Provost Sergt.
8 Office copy.
9 Signal Sergt.
10 War diary.

Vol

WAR DIARY

4th Yorkshire Regiment

MARCH – 1917.

Instructions regarding War Diaries and Intelligence Summaries are contained in F. S. Regs., Part II. and the Staff Manual respectively. Title Pages will be prepared in manuscript.

WAR DIARY
or
~~INTELLIGENCE SUMMARY~~
(Erase heading not required.)

Army Form C. 2118.

Vol 18

7th (S) Batt Yorkshire Regt

Place	Date	Hour	Summary of Events and Information	Remarks and references to Appendices
MEAULT.	1/3/17		Lt Col G.B. Mairis D.S.O. went on leave Major R.E Cotton in command of the Battn.	RSC
		9.20AM	Battn. marched to WARLOY + went into billets arriving about 2 P.M. No 14123 Pte R ARMSTRONG awarded the Military Medal.	
WARLOY	2/3/17 to 3/3/17		Company + platoon drill.	RSC
"	3/3/17		Church parades.	RSC
"	4/3/17			RSC
"	5/3/17		Training 6 hours per day 9AM – noon, 2 PM – 5 P.M Draft 2/Lt J H Palin + 13 O.R.	RSC
"	"	9AM	Battn training artillery formation &c	RSC
"	6/3/17		Draft 2/Lt. L A MULLANEY	RSC
"	8/3/17		" 64 O.R	RSC
"	11/3/17		" 2/Lt. G.S Townsend 2/Lt C S Hill, 2/Lt R R Humphrey. + 8. O.R.	RSC
"	6/3/17 to 13/3/17		Morning or afternoon Specialists training under their own Officers. The remainder of day, during this period, the Battn. practiced various forms of attack, patrol + did tactical schemes set by Coy and Battn. Commanders. A considerable amount of drill with + without arms + musketry was ~~also~~ also done. One night attack scheme carried out on 10/3/.	RSC
	12/3/17		Lt. Col Mairis D.S.O took over command of the Battn.	

2449 Wt. W14957/M90 750,000 1/16 J.B.C. & A. Forms/C.2118/12.

Instructions regarding War Diaries and Intelligence Summaries are contained in F. S. Regs., Part II. and the Staff Manual respectively. Title pages will be prepared in manuscript.

WAR DIARY
or
~~INTELLIGENCE SUMMARY.~~
(Erase heading not required.)

Army Form C. 2118.

Place	Date	Hour	7th (S) Battn Yorkshire Regt — Summary of Events and Information	Remarks and references to Appendices
WARLOY	14/3/17	7·35 AM	Battn marched with Bgde Group to BEAUVAL arriving at 1 P.M. + went into billets	R.E.C.
BEAUVAL	15/3/17	7·55 AM	March continued to BONNIERES + Battn arrived 2 P.M. + went into billets for the night	R.E.C.
BONNIERES	16/3/17	8 AM.	March continued to VIEIL HESDIN arriving at 1 P.M. The billets of the Battn were rather scattered but accomodation ample.	R.E.C.
VIEIL HESDIN	17/3/17		Coys had short parades. The Battn cleaning up making new latrines &c.	R.E.C.
"	18/3/17		Church Parades. Draft 60 O.R.	R.E.C.
"	19/3/17 to 22/3/17		Coy and Battn training for 6 hours daily. Practice attacks by Coys under C.O. &c.	
	21/3/17		Draft 2/Lt. J.T. MOWATT and 94 O.R.	R.E.C.
"	23/3/17	11 A.M.	Battn with Brigade Group went by "bus" to IVERGNY + went into billets arriving 5.45 P.M	R.E.C.
IVERGNY	24/3/17		Battn resting + re-organising new drafts. Draft 40 R	R.E.C.
"	25/3/17		Church Parades	R.E.C.
"	26/3/17 to 28/3/17		Coy + Battn training continued. Specialists under their own Officers for 3 hrs per day. 26/3/17. Lt. T. R. GROOM joined the Battn	R.E.C.
"	29/3/17		Brigade ~~field day~~ route march under Bgdier Genl. Yatman Commanding 50th Inf. Bgde.	R.E.C.
"	30/3/17		Brigade field day.	R.E.C.
"	31/3/17		Coys training under their own Officers. 2 Coys musketry on range. In the afternoon.	R.E.C.

A5834 Wt. W4973/M687 750,000 8/16 D. D. & L. Ltd. Forms/C.2118/13.

Instructions regarding War Diaries and Intelligence Summaries are contained in F. S. Regs., Part II. and the Staff Manual respectively. Title pages will be prepared in manuscript.

WAR DIARY
or
~~INTELLIGENCE SUMMARY.~~
(Erase heading not required.)

Army Form C. 2118.

Place	Date	Hour	7th (S) Battn Yorkshire Regt. Summary of Events and Information	Remarks and references to Appendices
IVERGNY	31/3/17		Bgde Staff Ride with C.O. 2nd-in-command & Coy Commanders. Subject taking up outpost position.	[illegible]
			Ration Strength: Officers 29, O.R. 643	
			Effective Strength: Officers 35, O.R. 994	

A5834 Wt. W4973/M687 750,000 8/16 D. D. & L. Ltd. Forms/C.2118/13.

1917. 187.

CONFIDENTIAL

Vol 19

WAR DIARY

FOR

APRIL

7th

YORKSHIRE REGT

Instructions regarding War Diaries and Intelligence Summaries are contained in F. S. Regs., Part II. and the Staff Manual respectively. Title pages will be prepared in manuscript.

WAR DIARY
or
~~INTELLIGENCE SUMMARY.~~
(Erase heading not required.)

Army Form C. 2118.

Place	Date	Hour	Summary of Events and Information — 7th (S) Battn. Yorkshire Regt.	Remarks and references to Appendices
IVERGNY	1/4/17		Church Parades. Battn. resting.	REC MAP. LENS.
"	2/4/17	1 PM	Brigade field day postponed at 3 PM on account of weather	REC
"	3/4/17		Preparations for move. Surplus kits + stores sent away. Training under Coy arrangements.	REC
"	4/4/17		Rear guard scheme for A + B Coys under C.O. C + D Coys Range musketry re 2/Lt. Eyre rejoined the Battn.	REC
"	5/4/17	9.35 AM	Marched to MAIZIERES arrived 12.30 P.M.	REC
MAIZIERES	6/4/17		Coys training under Coy Commanders.	REC
"	7/4/17	10 AM.	Marched to IZEL-LES-HAMEAUX. Arrived 12 noon + went into billets	REC
IZEL-LES-HAMEAUX.	8/4/17	11.15 AM	Marched to MONTENESCOURT. The Battn. was rather close billeted. The Battn. is still in 3rd Army XVIII Corps. The Division is under orders to move in support of 3rd Cavalry Corps in the forthcoming operations East of ~~[illegible]~~ ARRAS. On Z day (the day of the infantry assault) the Battn. is under orders to move at 4 hours notice, on Z + 4 hours at 50 min. notice on receipt of orders at Bgde H.Q. Final preparations for the move.	REC
MONTENES-COURT	9/4/17		"Z" day Infantry attack began at 5 AM on a 12 mile front S East, E + N.E of ARRAS	
		9 AM.	Battn. under orders to move at 50 mins notice	
		4.45 PM	The Battn. moved to the starting point of the Bgde Group at Cross Roads East	REC

A5834 Wt. W4973/M687 750,000 8/16 D. D. & L. Ltd. Forms/C.2118/13.

Army Form C. 2118.

WAR DIARY
or
~~INTELLIGENCE SUMMARY.~~
(Erase heading not required.)

Instructions regarding War Diaries and Intelligence Summaries are contained in F. S. Regs., Part II. and the Staff Manual respectively. Title pages will be prepared in manuscript.

7th (S) Batt. Yorkshire Regt.

Place	Date	Hour	Summary of Events and Information	Remarks and references to Appendices
			of AGNEZ LES DUISANS. The transport moved in 3 echelons. A. Echelon, under Battn. transport officer with the Battn, consisted of Lewis Gun G.S limber waggons, pack animals with SAA + tools. "B" Echelon moved behind the Brigade group + consisted of mess cart, maltese cart + water carts. "C" Echelon under orders of the Division moved ½ an hour later + consisted of 2 G.S waggons + Coy cookers. A proportion of Officers + N COs joined the Corp depôt for training drafts &c. A second group of Officers N COs + men as first reinforcements to replace casualties composed the Bgde Depôt under Capt. J. R. STONE and moved with "C" Echelon.	
			The 7th Battn E York Regt formed the advance guard of the Bgde Group. 7th Battn York Regt was the rearmost Battn in the column + left 1 Platoon to act as rear guard.	
			C. Echelon + Bgde Depôt stayed the night at AGNEZ LES DUISANS	RSC.
			Brigade halted outside ARRAS and at 8.30 pm received orders to bivouack in a field. Snowed all night.	
Bivouack West of ARRAS.	10/4/17	9.45AM.	Battn moved into cellars at ARRAS. with orders to move at 2 hours notice. Bgde Depôt moved at 10.30 AM to BERNEVILLE. Snowed most of the day.	RSC
ARRAS	11/4/17.	4P.M.	All previous orders cancelled with regard to the Division being in support of Cavalry Corps. New orders issued for the Division to relieve 15th Division in the line between Monchy and the River SCARPE. Battn marched from ARRAS at 4.20 PM route ARRAS-CAMBRAI Road.	MAPS. Sheet 51 B N.W. Edition 6 A. Sheet 51 B S W Edition 4 A RSC

A5834 Wt. W4973/M687 750,000 8/16 D. D. & L. Ltd. Forms/C.2118/13.

Instructions regarding War Diaries and Intelligence Summaries are contained in F. S. Regs., Part II. and the Staff Manual respectively. Title pages will be prepared in manuscript.

WAR DIARY

or

~~INTELLIGENCE SUMMARY.~~

(Erase heading not required.)

Army Form C. 2118.

Place	Date	Hour	7th (S) Batt. Yorkshire Regt. — Summary of Events and Information	Remarks and references to Appendices
	11/4/17 (contd)		The Battn lost 1 man killed 1 Officer + 6 men wounded outside the town by shell fire. Brigade halted at 9 P.M. in a blinding snow storm at H 27. b. Divn now in VI Corps.	REE
East of ARRAS	12/4/17	1 A.M.	Battn, in Brigade Reserve, moved to the old German Support line from H. 28. a. 7. 6 to just South of the SCARPE. A. B + C Coys in German Support line with D Coy a few yards in rear. 7th E Yorkshire Regt were in Support of 6th Dorset Regt and 10th W. Yorkshire Regt and 800 yds in front of us. The W. Yorkshire + Dorset Regts held the front line from a point just outside the N.W. corner of MONCHY-LE-PREUX along the road running N.W. in the direction of FAMPOUX to just S of the SCARPE at H. 23 the 29th Div on the Right and 4th Divn on the left North of the river SCARPE. Battn H.Q. in FEUCHY at H 21-d-5-0. The Battn relieved Scottish Rifles. Relief completed about 3 A.M. Quiet day	Maps 51B N.W. Edition 6A. and 51B S.W. Edition 4A. REE
FEUCHY	13/4/17		Quiet day	REE
"	14/4/17	1 A.M.	Hostile artillery fired over 1000 rounds of tear shells in the sector held by the Battn. Box respirators were adjusted but the shells had little effect owing to the damp state of the ground. No casualties. Quiet day	
		9.30 P.M.	Battn relieved by 12th Manchester Regt. D Coy moved to dug outs at "Railway Triangle" H. 19. c. A B + C Coys bivouacked in "Battery Valley" H 26.	REE
H. 19. c.	15/4/17		Quiet day.	
		5. P.M.	Battn moved to caves on the ARRAS-CAMBRAI Road at G 29. d.	REE

A5834 Wt. W4973/M687 750,000 8/16 D. D. & L. Ltd. Forms/C.2118/13.

Instructions regarding War Diaries and Intelligence Summaries are contained in F. S. Regs., Part II. and the Staff Manual respectively. Title pages will be prepared in manuscript.

WAR DIARY
or
~~INTELLIGENCE SUMMARY.~~
(Erase heading not required.)

Army Form C. 2118.

Place	Date	Hour	7th (S) Batt Yorkshire Regt. Summary of Events and Information	Remarks and references to Appendices
FAUBERGE ST. SAUVEUR G29.d.	16/4/17		Battn resting	
"	17/4/17		Baths + change of clothing.	
"	18/4/17	noon	Battn marched to trenches and relieved 10th Battn Sherwood Foresters in old German Suppt line. Relief completed 2 P.M. Battn H.Q. H.34.a.9.8 with 2 Coys on the Right + 2 Coys on the left. 1st Battn Dublin Fusls (29th Division) on the right. 7th Battn E Yorkshire Regt on left. Quiet day.	
"	19/4/17.	8P.M.	Relieved 8th Battn S. Staffordshire Regt in the left sector of the front line from H36.a.2.8 to H23.b.4.0 Relief completed 2 AM. 7th E York Regt relieved Border Regt on the right with our left on Scarpe. All 4 Coys in the front line D Coy on the right. Posts at H24.c.5.5 + H30.a.5.9.	Situation Map. 51B
Front line H26–H23	20/4/17		Quiet day Hostile shelling directed at valley H24c + H30.a. During the night a new post established at H30.b.4.2. A patrol established connection with 51st Divn on our left north of the Scarpe at H24.a.4.7. Another patrol went round the lake in H24.d met with considerable machine gun fire + retired.	
"	21/4/17.		Quiet day. During the night D Coy provided a covering party for the York + Lancaster Regt but the working party did not arrive. 12 casualties in D Coy. Bgde Depôt moved to ARRAS	
"	22/4/17	2.AM.	Relieved by 8th S. Staffordshire Regt. Battn returned to Railway Triangle H.17 central + were accomodated in old German dug outs. Battn resting	
Railway Triangle	23/4/17	2 AM.	Battn moved to old German Support line. Batt H.Q at H28. 7th E York Regt on the Right Battn in Bgde Support.	

A5834 Wt. W4973/M687 750,000 8/16 D. D. & L. Ltd. Forms/C.2118/13.

Instructions regarding War Diaries and Intelligence Summaries are contained in F. S. Regs., Part II. and the Staff Manual respectively. Title pages will be prepared in manuscript.

WAR DIARY
or
~~INTELLIGENCE SUMMARY.~~
(Erase heading not required.)

Army Form C. 2118.

Place	Date	Hour	7th (S) Battn. Yorkshire Regt. — Summary of Events and Information	Remarks and references to Appendices
N.W. German Support line H.28.a.5.8.	23/4/17	3.40 AM	A General attack was delivered on a frontage of several miles. The 51st Bgde. assaulted on the frontage allotted to the Divn. with 50th Bgde in Support + 52nd Bgde in Reserve. This attack failed + was renewed by 6th Battn. Dorset Regt + 10th Battn. W. Yorkshire Regt. The Battn. took the place of these 2 Battns. in the front line. This 2nd attack also failed. Subsequently the Battn. dug in 200 yards in front of the line from which the attacks were launched. This new line was occupied by C, B + A Coy with D Coy in a trench near Lone Copse. D Coy also held 2 posts at H 30 b. 4.2 + H30.b.4.6. Battn. H.Q. at H 29. b. 6.7. 7th E. York Regt on the right.	Divl. front H.36.a – H.25.b 3.4. Battn. front H 30 d. 5.0 – H 30. b. 7.8. REC
H29.b.6.7.	24/4/17.		Enemy shelled new front line all day. Slight casualties.	REC
"	25/4/17.	3.30 AM.	"A" Coy made a demonstration against N. end of BAYONET Trench in order to assist bombing attack by 7th E. York Regt. At 9 P.M. all 4 Coys pushed forward patrols and reported BAYONET trench occupied by enemy. Shelling continued all day. During the night the Battn. was relieved by 5th Battn. Berkshire Regt 12th Divn. Quiet relief. Battn. returned to "Railway Triangle"	REC
RAILWAY TRIANGLE	26/4/17	7 AM	Battn. marched to Bgde Depôt Camp on the outskirts of ARRAS and at 1 PM proceeded in lorries to FOSSEUX + went into huts.	REC
FOSSEUX	27/4/17		Battn. resting. Total casualties from 9/4/17 – 25/4/17. 5 Officers wounded. O.R. 14 killed 113 wounded 14 missing. Draft. 1 Off. Lt. Clarke + 59 O.R. 2/Lt Thacker re-joins	REC

A5834 Wt. W4973/M687 750,000 8/16 D. D. & L. Ltd. Forms/C.2118/13.

Army Form C. 2118.

Instructions regarding War Diaries and Intelligence Summaries are contained in F. S. Regs., Part II. and the Staff Manual respectively. Title pages will be prepared in manuscript.

WAR DIARY
or
~~INTELLIGENCE SUMMARY.~~

(Erase heading not required.)

Place	Date	Hour	7th (S) Battn. Yorkshire Regt. Summary of Events and Information	Remarks and references to Appendices
FOSSEUX.	28/4/17		Parades under Coy arrangements.	REC MAP LENS.
"	29/4/17		Church parades. Orders for Bgde Group to be prepared to move on 1st May to HAUTE-AVESNES, LARESSET area. 2nd Lt. F. D. Harling joined the Battn.	REC
"	30/4/17		Training continued	
			Effective Strength: Officers 30, O.R. 861. Ration Strength: Officers 25, O.R. 688	REC.

A5834 Wt. W4973/M687 750,000 8/16 D. D. & L. Ltd. Forms/C.2118/13.

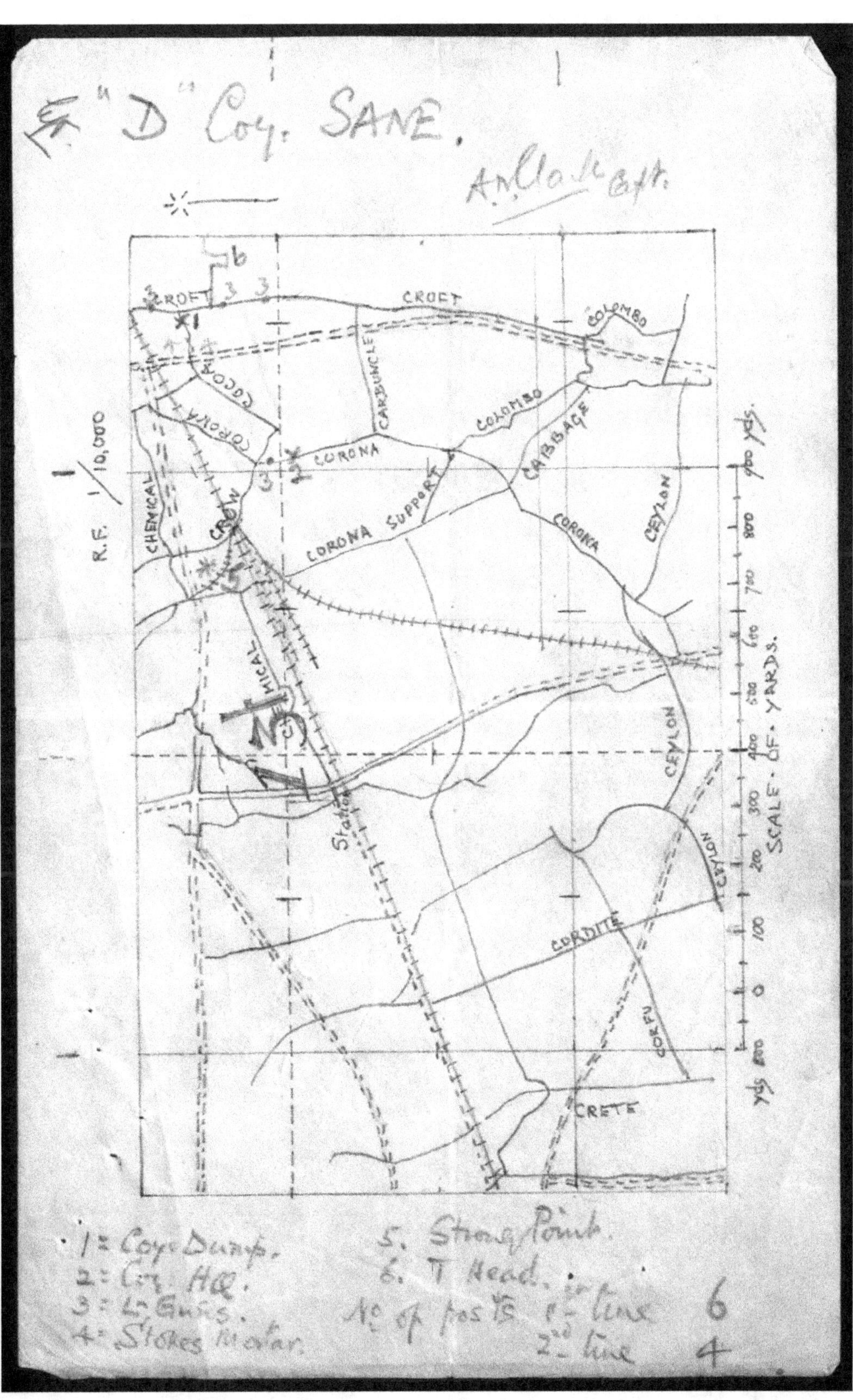
"D" Coy. SANE.
A. N. Clark Capt.
R.F. 1/10,000
CROFT
COLOMBO
CARBUNCLE
CORONA
COLOMBO
CABBAGE
CHEMICAL
CROW
CORONA SUPPORT
CORONA
CEYLON
Station
CEYLON
CEYLON
CORDITE
CORFU
CRETE
SCALE OF YARDS.
1 = Coy. Dump.
2 = Coy. HQ.
3 = L. Guns.
4 = Stokes Mortar.
5. Strong Point.
6. T Head.
No. of posts 1st line 6
2nd line 4

SAME

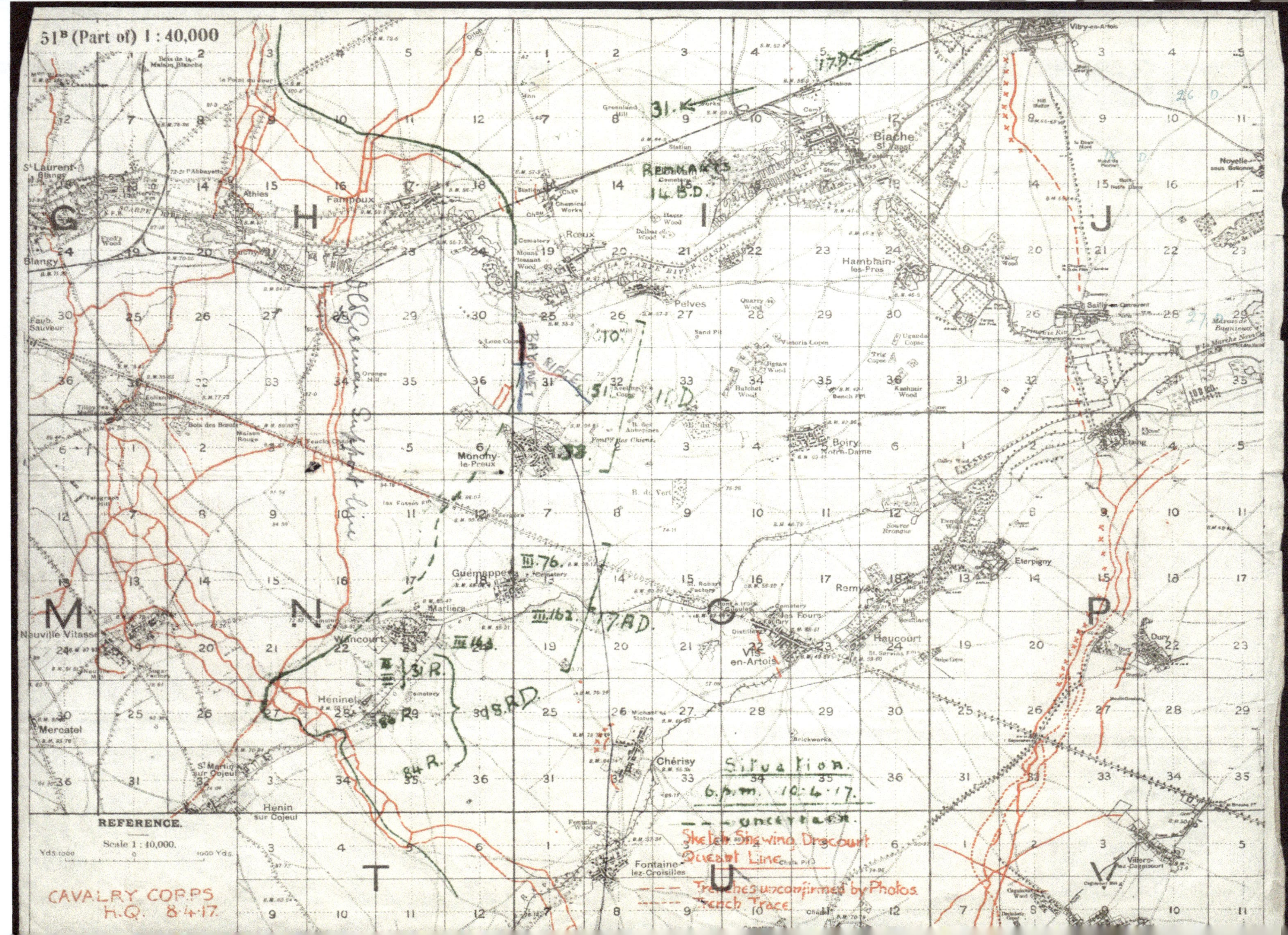
51B (Part of) 1 : 40,000
REFERENCE.
Scale 1 : 40,000.
Yds 1000
1000 Yds.
CAVALRY CORPS
H.Q. 8.4.17.
Situation.
6.p.m. 10.4.17.
uncertain.
Sketch Showing Drocourt
Queant Line
Trenches unconfirmed by Photos.
Trench Trace
St Laurent-Blangy
Blangy
Athies
Fampoux
Feuchy
Roeux
Pelves
Biache St Vaast
Hamblain-les-Prés
Vitry-en-Artois
Sailly-en-Ostrevent
Noyelle-sous-Bellonne
Monchy-le-Preux
Boiry-Notre-Dame
Guémappe
Wancourt
Héninel
Vis-en-Artois
Haucourt
Rémy
Etaing
Dury
Eterpigny
Chérisy
Fontaine-lez-Croisilles
Hénin sur Cojeul
St Martin sur Cojeul
Mercatel
Neuville Vitasse
Tilloy
Faub. St Sauveur
Greenland Hill
Remnants 14 B.D.
31.
17D.
Old German Support line
Bayonet
Rifle
51
10.
11 D.
38
III.76.
III.162.
17 A.D.
III 44.
III 3 R.
29
30 S.R.D.
84 R.
G
H
I
J
M
N
O
P
T
U
V

19 ¼
3 sketches
2 maps

WAR
DIARY
MAY. 1917.

50/17

Vol 20

7th
(S) Bn. A.P.W.O.
(The Yorkshire Regt)

Instructions regarding War Diaries and Intelligence Summaries are contained in F. S. Regs., Part II. and the Staff Manual respectively. Title pages will be prepared in manuscript.

WAR DIARY
or
~~INTELLIGENCE SUMMARY.~~
(Erase heading not required.)

Army Form C. 2118.

Place	Date	Hour	7th (S.) Battn. Yorkshire Regt. Summary of Events and Information	Remarks and references to Appendices
FOSSEUX.	1/5/17.		Training continued. Division began moving in direction of ARRAS. Div is now in XVII Corps. 3rd Army.	MAP. LENS 11. 1/100,000
"	2/5/17.	8.30 AM.	Battn. marched about 1 mile in direction of HAUTEVILLE and left in lorries + buses for Arras. Arrived in the suburb of ~~St~~ Nicholas about 11 AM + went into billets. 50th Bgde Depôt formed at LARESSET. Capt. Stone 7th Yorkshire Regt OC Depôt	REC.
SAN NICHOLAS ARRAS	3/5/17		Battn. remained in billets with orders to be ready to move at 2 hours notice. General attack N. + S. of the Scarpe	REC.
"	4/5/17.	8.30 PM.	A large dump of shells + S.A.A. close to billets occupied by 7th E. York Regt + 6th Dorset Regt caught fire. Two men wounded in the Battn. in consequence.	
		11 PM.	Battn. moved back to Y hutments on the Arras - St Pol road N. E. of AGNES-lez-DUISANS	REC
Y. Hutments AGNES-LEZ-DUISANS.	5/5/17.	4 AM.	Battn. arrived + accomodated in huts.	REC
"	6/5/17 to 7/5/17.		Battn. training continued under Coy arrangements. Attacks from trenches + c practiced by Platoons + Companies.	REC
"	8/5/17.		Training continued. Advance parties 1 Officer + 3 O.R per Coy. + 1 Officer + 5 O.R. for H.Q. left to reconnoitre the trenches to be taken over by the Bgde. These parties remained in the trenches that night. Sector to be taken over by 50th Bgde from 12th Bgde to come into force after relief 10th/11th May, front line about I.13.a.8.5 to I.7.a.0.7	Trench Map 51 B N.W. REC

A5834 Wt. W4973/M687 750,000 8/16 D. D. & L. Ltd. Forms/C.2118/13.

Instructions regarding War Diaries and Intelligence Summaries are contained in F. S. Regs., Part II. and the Staff Manual respectively. Title pages will be prepared in manuscript.

WAR DIARY
or
~~INTELLIGENCE SUMMARY.~~
(Erase heading not required.)

Army Form C. 2118.

7th (S) Battn Yorkshire Regt.

Place	Date	Hour	Summary of Events and Information	Remarks and references to Appendices
Y Hutments AGNES-LEZ-DUISENS	9/5/17	9AM.	Battalion marched to the Candle factory at ~~…~~ ST NICHOLAS North E of ARRAS G.17.A. and rested during the day. At 7 PM continued march to the trenches + took over as follows from 12th Brigade 4th Division. A Coy in front line CLOVER TRENCH relieving 2nd Battn Lancashire Fusilrs. D Coy in support in CUSHION Trench relieving 2nd Battn West Riding Regt. C + B Coys relieved 1st Battn Kings Own Royal Lancaster Regt in COPPER trench. Battn H.Q in CADIZ. Quiet relief. 9th Division on the left. 11th Brigade on the right. Battn under orders of G.O.C. 12th Bgde.	Trench Map 51B NW Edition 6A. Map. Bianche Edition 6 K (attached) DSC
Trenches North of ROEUX	10/5/17		Hostile artillery shelled CADIZ. Our heavy artillery active especially against Chemical Works I.13.d. During the night 7th E. Yorkshire Regt ~~was~~ relieved 9th Division on the left of the Battn.	DSC
"	11/5/17.		Fairly quiet day. At 10 AM. Battn reverted to Command of G.O.C. 50th Brigade.	DSC
		7.30PM.	2 Coys of Attack on the Chemical Works and trenches to the N of it carried out by 11th Bgde and 6th Battn Dorset Regt was successful. Slight casualties. A Coy held CLOVER trench. D Coy CUSHION trench. B + C Coys Copper trench. Battn H Q CADIZ. Capt H.K.C. HARE commanding B Coy was wounded in his dug out by a shell in COPPER trench. B + C Coys moved to CLOVER trench + A Coy moved to the Right of D Coy in CUSHION trench. The XVII Div took over the line from 12th Division during the day.	DSC
"	12/5/17.	2.30AM.	B + C Coys moved forward + occupied the new assembly trenches completed during the night by 7th Pioneer Battn York + Lancaster Regt. These trenches ran from CROOK trench to South end of CUBA trench. A + D Coys took the place of B + C Coys in CLOVER. 2 Coys of 6th Dorset Regt occupied the trenches vacated by the Battn.	Copies of 50th Bgde + Battn orders attached.
		6.30AM.	A general assault by 4th + 17th Divisions began in accordance with Brigade + Battn orders.	

A5834 Wt. W4973/M687 750,000 8/16 D. D. & L. Ltd. Forms/C.2118/13.

Instructions regarding War Diaries and Intelligence Summaries are contained in F. S. Regs., Part II. and the Staff Manual respectively. Title pages will be prepared in manuscript.

WAR DIARY
or
~~INTELLIGENCE SUMMARY.~~
(Erase heading not required.)

Army Form C. 2118.

Place	Date	Hour	7th (S) Batt. Yorkshire Regt — Summary of Events and Information	Remarks and references to Appendices
Trenches N. of ROEUX	12.5.17 (contd)		IV Division's objective. South end of "Cupid" trench S of the railway inclusive. XVII Division attacked with 50th Bgde on the right + 52nd Bgde on the left. The former assaulted on a frontage of 2 Battns, 7th Yorkshire Regt on the right + 7th E. Yorkshire Regt on the left. Objectives CUPID trench from a point 100 yards N of the railway to points Charlie - CUTHBERT line E of X roads I.7.a. The latter on a frontage of one Battn assaulted with objective Charlie + Cuthbert + to be carried out by Lancashire Fusrs. A line of posts will be ~~established in~~ CUTHBERT and COD the Battn attacked, under an effective shrapnel barrage, in 2 waves of 2 Coys each. B Coy on the right in the 1st wave and A Coy on the right in the 2nd wave. Each wave consisted of 2 lines. A + D Coys also furnished 20 men each under two officers to "mop up" CROOK trench. The 1st Battn Rifle Bgde on the right of the Battn + 7th E York Regt on the left. Dust from the artillery barrage made observation impossible after the commencement of the attack. 1 Sect. M.G. attached to Battn.	50th Bgde Orders No 142 + 143 attached to fast sheet
		7.30 AM	Message received from Lt H A Wilkinson A Coy, who had taken command of the assaulting troops when Capt Croft of C Coy had been killed, stated that all objectives had been gained with the exception of junction of CURLY. CUPID + CROOK trenches. Touch had been maintained with 1st Battn Rifle Bgde on the right but not with 7th Battn E York Regt on the left. The last mentioned Battn had not gained their objective + the enemy still held CURLY leaving the left of the Battn greatly exposed. Orders were sent to secure the junction above mentioned but after heavy fighting this important point was not occupied by either side at dusk.	AEROPLANE Photograph attached.
		12.30 PM	A reconnaisance by 2/Lt Collins established the fact that this junction of trenches was not occupied by the enemy nor was the Eastern end of CROOK trench	
		10.30 PM	Lt H A. Wilkinson sent a party under 2/Lt Fox to establish a block in Curly. This was made about 40 yards N of the junction and the junction itself occupied after considerable opposition	
"	13.5.17		Incessant fighting continued all day in the neighbourhood of the block in CURLY but the Battn held its own + was assisted by Stokes mortar battery &c from CROOK.	

A5834 Wt. W4973/M687 750,000 8/16 D. D. & L. Ltd. Forms/C.2118/13.

Instructions regarding War Diaries and Intelligence Summaries are contained in F. S. Regs., Part II. and the Staff Manual respectively. Title pages will be prepared in manuscript.

WAR DIARY
or
~~INTELLIGENCE SUMMARY.~~
(Erase heading not required.)

Army Form C. 2118.

Place	Date	Hour	7th (S) Battn Yorkshire Regt. Summary of Events and Information	Remarks and references to Appendices
Trenches N. of ROEUX.	13.5.17 (contd)	11 P.M.	The Battn attempted to push northwards in CURLY trench in co-operation with a frontal overland attack on the northern part of the trench by 7th East Yorkshire Regt. Both Battns met with strong opposition. The attack of the left Battn failed and the Yorkshire Regt only succeeded in, eventually, advancing the stop 20-25 yards. 2/Lt Fox was in command of the bombing party & both he & Lt Wilkinson were severely wounded. At one period of the fight they got 100 yards up the trench but had to give way. The men were all very tired & it was impossible, owing to the failure of the attack on the left, to do more. There was a shortage of water. Only 3 Coy Officers were left after this operation. 2 Coys 6th Dorset were sent up about midnight to re-inforce front line.	SSC
"	14.5.17.	4 AM	A Coy in the front line & Battn H.Q were relieved by 6th Battn Dorset Regt & withdrew to H.11.A.3.1. B C & D Coys occupied CLOVER trench and were attached to the Dorset Regt They were heavily shelled all day with 5.9" & 4.2" shells.	SSC
"	15/5/17		At 2.30 AM. B C & D Coys were relieved by a Coy of 7th Battn Lincolnshire Regt & rejoined A Coy & H.Q in camp at St Nicholas G.17.A. at 6 A.M. where the latter had arrived during the night. Total Casualties	SSC

Officers Killed	Officers Wounded.	Officers Missing	NCOs & Men Killed	NCOs & Men Wounded	NCOs & Men Missing	
Capt R W S Croft 2/Lt. G S R Roper MC " W A. Thacker	9	1	23	130	42.	Total 13 Officers & 195 OR

The Battn went into the line on 9/5/17 18 Officers 436 O.R & came out with 5 Officers and ~~241~~ O.R Only 1 Coy Officer remained out of 14

SSC

A5834 Wt. W4973/M687 750,000 8/16 D. D. & L. Ltd. Forms/C.2118/13.

Instructions regarding War Diaries and Intelligence Summaries are contained in F. S. Regs., Part II. and the Staff Manual respectively. Title pages will be prepared in manuscript.

WAR DIARY

or

~~INTELLIGENCE SUMMARY.~~

(Erase heading not required.)

Army Form C. 2118.

Place	Date	Hour	7th (S) Battn Yorkshire Regt — Summary of Events and Information	Remarks and references to Appendices
St NICHOLAS. G.17.a.	16/5/17 to 20/5/17		Battn resting and re-organising. Two Coys were formed out of the remains of the Battn with the addition of Capt. Bastium and details from the Bgde Depot at LARESSET making a total of 6 Officers and O.R. One Lewis Gun had been destroyed by shell fire.	RSC
"	21/5/17	10PM	Battn relieved 10th Battn West York Regt in HERON + HUDSON trenches H11.A + H11.b. + came under the orders of GOC 51st Bgde. One Coy carried water, rations + RE material all night until after dawn. During the evening 3, 2nd/Lts joined the Battn from Corps depot. Battn H.Q. H.10.d.4.6. 2/Lts Sherwood + Nicholson joined the Battn	French Map 51B NW.
~~H.11.A~~ H.10.d.4.6	22/5/17	9.30PM	A + D Coy amalgamated (No 1 Coy) moved to CADIZ north of CLYDE + came under the orders of 7th E. York Regt in support of front line. No 2 Coy (B + C Coys) carrying RE stores, water + rations worked all night.	RSC
"	23/5/17	9.30PM	Relieved 7th Battn E York Regt in front line. Relief completed 3 AM 24th. Battn H Q in HUDSON H.11.b.0.4.	RSC
H.11.b.0.4	24/5/17		Both Coys in Cuba trench. Right boundary Cash + Cuba trench junction. Left boundary I.7.b.0.6. 10th W. Yorkshire Regt attached to 51st Bgde on the right of the Battn + 52nd Bgde on the left. Front line heavily shelled all day.	RSC
"	25/5/17		During the night wiring parties worked in front of CUBA + succeeded in wiring the whole front line. Hostile artillery continued to shell the trench all day with 5.9in + 4.2in howitzers. Several casualties occurred.	RSC

A5834 Wt. W4973/M687 750,000 8/16 D. D. & L. Ltd. Forms/C.2118/13.

Instructions regarding War Diaries and Intelligence Summaries are contained in F. S. Regs., Part II. and the Staff Manual respectively. Title pages will be prepared in manuscript.

WAR DIARY
or
~~INTELLIGENCE SUMMARY.~~
(Erase heading not required.)

Army Form C. 2118.

Place	Date	Hour	Summary of Events and Information — 7th (S) Batt Yorkshire Regt	Remarks and references to Appendices
H.11.b.0.4	26.5.17	12 midnight	The Battn was relieved by 8th Batt. S. Staffordshire Regt. and moved back to HERON trench. HQ in sunken road H.11.A.6.3. All day the front line was heavily shelled. Several casualties.	JEC
HERON Trench	27.5.17		Intermittant shelling all day. At 10.30 PM the Battn was relieved by 10th Battn Sherwood Foresters and returned to the camp occupied by the Battn 16th/20th at St Nicholas. Details left at Bgde Depot rejoined the Batt.	JEC
St Nicholas	28/5/17	4.PM	The Battn entrained at Arras + went into billet at HALLOY. arriving about 7.30 PM. Draft 24. O.R	JEC
HALLOY.	29/5/17		Resting + cleaning up. Casualties last tour in the trenches 21/5/17 – 27/5/17. Other Ranks 6 Killed, 19 wounded.	JEC
"	30/5/17		Battn inoculated + cleaning up. 2 Officers + 30 men left at Arras with tunnelling Coy re-joined about 8 PM.	JEC
"	31/5/17		Battn recovering from effects of inoculation. Lt Col. Mairis D.S.O went on leave Major R.E. Cotton taking command during his absence Effective strength of the Battn — Officers 20, O.R 619. Ration " " " — 19. 503. Draft recd late ~~last~~ at night from Corps Depôt 3 Officers 40 O.R. + 2 Off re-joined from Depôt	JEC

A5834 Wt. W4973/M687 750,000 8/16 D. D. & L. Ltd. Forms/C.2118/13.

Secret

50th Infantry Brigade Operation Order No. 142.

Ref Trench Map. 1/20.000. BIACHE. 10th May. 1917

1. 4th Div. will capture the Chemical Works and Station Group of buildings up to and inclusive of the junction of CROOK and CROW trenches with CAM Trench on evening of May 11. Zero will be notified later.

2. 6th Dorsetshire Regt. less two Companies will be attached to 11th Brigade, 4th Division for this operation. OC 6th Dorsetshire Regt. will report direct to GOC 11th Brigade for orders on morning of 10th.

3. The objective of 6th Dorsetshire Regt less 2 Coys. is the junction of CAM, CROW and CROOK trenches and the portion of CROOK trench which runs north to I. 13. b. 12. 8. double block CROOK and CROW and establish a post between CROOK and a post in CLOVER at I. 13 a. 80. 95. to cover the left flank of 4th Divn. as ordered by GOC 11th Brigade.

4. To assist in this attack and to cover consolidation OC 50th Trench Mortar Battery will establish two guns at I. 7 c. 8. 2. in CLOVER to keep up a slow fire on strong point CROW - CROOK - CAM till front wave of 6th Dorsetshire Regt. cross the Cemetery - Gavrelle Road.

The section of 50th Machine Gun Company attached to 7th Yorkshire Regt. will co-operate by covering the left flank of 6th Dorsetshire Regt. with direct fire from trenches in I. 7 c. with 2 guns and to enfilade counter attack from N.E. Two guns will be established in strong point at junction of CROW - CROOK and CAM. to deal with counter attack from East or from Railway.

O.C. 7th Yorkshire Regt. and 7th East Yorkshire Regt. will cooperate with rifle and Lewis gun fire to attract attention of enemy opposite their fronts and keep enemy fire off the front of attack.

5. Tonight 10th/11th May, 2 Coys. 6th Dorsetshire Regt assemble in CLARK trench from CAM at I. 13. a. 3. 5 northward. Headquarters 6th Dorsetshire Regt. will be as ordered by G.O.C. 11th Brigade.

6. 7th Yorkshire Regt. will thin out garrisons of CLOVER and CUSHION so as to be able to clear these trenches entirely as far north as I.7.c.6.1 and I.7.c.8.1 by zero.

7th East Yorkshire Regt. will arrange to let 7th Yorkshire Regt move into these trenches as far north as CLYDE-CUT exclusive.

7. 7th Yorkshire Regt. will place 15 ladders in the broader parts of CUSHION and CLOVER for a distance of 150 yds north from CAM. These ladders will be placed against the western sides of each trench inside the trenches so that they may be pulled up and used as bridges by assaulting Coys. of 6th Dorsetshire Regt.

8. Os. C. Battalions and O.C. 50th Machine Gun Coy. will take special precautions to prevent low flying aeroplanes from reconnoitring our lines from dawn on 11th.

9. The assault will be made behind an intense barrage which will come down about the line of CUSHION trench and creep Eastward at the rate of 100 yds in four minutes.

(sd) H. J. Simson Capt.
Brigade Major 50th Brigade.

Issued through Signals
at 2pm.

Secret.

50th Infantry Brigade Operation Orders No. 143.

10th May. 1917

Ref. 1/20.000. Map. 51 b.N.W.
and 1/20.000 Trench Map, BIACHE.

General Plan and objectives.

1. If the attack of 4th Division (vide O.O.142) is successful an attack will be delivered by the 4th and 17th Divisions at 6/30 am on May 12th.

The objectives will be CORNOA - Railway Cutting at the point where CUPID meets it - CURLY - CHARLIE to its junction with CUTHBERT thence back to front line at I.7.b.7.0.

A line of posts will be established in CUTHBERT and COD, the final artillery barrage halting beyond these trenches.

Roll of 50th Brigade.

2. The 50th Brigade will attack between a line joining the junction of CLOVER and CAM to the point where CUPID joins the railway and an East and West line just North of cross roads in I.7.a (inclusive to 50th Brigade)

4th Division will attack on right and 52nd Brigade on left.

Assaulting Battalions.

3. The attack will be delivered by 7th Yorkshire Regt. on right and 7th East Yorkshire Regt on left.

The dividing line between Battalions will be junction of CUPID and CROOK I.7.D.9.1. (inclusive to 7th Yorkshire Regt.) to South end of CUBA I.7.D.2.3 thence due West.

10th West Yorkshire Regt. will be in GREEN line LUCID and HUDSON, 2 Companies will be ready to move forward to COPPER trench.

6th Dorsetshire Regt. less 2 Coys. revert to Command of G.O.C. 50th Brigade at 9pm. 11th May. During the night 11/12th May, 6th Dorsetshire Regt. will thin out in CROW - CROOK - CAM leaving an adequate garrison for defence. The remainder will move back to trenches in H9.

Section 50th Machine Gun Coy. with 2 guns in CUBA and 2 guns in strong point CAM-CROOK-CROW will standfast.

The trench garrison of 6th Dorsetshire Regt and one section 50th Machine Gun Coy. will come under orders of O.C. 7th Yorkshire Regt. from midnight 11/12th May.

Preliminary Work. 4. A trench will be dug by two Coys. 7th York and Lancs Regt. to extend CUBA southward to join CROOK. This work will be reconnoitred and carried out under orders of O.C. 78th Field Company R.E.

Assembly. 5 Battalions will assemble as follows by 2/30am
(a) 7th Yorkshire Regt in CLOVER and CUSHION. If southern extension of CUBA is reported complete at 2/30am. 7th Yorkshire Regt. will assemble in CUBA-CROOK and CLOVER, O.C. 78th Field Company R.E. will arrange to report progress at 1am. and 2am to O.C. 7th Yorkshire Regt. repeating to Brigade H.Q.
(b) 7th East Yorkshire Regt. will assemble in CUBA and CLASP.

The enemy is in the habit of reconnoitring about dawn with low flying aeroplanes. Every precaution will be taken to prevent assembly being discovered. Where the trenches are shallow they must be camouflaged. Bayonets will not be fixed before zero minus ten minutes

Plan of Attack. 6. At Zero the shrapnel barrage will come down 150 yards from our front line trench and remains stationary for 3 minutes and then moves at rate of 100 yards in 2 minutes by lifts of 50 yards. The assault will be delivered in 2 waves each of 2 lines close behind the barrage.

In the event of the extension of CUBA being unfit for occupation O.C 7th Yorkshire Regt. will arrange to bring his waves into the same alignment as 7th East Yorkshire Regt. on his left under cover of the barrage.

The second wave will close up to 60 yards behind the first wave.

Moppers up must have reliable commanders told off in each Company. They will move behind the first wave.

On reaching final limit the barrage will continue intense for 15 minutes and then stops altogether. Under cover of this barrage posts will be established in CUTHBERT and COD by 7th East Yorkshire Regiment and on Railway cutting and just beyond CUPID by 7th Yorkshire Regt.

4.5 Hows. will fire on trenches in advance of the shrapnel barrage. After the shrapnel barrage stops one battery per artillery brigade will continue searching for machine guns in the open.

The railway embankment will be dealt with by 60 pounder batteries firing cross fire. Smoke shell will be used.

Machine Guns. 7 One section 50th Machine Gun Company will be attached to each assaulting battalion.

The section co-operating with attack of 6th Dorsetshire Regt. on evening of May 11th will standfast and on 12th will engage any enemy machine gun or rifle fire directed against assaulting battalions. Fire will be maintained till the first wave reaches our Machine Gun positions. This section will then withdraw into reserve into LUCID trench.

One section will be ready to turn on a barrage East of COD.

Trench Mortar Battery

8. 2 Guns will take up a position in CROOK trench by 3 am. I 13. b. 1. 7 these guns will cover the right flank and deal with the railway.

2 Guns will be in CUBA to deal with enemy strong point in CASH or machine gun fire from the most westerly half of CHARLIE.

Stokes will open fire immediately on an enemy machine gun or riflemen missed by our barrage.

Flanks.

The flank companies of battalions will get in touch with the companies of the battalions next to them to discuss co-operation before Zero. It is most important that the right company of 7th Yorkshire Regiment should get in touch with the left of 4th Division through 6 Dorsetshire Regt. on night 11th/12th May to ensure that no gap is left in the first wave.

As the right flank is exposed, 7th Yorkshire Regiment will be prepared to occupy the line of CROOK to its junction with CURLY with the second wave should the first wave fail to make progress, and form a defensive flank facing S.E.

Consolidation

10. The line CUPID-CURLY-CHARLIE will be held as the main line of defence. A line of posts will be established in COD and CUTHBERT trenches.

CROOK and CASH will be opened up to form C.Ts. back to the present trench system. A new C.T will be dug joining CHARLIE to CUBA. These will be dug as early as possible.

Machine guns will be placed in depth, guns being established in CROOK, CASH, and CUBA as well as in main line of defence.

Liaison.

11. Battalions will send Liaison Officers to the battalions on their right and left.

Lieut Wilson, 10th West Yorkshire Regt. will report to 11th Brigade H.Q., 12 NOON tomorrow as Liaison Officer, reporting first to 50th Brigade Headquarters.

Flags. 12. 7th Yorkshire Regt. will use pairs of small blue signalling flags to mark their flanks, 7th East Yorkshire Regt. will use pairs of yellow and black flags.

Flares. 13. Green flares will be lit when called for by Klaxon Horns or Very light by the contact aeroplane after zero which has one black band under left lower plane.

Reports. 14. Reports will be sent in hourly from commencement of operations.

15. Movement of Brigade H.Q. will be notified later. Till then Headquarters will be in Railway Cutting.

(sd) H. J. Simson. Captain
Brigade Major. 50th Brigade

Issued through Signals
at 9-30 pm to.

Copy No. 1 and 2 - War Diary
3 - File
4 - Brigadier.
5 - 10th West York.
6 - 7th East York.
7 - 7th York
8 - 6th Dorset
9 - 50th M.G. Coy.
10 - 50th T. M. Bty.
11 - 78th Field Company.
12 - 53rd Field Amb.
13 - No. 2 Coy. Train.
14 - Staff Captain.
15 - Sig. Offr.
16 - B. T. O.
17 - 17th Div. G.
18 - 51st Bde.
19 - 52nd Bde.
20 - 81st Bde.

LA356
CASH
NEW TRENCH
COTE
CUBA
CURLY
CROOK
CROOK
CROW
CUPID

behind C on the left.
Each Coy will be on a frontage of 2 platoons B & C Coy at 4 paces interval. Distances between each line of each wave 20 yds and 60 yds between 1st and 2nd waves

8 A and D Coys will each furnish an Officer and 50 men as moppers up. These parties will join B & C Coys respectively during the night 11/12 on their arrival in the assembly trench. They will wear white bands on left forearms and be provided with 10 bombs each by B and C Coy.

9 At zero the shrapnel barrage will come down 150 yds from our front line trench and remain stationary for 3 mins and then move at rate of 100 yds in 2 minutes by lifts of 50 yds.
The assault will be delivered behind the barrage
In the event of the extension of CUBA being unfit for occupation waves will be brought into the same alignment as the 7th E. York

on the left under cover of the barrage.

On reaching final limit barrage will continue intense for 15 mins and then stop altogether. Under cover of this barrage posts will be established in CUTHBERT and COD by 7th E. Yorks and on the Railway at about I 14 A 55 and at about I 14 A 37 by B Coy and at about I 8 D 22 by C Coy.

10. The Railway embankment will be shelled by 60 pounder batteries using smoke shells.

11. The boundary line between Coys will be from I 13 A 85 80 due East to CROOK at I 13 B 15 along CROOK to I 13 B 48 thence a straight line to I 14 A 37. The whole of this line is inclusive to B. Coy.

12. As the right flank is exposed the second wave (A & D Coys) will be prepared to occupy the line of CROOK to its junction with CURLY should the first wave fail to make progress and form a defensive flank facing South East.

13. If the first wave is successful the second wave will go straight on and join it in the objective.
The moppers up will be responsible for clearing all trenches passed over by the first wave.

14. The line CUPID-CURLY-CHARLIE will be held as the main line of defence. CROOK and CASH will be opened up to form C.Ts back to present trench system.

15. Machine guns will be brought up to assist in consolidation and be placed approximately two guns on right of CUPID one on left near the junction with CROOK and a fourth at about I.13.B.4.3.

16. Each of B & C Coys. will be provided with a pair of small blue signal flags to mark their outer flank. C Coy. will use yellow and black.

17. Reports will be sent hourly to Battn. HQ after zero and directly after capture of objectives.

1/5/17.

Capt
Adjt. 7 York R

"A" Form.

Army Form C. 2121.
(In pads of 100.)

MESSAGES AND SIGNALS.

No. of Message..............

Prefix........ Code............m	Words.	Charge.	This message is on a/c of:	Recd. at..........m.
Office of Origin and Service Instructions.	Sent		Service.	Date
	At............m.		SECRET.	From
	To			
	By		(Signature of "Franking Officer.")	By

TO { O.O. No S.3. by Lieut Col G.B. McMains commdg 7th Yorkshire Regt.

Sender's Number.	Day of Month.	In reply to Number.	AAA
* AA.52.	11		

(1) If the attack tonight of the 4th Division is successful an attack will be delivered by the 4th & 17th divisions at 6.30. a.m. on May 12th

The objectives will be CORONA Railway cutting at point where CUPID meets it – CURLY – CHARLIE to its junction with CUTHBERT thence back to front line at I 1870.

A line of posts will be established in CUTHBERT and COD, the final artillery barrage halting beyond these trenches.

(2) The 50th Brigade will attack between a line joining the junction of CLOVER and CAM to the point where CUPID joins the railway and an East and West line just North of Cross roads in I 7 a.

From

Place

Time

The above may be forwarded as now corrected. (Z)

Censor. Signature of Addressor or person authorised to telegraph in his name.

* This line should be erased if not required.

(3198.) Wt. W 1395/M1294. 375,000 Pads. 1/17. H. W. & V., Ld. (E. 818.)

"A" Form.

Army Form C. 2121.
(In pads of 100.)

MESSAGES AND SIGNALS.

No. of Message..............

Prefix .... Code .... m | Words. | Charge. | This message is on a/c of: | Recd. at .... m.

Office of Origin and Service Instructions.

Sent At .... m. To .... By ....

.... Service.

(Signature of "Franking Officer.")

Date .... From .... By ....

TO

Sender's Number. | Day of Month. | In reply to Number. | AAA

and I7C91 ~~respectively~~ after zero.
They must be in position within
these limits by zero.

(5) Zero hour will be notified later

(6). From dawn on the 11th special
precautions will be taken by A & D Coys to
prevent low flying aeroplanes reconnoitring
our lines. They will be fired on by
Lewis and Vickers guns as soon as
they are within range. Riflemen will
keep as low as possible in the trenches.

(7) The assault will be made behind
an intense barrage which will
come down about the line of Cushion
Trench and creep Eastward at the
rate of 100 yards in four minutes.

From
Place
Time

[illegible] Capt
adjt [illegible]

The above may be forwarded as now corrected. (Z)

Censor. Signature of Addressor or person authorised to telegraph in his name.

* This line should be erased if not required.

Wt. W 12952/M1294. 375,000 Pads. 1/17. H. W. & V., Ld. (E. 818.)

"A" Form.

Army Form C. 2121.
(In pads of 100.)

MESSAGES AND SIGNALS.

No. of Message..............

Prefix.......Code............m	Words.	Charge.	This message is on a/c of:	Recd. at.........m.
Office of Origin and Service Instructions.	Sent		Rifleman ....Service.	Date
	At...........m.			From
	To			
	By		(Signature of "Franking Officer.")	By

TO Operation order No 52 by Lt Col G. R. Mairis DSO. Y[orks]R.

Sender's Number.	Day of Month.	In reply to Number.	AAA
AAH2	10		

(1) Ref O.O. No 51 of today para 2. Objectives of 6th Dorset less 2 Coys are the junction of CAM CROW & CROOK trenches and the portion of CROOK Trench which runs N. to I.13.B 1½.8. double block CROOK and CROW and establish a post between Crook and a post in CLOVER at I 13 A80.95. to cover left flank of the [illegible] Division.

(2) To assist in this attack and to cover consolidation O.C. 50 TMB will establish 2 guns at I 7 C 8 2 in Clover to keep up a slow fire on strong point CROW CROOK CAM till front wave 6th Dorset crosses the Cemetery Gavrelle road.

The section of 50 M G Coy.

From SASH

Place

Time

The above may be forwarded as now corrected. (Z)

Capt

Censor. Signature of Addressor or person authorised to telegraph in his name.

* This line should be erased if not required.

(3198.) Wt. W 1295/M1294. 375,000 Pads. 1/17. H. W. & V., Ld. (E. 818.)

"A" Form.

Army Form C. 2121.
(In pads of 100.)

MESSAGES AND SIGNALS.

No. of Message..............

Prefix....... Code........ m	Words.	Charge.	This message is on a/c of:	Recd. at .... m.
Office of Origin and Service Instructions.	Sent At.......m. To....... By.......		..................Service. (Signature of "Franking Officer.")	Date....... From....... By.......

TO

Sender's Number.	Day of Month.	In reply to Number.	AAA

attached to 7th Yorkshire Regt will cooperate by covering the left flank of 6th Dorsetshire Regt with direct fire from Trenches in I 7 C with 2 guns and to enfilade counter attack from North East. 2 Guns will be established in strong point at junction of CROW CROOK and CAM to deal with counter attack from East or from Railway

(3) OC A Coy will cooperate with rifle and Lewis gun fire to attract attention of any enemy in front and keep enemy's fire off front of attack

(4) Ref Para 4 of O.O. 51. A and D Coy may occupy CLOVER and CUSHION between CLYDE and CUT and I 7 C 6 1

From

Place

Time

The above may be forwarded as now corrected. (Z)

Censor. Signature of Addressor or person authorised to telegraph in his name.

* This line should be erased if not required.

(3198.) Wt. W 12952/M1294. 375,000 Pads. 1/17. H. W. & V., Ld. (E. 818.)

for 100 yards North of CAM. on the night 10/11th May.

4 O.C. A & D Coys will clear CLOVER and CUSHION trenches up to I.7.C.6.1 and I.7.C.9.1 by daylight on 11th May.

This will be done by moving their companies into the northern portion of CLOVER and CUSHION Trenches respectively in order to clear our barrage which will begin 100 yards West of the Road W of CLOVER TRENCH.

5 On completion of Operation A the 2 Coys. 6th Dorset Regt should be disposed in the portion of CROOK Trench which runs N and S and loop junction with CAM. total 150 yards. with supports in S. portion of CLOVER.

Operation B

6 The capture on the morning of 12th May by the 4th and 17th Divisions of The Cemetery I.19.b. – CORONA trench and CUPID trench to junction with railway – CURLEY and CHARLIE to junction of CHARLIE

with WHIP and WISH.

7 During the night 11/12th the pioneers will join up CUBA and CROOK Trench and the line from about I 7.d 2.3 to I 13.b.1.6. will be taken over by B + C Coys (B on right and C on left). This line will form the Battn. assembly trench for the first wave in Operation B. The second wave consisting of A Coy on the right and D Coy on the left will assemble in CLOVER Trench the same night between I. 13 a 80.45 and I. 7c. 8.3.

8 Further orders for both oper-ations will be issued later.

10/5/17 (Signed) L.V.C. Hawkes Cpt
Capt 7th York R.

"A" Form.
Army Form C. 2121.
(In pads of 100.)

MESSAGES AND SIGNALS.

No. of Message..............

Prefix...... Code...... m	Words.	Charge.	This message is on a/c of:	Recd. at ...... m.
Office of Origin and Service Instructions.	Sent		.... Service.	Date ....
	At............m.			From ....
	To............			
	By............		(Signature of "Franking Officer.")	By............

TO

Sender's Number.	Day of Month.	In reply to Number.	AAA
*			

4th Division will attack on right and 52nd Brigade on left.

(3) The 7th Yorkshire will attack with East Yorkshire on its left. The dividing line between battns. will be the junction of CUPID and CROOK, I7O91 (inclusive to 7th York) to South end of CUBA, I7D23, thence due west

(4) During the night of 11th/12th May 6th Dorset will thin out in CROW, CROOK CAM having an adequate garrison for defence. The remainder will move back to HQ.

2 guns MG Coy in strongpoint CAM CROOK CROW will stand fast and from midnight 11/12 May garrison of these trenches comes under orders of O.C. 7 York R.

From

Place

Time

The above may be forwarded as now corrected. **(Z)**

Censor. Signature of Addressor or person authorised to telegraph in his name.

* This line should be erased if not required.

(3198.) Wt. W 1295?/M1294. 375,000 Pads. 1/17. H. W. & V., Ld. (E. 818.)

"A" Form.

Army Form C. 2121.
(In pads of 100.)

MESSAGES AND SIGNALS.

No. of Message..............

Prefix .... Code .... m	Words.	Charge.	This message is on a/c of:	Recd. at .... m.
Office of Origin and Service Instructions.	Sent		.... Service.	Date
	At .... m.			From
	To			
	By		(Signature of "Franking Officer.")	By

TO

Sender's Number.	Day of Month.	In reply to Number.	AAA

*

(5). A Trench will be dug by two companies 7th York and Lancaster Regt to extend CUBA southward to join CROOK.

(6). Assembly. By 12 midnight the Battalion will be assembled as follows B and C Coys in Clover A and D in CUSHION the rights of B and A Coys both resting on CAM.

The left of C & D Coys will rest on an East and West line through I 7 D 2 3

If southern extension of CUBA is reported complete by 2.30 orders will be sent to Coys to move forward, so that B & C Coys occupy the same front in this Trench and A and D company in CLOVER. In this case B and C Coy assemble in CUBA & CROOK with right on CROW at about I 13 B 1 6

From

Place

Time

The above may be forwarded as now corrected. (Z)

Censor. Signature of Addressor or person authorised to telegraph in his name.

* This line should be erased if not required.

(3198.) Wt. W 12952/M1294. 375,000 Pads. 1/17. H. W. & V., Ld. (E. 818.)

"A" Form.

Army Form C. 2121.
(In pads of 100.)

MESSAGES AND SIGNALS.

No. of Message..............

Prefix........ Code............ m	Words.	Charge.	This message is on a/c of:	Recd. at........ m.
Office of Origin and Service Instructions.	Sent		.... Service.	Date............
6 (cont)	At........ m.			From............
	To........			
	By........		(Signature of "Franking Officer.")	By............

TO

Sender's Number.	Day of Month.	In reply to Number.	AAA
*			

In the event of this forward move being made A & D Coys will take forward to CLOVER all the scaling ladders now in CUSHION

The East York regt. will assemble in CUBA and CLASP.

(8) Every precaution will be taken to prevent the assembly being discovered and if required for the new Trench CUBA-CROOK there are 3 rolls camouflage at the junction CLOVER CAM.

(9) ~~At Zero~~ B and C Coy will form the first wave B on the right and C on the left. A and D Coy will form the second wave A Coy behind B on the right and D Coy behind C on the left

From

Place

Time

The above may be forwarded as now corrected. (Z)

Censor. Signature of Addressor or person authorised to telegraph in his name.

* This line should be erased if not required.

(3198.) Wt. W 1295./M1294. 375,000 Pads. 1/17. H. W. & V., Ld. (E. 818.)

"A" Form.

Army Form C. 2121.
(In pads of 100.)

MESSAGES AND SIGNALS.

No. of Message..............

Prefix......... Code......... m	Words.	Charge.	This message is on a/c of:	Recd. at .... m.
Office of Origin and Service Instructions.	Sent		.... Service.	Date ....
	At .... m.			From ....
	To			
	By		(Signature of "Franking Officer.")	By ....

TO

Sender's Number.	Day of Month.	In reply to Number.	AAA
*			

Each coy will be on a frontage of 2 platoons
B and C coy at 4 paces interval
Distances between each line of each
wave 20 yards and 60 yards
between 1st and 2nd waves.

(8) A and D Coys will each furnish an
Officer and 20 men as moppers up
these parties will join B and C Coys
respectively during the night 11/12 ~~and~~
~~and will~~ on their arrival in the assembly
Trench, they will wear white bands on left
forearm and be provided with 10 bombs
each by B and C Coys.

(9) At Zero the Shrapnel barrage will
come down 150 yards from our front
line Trench and remain stationary for
3 minutes and then moves at rate of
100 yards in two minutes by lifts of
50 yards.

From

Place

Time

The above may be forwarded as now corrected. (Z)

Censor. Signature of Addressor or person authorised to telegraph in his name.

* This line should be erased if not required.

(3198.) Wt. W 12952/M1294. 375,000 Pads. 1/17. H. W. & V., Ld. (E. 818.)

"A" Form.

Army Form C. 2121.
(In pads of 100.)

MESSAGES AND SIGNALS.

No. of Message..............

Prefix.......... Code.............. m	Words.	Charge.	*This message is on a/c of:*	Recd. at .... m.
Office of Origin and Service Instructions.	Sent		.... *Service.*	Date..............
	At.............m.			From ....
	To..............			
	By..............		(Signature of "Franking Officer.")	By................

TO

Sender's Number.	Day of Month.	In reply to Number.	AAA

The assault will be delivered behind the barrage.

In the event of the extension of CUBA being unfit for occupation waves will be brought into the same alignment as the 7th East York on the left under cover of the barrage.

On reaching final limit barrage will continue intense for 15 minutes and then stop altogether. Under cover of this barrage posts will be established in CUTHBERT & COD by 7th East York and on the Railway at about I 14 A 55 and at about I 14 A 37 by B Coy and at about I 8 D 22 by C Coy.

(10) The railway embankment will be shelled by 60 pounder batteries using smoke shells.

From

Place

Time

The above may be forwarded as now corrected. **(Z)**

Censor. Signature of Addressor or person authorised to telegraph in his name.

* This line should be erased if not required.

(3198.) Wt. W 12953/M1294. 375,000 Pads. 1/17. H. W. & V., Ld. (E. 818.)

"A" Form.

Army Form C. 2121.
(In pads of 100.)

MESSAGES AND SIGNALS.

No. of Message..............

Prefix........ Code............ m	Words.	Charge.	This message is on a/c of:	Recd. at .... m.
Office of Origin and Service Instructions.	Sent		.... Service.	Date ....
	At............m.			From ....
	To..............			
	By..............		(Signature of "Franking Officer.")	By..............

TO

Sender's Number.	Day of Month.	In reply to Number.	AAA
*			

(11). The boundary line between Coys will be from *~~I 7 C 85 30~~ due East to CROOK at I 13 B 18 along CROOK to I 13 B 48 thence a straight line to I 14 A 37. The whole of this line is inclusive to B Coy.

*I 13 A 85 80

(12) As the Right flank is exposed the Second wave (A+D Coys) will be prepared to occupy the line of CROOK to its junction with Curly should the first wave fail to make progress and form a defensive flank facing South East.

(13) If the first wave is successful the Second wave will go straight on and join it in the objective.

The moppers up will be responsible

From

Place

Time

The above may be forwarded as now corrected. (Z)

.... Censor. Signature of Addressor or person authorised to telegraph in his name.

* This line should be erased if not required.

(3198.) Wt. W 1395.2/M1294. 375,000 Pads. 1/17. H. W. & V., Ld. (E. 818.)

"A" Form.

MESSAGES AND SIGNALS.

Army Form C. 2121.
(In pads of 100.)

No. of Message..............

Prefix......... Code............ m	Words.	Charge.	This message is on a/c of:	Recd. at.........m.
Office of Origin and Service Instructions.	Sent		.... Service.	Date............
	At..........m.			From ....
	To..........			
	By..........		(Signature of "Franking Officer.")	By............

TO

Sender's Number.	Day of Month.	In reply to Number.	AAA

for clearing all trenches passed over by the first wave

(14). The line CUPID-CURLY-CHARLIE will be held as the main line of defense. CROOK and CASH will be opened up to form CTS back to present trench system

(15) Machine guns will be brought up to assist in consolidation and placed approximately at two guns on right of Cupid one on left near its junction with CROOK and a fourth at about I 13 B 4 8.

(16) Each of B and C Coys will be provided with a pair of small blue signal flags to mark its outer flank. East Yorks use yellow & black.

(17) Reports will be sent hourly to Battn HQ

From

Place

Time

The above may be forwarded as now corrected. (Z)

Censor. Signature of Addressor or person authorised to telegraph in his name.

* This line should be erased if not required.

(3198.) Wt. W 12952/M1294. 375,000 Pads. 1/17. H. W. & V., Ld. (E. 818.)

Secret

Operation Order 51.

The following operations will be carried out on the 11th and 12th May respectively.

Operation A.

1 The capture by 4 Division of Chemical Works and Station Group of buildings up to and inclusive of the junction of CROOK and CROW Trenches with CAM Trench.

2 This operation will take place on the evening of 11 May before dusk.
For this operation 2 Coys 6 Dorset Regt will be placed at disposal of 4 Division to assist in capture of junction of CAM, CROW and CROOK Trenches and the portion of CROOK Trench which runs N NE.

3 These 2 Coys will assemble in the newly constructed trench in rear of CUSHION running North from CAM Trench at I.13 a 3.5 and CADIZ

Operation Order No 53

by

Lieut Col. Edgar [illegible] DSO
Commdg 9th Bn [illegible]

If the attack tonight of the 1st Division is successful an attack will be delivered by the 4th and 17th Divisions at 1.30am on May 12th.

The objectives will be CORONA railway cutting at point where CUPID meets it – CURLY – CHARLIE to its junction with CUTHBERT thence back to front line at I 18 70.

A line of posts will be established in CUTHBERT and COD the final artillery barrage falling beyond these trenches.

The 50th Bde will attack between [illegible] running from the junction of CLOVER and CRAB to the point where CUPID [illegible] the Railway and [illegible] [illegible] just North of [illegible] [illegible]

[illegible] Division will attack on right and [illegible] Bde on left.

The 9th [illegible] will attack

[illegible] East Yorkshires and left [illegible]
[illegible] dividing line between [illegible]
will be the junction of CUPID [illegible]
CROOK. [illegible] 9th [illegible] to [illegible]
[illegible] side of CUBA [illegible] [illegible]
due west

4. During the night of 11th/12th May
1st Bord. will [illegible] out to CROW
CROOK CAM [illegible] an adequate
garrison for defence. [illegible] remainder
will [illegible] back to HQ.

2 [illegible] M.G. Coy in STRONG
Point CAM CROOK CROW will
stand fast and from midnight 11/12th
May garrison of these [illegible]
under [illegible] orders of O.C. 9th [illegible]

5. [illegible] will be [illegible] by 2 Coys
9th [illegible] [illegible] Regt to extend
CUBA Southward to join CROOK.

6. Assembly. By 12 midnight the
[illegible] will be assembled as
follows: B and C Coys [illegible]
A and D in CUSHION [illegible]
[illegible] A Coy. [illegible]
AM.
[illegible] of C and D Coys

[illegible] are [illegible] [illegible]
[illegible] 190 73.
[illegible] [illegible] [illegible] [illegible]
CUBA [illegible] completed by [illegible]
order will be sent [illegible] Coy to
move forward [illegible] B & C Coy
occupy the same front [illegible] the
trenches and C and D Coy in CLOVER
[illegible] A and D Coy assemble
[illegible] CUBA & CROOK [illegible]
[illegible] about 1 1 3 E 1 b.

[illegible] of [illegible] forward [illegible]
being made A and D Coy will
[illegible] forward to CLOVER [illegible] the
[illegible] ladders [illegible] CUSHION.

[illegible] R. will assemble
[illegible] CUBA and CLASP

[illegible] precaution will be
taken [illegible] the assembly being
[illegible] and if required for the
[illegible] CUBA - CROOK there are
[illegible] camouflage at the junction
CLOVER CAM.

[illegible] & C Coy will form the
first wave B on the right and
C on the left. A and D Coy
will form the second wave, A Coy
behind B on the right and D Coy

Vol 21

20 Y
4 sheets
map.

WAR
DIARY
JUNE.

7th
YORKSHIRE
REGt

Army Form C. 2118.

Instructions regarding War Diaries and Intelligence Summaries are contained in F. S. Regs., Part II. and the Staff Manual respectively. Title pages will be prepared in manuscript.

WAR DIARY ~~or~~ INTELLIGENCE SUMMARY.

(*Erase heading not required.*)

Place	Date	Hour	7th (S) Battn Yorkshire Regt. Summary of Events and Information	Remarks and references to Appendices
HALLOY	1/6/17		Battn doing light duty only on account of recent inoculations Effective Strength 20 Officers 614 OR Ration Strength 17 " 493 " Divisional Conference at H.Q. for C.Os	LENS MAP
"	2/6/17		First day of training. Drill, bayonet fighting musketry on the range &c	
"	3/6/17		Church Parades	
"	4/6/17		Training continued. Lt. Mulholland appointed Batt Intelligence Officer, 2/Lt Hume Lewis Gun Officer. The four Coys have only sufficient men to form 2 platoons each. D Coy being much the weakest. Lt Col R D'A Fife CMG awarded DSO in King's Birthday Honours	
"	5/6/17		Training. Preliminary heats run off for Cross Country race of 4 miles at 6 PM.	
"	6/6/17		Training	
"	7/6/17		Training in the morning. Divsl Horse Show. Battn gained 1st prize for pair of pack mules.	
"	8/6/17		Training continued. 2nd period from 9th–16th including Coy drill, attacks &c	
	9/6/17		Brigade Sports 3 pm 9th. Draft 3 officers 2nd Lts, Hodgson, Barker, Sykes, and 18 OR arrived on 8th	

A5834 Wt. W4973/M687 750,000 8/16 D. D. & L. Ltd. Forms/C.2118/13.

Instructions regarding War Diaries and Intelligence Summaries are contained in F. S. Regs., Part II. and the Staff Manual respectively. Title pages will be prepared in manuscript.

WAR DIARY
or
~~INTELLIGENCE SUMMARY.~~
(Erase heading not required.)

Army Form C. 2118.

Place	Date	Hour	7th (S) Battn Yorkshire Regt. Summary of Events and Information	Remarks and references to Appendices
HALLOY	10/6/17		Church Parades. Bgde Boxing Competition in the afternoon. Battn obtained 1st Prize in the heavyweight competition + 2nd in middle weight + catch weight competitions. Draft 1 Officer 2/Lt Batt + 11 O.R.	DRC
"	11/6/17		Training continued. Draft 9 O.R.	DRC
"	12/6/17		The Commanding Officer returned from leave and assumed command of the Bgde during Genl Yatman's absence at Divl HQ	DRC
"	13/6/17 to 14/6/17		Training continued. Tactical Scheme set by C.O. for Coy Commanders without troops.	DRC
	15/6/17		"Evelyn Wood" Competition held by the 50th Bgde. Teams of 20 from each platoon in the Battn competing. After a six mile march teams shot at 2 unknown ranges. Result, Battn did not get more than 3rd place. Rest of the day training continued.	DRC
	16/6/17	7 AM.	Battn practised an attack on the training area under Battn arrangements in conjunction with 10th Battn West Yorkshire Regt. The remaining 2 hours training devoted to Specialists + bayonet fighting &c. 8 Officers + 129 O.R. inoculated. This completes the inoculation of the Battn.	DRC
	17/6/17		Church parades. Lt Col Mairis D.S.O. returned from the Bgde + assumed command of the Battn.	DRC
	18/6/17	6 AM.	Practice attack on a S. Point near HURTEBISE Farm by the Battn. Preparations for a move to the line tomorrow.	DRC

A5834 Wt. W4973/M687 750,000 8/16 D. D. & L. Ltd. Forms/C.2118/13.

Instructions regarding War Diaries and Intelligence Summaries are contained in F. S. Regs., Part II. and the Staff Manual respectively. Title pages will be prepared in manuscript.

WAR DIARY

or

~~INTELLIGENCE SUMMARY.~~

(Erase heading not required.)

Army Form C. 2118.

Place	Date	Hour	7th (S) Batt. Yorkshire Regt — Summary of Events and Information	Remarks and references to Appendices
HALLOY	19/6/17	7.30AM	Batt. marched to MONDICOURT and went by bus to St. NICHOLAS where it arrived about 12 noon the Batt. occupied tents in almost the same place as in May (C.17.a). The following have been awarded decorations for gallantry in the May operations N of the Chemical Works. Military Medals. Sgt. J.G. MADDISON. L/Cpl. T. CARNEY. L/Cpl. F. MARSDEN (previously awarded D.C.M.) Pte M. RILEY. + Pte J. WILLIAMS.	Trench Map Sheet 51B N.W. RSC
ST. NICHOLAS C.17.a.	20/6/17.	6 P.M.	Batt. moved up to the Support line in the Railway cutting H.7.d and relieved 22nd Batt. Northumberland Fusiliers belonging to 102 Bgde. Reserve Batt. 6th Dorset in sunken road H7.a moved up to the same ~~day~~ line. During the night 7th E. York Regt + 10th W. York Regt relieved 2 Batts of 102nd Bgde on the right + left respectively in the front line H.6. and I.1. Bgde depot joined 'B' Echelon + bivouacked at H.11.c under a Capt of 7th E York Regt. Capt de Quetteville to 3rd Army School. Major GOTTON in command of Batt. details at Bgde Depot.	RSC
Railway Cutting H.7.d	21/6/17.		50th Inf Bgde took over the line from 102nd Bgde. Working + carrying parties to the front line at night	RSC
"	22/6/17		200 men on working + carrying parties all night	RSC
"	23/6/17			
"	24/6/17	9.45PM	Batt. moved up to the front line + relieved the 7th Batt. E. Yorkshire Regt. Relief completed 2 AM. 25th	RSC

A5834 Wt. W4973/M687 750,000 8/16 D. D. & L. Ltd. Forms/C.2118/13

Instructions regarding War Diaries and Intelligence Summaries are contained in F. S. Regs., Part II. and the Staff Manual respectively. Title pages will be prepared in manuscript.

WAR DIARY
or
~~INTELLIGENCE SUMMARY.~~
(Erase heading not required.)

Army Form C. 2118.

7(s) Batt[n] Yorkshire Regt

Place	Date	Hour	Summary of Events and Information	Remarks and references to Appendices
HURRUM Trench. ~~H 6 d~~ H.6.c.1.5.	25/6/17		Bgde was occupying the left sector held by the Division (Div[l] front I.14.c.5.2 – I.1.b.1.8) The Batt[n] holding the right sector of left Bgde. (Bgde front I.7.d.6.5 to I.1.b.1.8) Batt[n] front ~~I.7.d.6.5~~ – I.7.b.8.9 – I.1.d.65.80. Batt[n] was holding the line as follows:– A Coy 1 platoon in front line in COKE with 1 platoon in Support in CRY B Coy 1 platoon in front line in COLIN + one platoon in Support in CURSE and CONRAD. C Coy in Support line in ~~[illegible]~~ CORK + CALEDONIAN. D Coy in "Green Line" HURRUM. Each Coy had only 2 platoons of about 40 strong per platoon Batt[n] H.Q. in HURRUM. 9th Batt[n] (52nd Bgde) on Right + 6th Batt[n] Dorset Regt on left.	Trench Map 1/20,000 attached BIACHE Edition 6[A].
			Intermittent shelling in the forward area all day. Reserve line being heavily shelled at intervals with 5.9" + 4.5" shells.	[initials]
"	26/6/17		During the night 26/27 the Batt[n] moved further South + took over line held by Northumberland Fusl[s] + portion of the line held by West Riding Regt. New Batt[n] front I.7.d.9.9 to I.1.d.7.2. distributed as follows A Coy front line CUTHBERT. B + C Coys CHARLIE (Support). D Coy in reserve in CUBA. Batt[n] H.Q. in CHILI at ~~H.12.c.~~ H.12.b.2.8. Dorset Regt taking over trenches the Batt[n] ~~[illegible]~~ vacated on left. Relief took all night. Manchester Regt prolonged line on the Right.	[initials]
CHILI. H.12.b.2.8.	27/6/17		All trenches shelled intermittently with gas + tear shells.	[initials]
"	28/6/17.		Attack on left by ~~other~~ another Division brought down a barrage at 7.18 PM on all trenches held by Batt[n].	[initials]

A5834 Wt. W4973/M687 750,000 8/16 D. D. & L. Ltd. Forms/C.2118/13

Instructions regarding War Diaries and Intelligence Summaries are contained in F. S. Regs., Part II. and the Staff Manual respectively. Title pages will be prepared in manuscript.

WAR DIARY
or
~~INTELLIGENCE~~ SUMMARY.

(Erase heading not required.)

Army Form C. 2118.

7th (S) Battn. Yorkshire Regt.

Place	Date	Hour	Summary of Events and Information	Remarks and references to Appendices
CHILI Trench H.12.b.2.8.	29/6/17		The Battn. was relieved by 8th Battn. S. Staffordshire Regt. Relief completed 4. AM. Heavy shelling on all trenches during the relief + hostile trench mortars active. Battn. reached camp at St. Nicholas about 7.30 AM. 2nd Lt. SYKES was killed on the way out. 2 Lt. Hodgson gassed and several men gassed during the relief. The enemy were particularly active with artillery, trench mortars and gas shells during the ~~whole~~ night and early morning.	REC
CAMP. ST. NICHOLAS C.17.a.	30/6/17		Battn. resting. During the tour in the trenches the casualties were as follows:- 1 Officer Killed + 2. O.R. 1 Officer + 2 O.R. gassed, Wounded 6. O.R. On 26th Lt. H A Wilkinson + 2/Lt. Fox awarded the Military Cross for gallantry in the action of 12th + 13th May/17. No 242697 Pte. TOM DRESSER of D. Coy was awarded the VICTORIA CROSS for bravery on 12th May. "For most conspicuous bravery and devotion to duty. Pte. Dresser, in spite of being twice wounded on the way, and suffering great pain, succeeded in conveying an important message from Battn. Headquarters to the front line trenches, which he eventually reached in an exhausted condition. His fearlessness + determination to deliver this message at any cost proved of the greatest value to his Battalion at a critical period"	
			Effective strength: Officers 28, O.R. 617. Ration Strength: Officers 21, O.R. 533	REC

A5834 Wt. W4973/M687 750,000 8/16 D. D. & L. Ltd. Forms/C.2118/13.

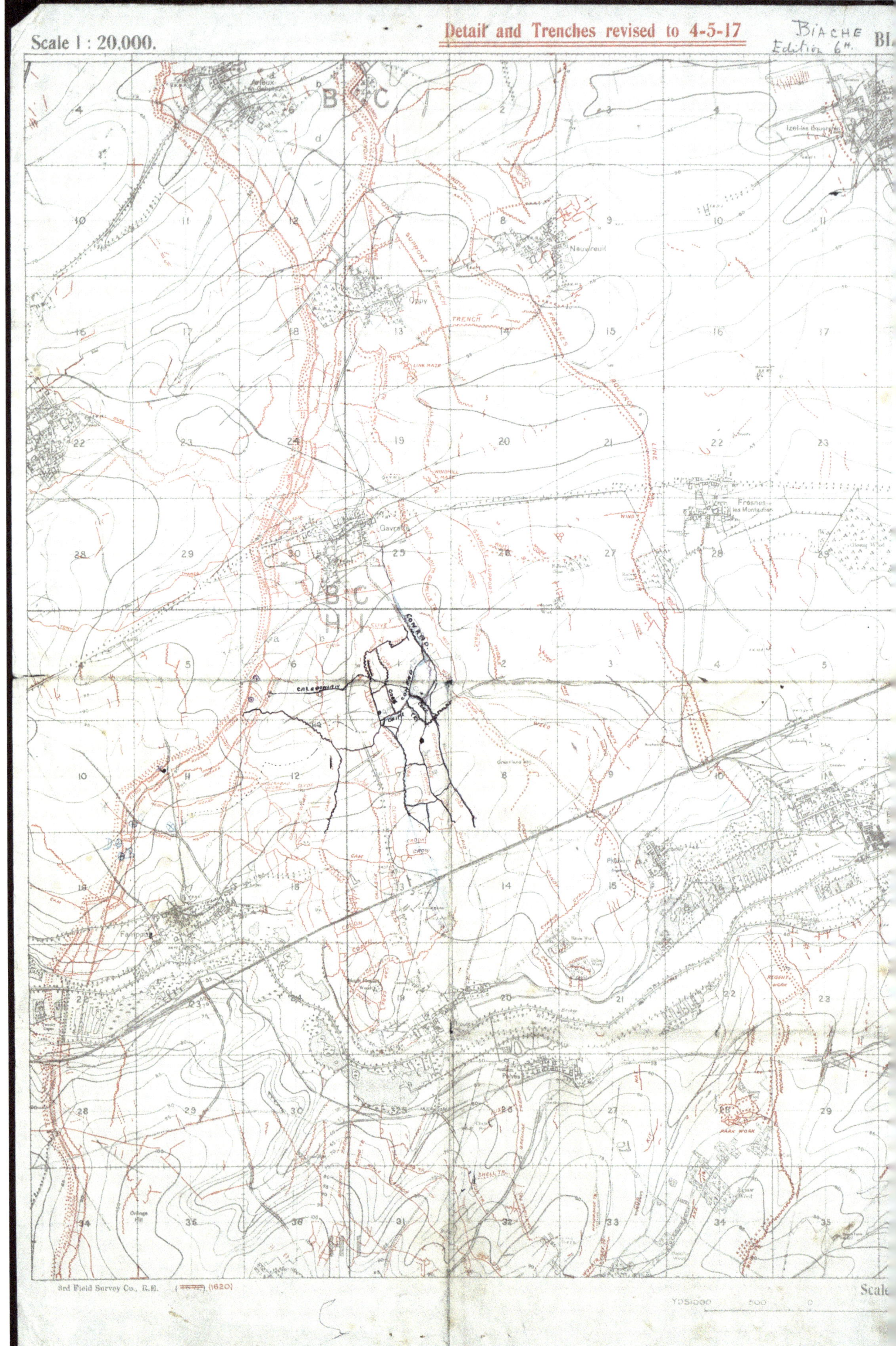

Scale 1 : 20,000.
Detail and Trenches revised to 4-5-17
BIACHE
Edition 6th.
Izel-les Equerchin
Nauvreuil
Oppy
Gavrelle
Fresnes les Montauban
Fampoux
Plouvain
Roeux
Pelves
Greenland Hill
Bradford Copse
Bois Rossignol
Rau Wood
Lone Wood
Orange Hill
Park Work
Regent Work
Link Trench
Support Trench
Fresnes
Windmill
Caledonian
3rd Field Survey Co., R.E.
(1620)
Scale

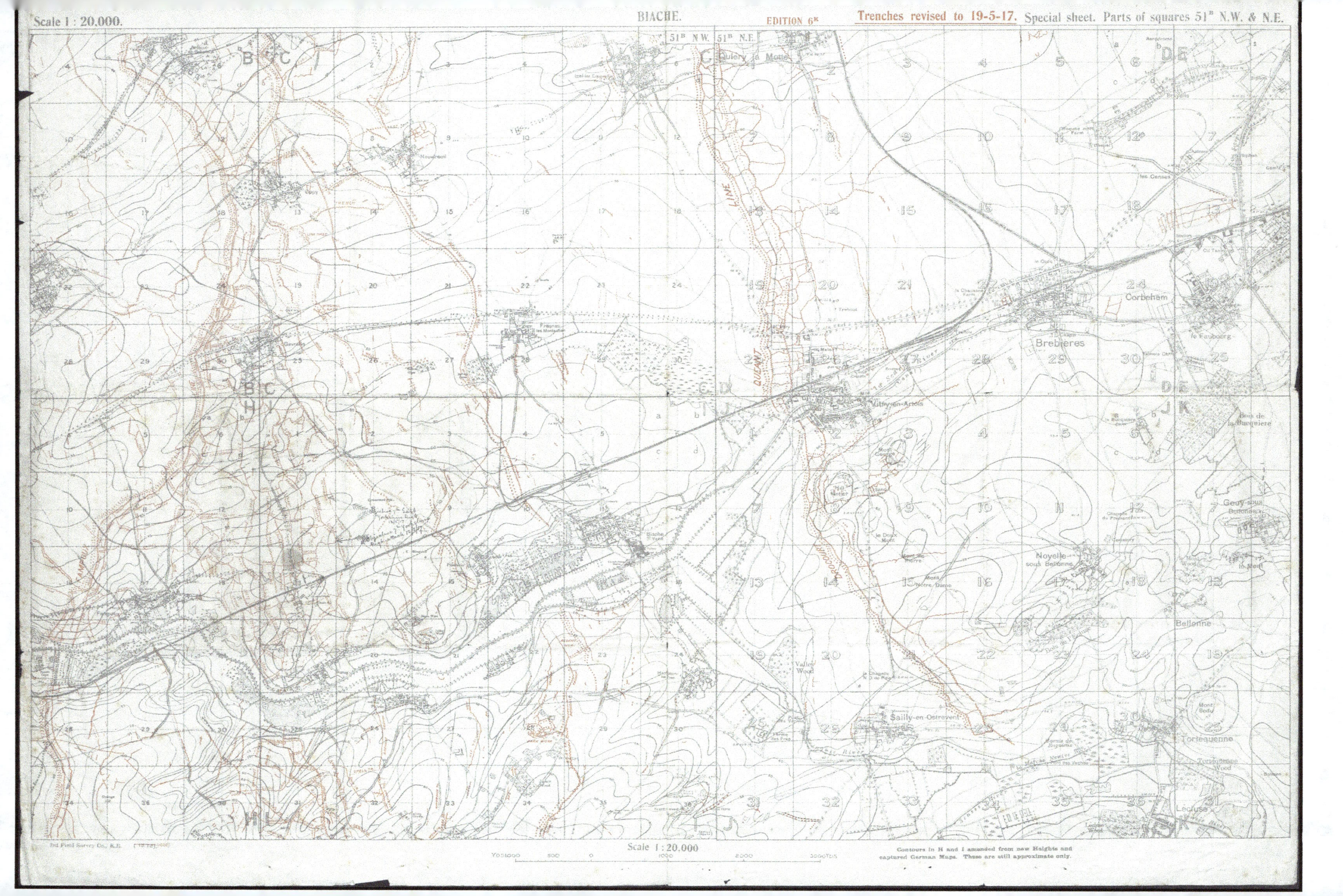

Scale 1 : 20,000.
BIACHE.
EDITION 6[B]
Trenches revised to 19-5-17. Special sheet. Parts of squares 51[B] N.W. & N.E.
51[B] N.W.
51[B] N.E.
Quiery la Motte
Corbehem
Brebières
Vitry-en-Artois
Noyelle sous Bellonne
Bellonne
Sailly-en-Ostrevent
Tortequenne
Lécluse
Valley Wood
LINE
QUEANT
DROCOURT
Scale 1 : 20,000
Contours in H and I amended from new Heights and captured German Maps. These are still approximate only.

WAR
DIARY
JULY
1914

N/

YORKSHIRE
REGT

Vol 22

Instructions regarding War Diaries and Intelligence Summaries are contained in F. S. Regs., Part II. and the Staff Manual respectively. Title pages will be prepared in manuscript.

WAR DIARY
or
~~INTELLIGENCE SUMMARY.~~
(Erase heading not required.)

Army Form C. 2118.

Place	Date	Hour	7th (S) Battn Yorkshire Regt. Summary of Events and Information	Remarks and references to Appendices
St. NICHOLAS Camp. G.17	1/7/17		Church parades.	MAP. 51B NW Edition 6A JSC
"	2/7/17 to 6/7/17		Battn training, special instruction in wiring, revetting & digging trenches. Coy commanders exercised in writing orders for a trench raid. Every night from 2nd to 5th 3 Officers + 125 O.R from each Battn in the Bgde worked on a trench for cable on S side of the River Scarpe, Opposite FAMPOUX in the direction of MONCHY a few casualties the 2nd night but none in the Battn.	
"			C.O. visited front line trenches on 5th N of ROEUX. Coy Commanders doing the same the following day.	JSC
"	7/7/17		Preparations for going into the trenches during the morning.	
		8.45PM	Battn left camp for the front line trenches. Bdge Depot 3 Officers + 55 OR. Major Cotton in command of Battn details. The Divisional front is from I.14.c to I.1.b about 2850 yds. Two Bgdes in the line the Battn holds the left sector of the Right Bgde. from ARRAS – DOUAI Rly inclusive to junction of Cash and Cuthbert trenches inclusive. The Battn relieved 12th Batt. Manchester Regt in the line. Relief completed at 2AM 8th. Line held as follows, Each Coy consisting of 2 platoons. D Coy 1 platoon "COCKBURN" with post in "COAL". 1 Platoon in immediate support in "Cupid". C Coy 1 Platoon in "COCKBURN" prolonging D Coy on the left in the front line ½ platoon in immediate support in "CUPID" on the left of D Coy. ½ platoon in "CINEMA". B Coy 1 platoon in "CUTHBERT" prolonging C Coy's line to the left. ½ platoon in "CURLY" in immediate support, ½ platoon in Strong Point. Junction of "Cash, CODAIGAMBRIAN". A. Coy 1 platoon in Quarry I.13.a + ½ platoon in "CRUSH". Batt H.Q. in CADIZ. H.18.b just N of junction of CAMEL + CADIZ. 10th Battn W. Yorkshire Regt on the Right. 51st Bgde on the left.	I MAP (attached) PLOUVAIN 1/10,000 Parts of 51B NW + N 12

A5834 Wt. W4973/M687 750,000 8/16 D. D. & L. Ltd. Forms/C.2118/13.

Instructions regarding War Diaries and Intelligence Summaries are contained in F. S. Regs., Part II. and the Staff Manual respectively. Title pages will be prepared in manuscript.

WAR DIARY
or
~~INTELLIGENCE SUMMARY.~~
(Erase heading not required.)

Army Form C. 2118.

Place	Date	Hour	7th (S) Battn Yorkshire Regt — Summary of Events and Information	Remarks and references to Appendices
CADIZ trench H.18.b.50.75	8/7/17 to 10/7/17		Enemy trench mortars were particularly active every night on the front line, especially the bombardment heavy at the junction of Cute & Clyde trenches – in that neighbourhood both with trench mortars & shells. Patrols went out each night to examine & locate enemy wire and discover if enemy were holding outlying shell craters.	REC
H11.a.6.1	11/7/17	2 AM	The Battn was relieved in the front line by 7th E. Yorkshire Regt and moved back to the GAVRELLE line. Battn H.Q at H11.a.6.1 with the Battn on the right in HERON Trench. Casualties 1 man killed by a trench mortar shell and 3 wounded. During the relief 2 men were wounded by a bag of German grenades by one man standing on them in a trench	REC
	12/7/17 to 14/7/17		Carrying & working parties found every night by the Battn. Trenches improved & duck walks laid. Training continued at Bgde Depôt	
			On 13th Draft recd of 22 O.R. and 2/Lt C. J. FREESTON.	
	15/7/17		Preparations for going into the line again	REC
		7 PM	Major R E Cotton took over the command of the Battn. Lt Col. Mains D.S.O went back to Bgde Depôt at St Nicholas. Two platoons of 3/10th Batt. Middlesex Regt attached to the Battn for instruction in the trenches	
		10.30 PM	Battn left for the trenches and relieved 7th Batt. East Yorkshire Regt in the same trenches held by the Battn 7th – 11th July. Quiet night.	
Battn H.Q CADIZ H18.b.50.75	16/7/17	2.45 AM	Relief completed. Battn dispositions as follows. A Coy 2 Sections in COAL on N of Rly cutting with L. Gun & bombing post S of the cutting, 2 Sections in COCKBURN, in immediate support 2 Sections in CUPID. C Coy on the left of A Coy. 1 Platoon in COCKBURN with 2 Sections from 3/10th Batt Middlesex Regt. 2 Sections in CUPID with 2 Sections + Lewis gun of Middlesex Regt. 2 Sections in Strong Point "C" (junction of CROOK & CINEMA). D Coy on the left of C Coy. 1 Platoon in COD with 2 sections of Middlesex Regt attached. 2 Sections in Curley + 2 Sections + 1 L Gun from Middlesex Regt in Strong Point "D" (junction of Cash + Cuba) 2 Sections. The 10th Batt W Yorkshire Regt on the Right of the Battn and Lancashire Fuslrs (52nd Brigade) on the left. B. Coy in Reserve. 1 Platoon in Quarry I.13.a.2.2 + 1 platoon in CRUSH. Two L Guns employed in aircraft defence were stationed	Trench map attached. I

A834 Wt. W4973/M687 750,000 8/16 D. D. & L. Ltd. Forms/C.2118/13.

Instructions regarding War Diaries and Intelligence Summaries are contained in F. S. Regs., Part II. and the Staff Manual respectively. Title pages will be prepared in manuscript.

WAR DIARY
or
~~INTELLIGENCE SUMMARY.~~
(Erase heading not required.)

Army Form C. 2118.

Place	Date	Hour	7th (S) Battn Yorkshire Regt — Summary of Events and Information	Remarks and references to Appendices
CADIZ H·18·G·50·75	16/7/17	(contd)	one in CADIZ on the left of Battn H.Q + one in QUARRY. Quiet relief. Trench Strength (including 80 men of the Middlesex Regt & 2 Officers) ~~414 O.R.~~ 15 Officers + 414 O.R. 2 patrols went out from each Coy ^competition^ The Officer patrol from D Coy on the left was bombed by the enemy. One man was killed + 2/Lt Applegard wounded. The hostile trench mortars were very active during the night and early morning on our right (A Coy's front). Forty men from B. Coy were working on new C.T. between "Coal + Cockburn". 2/Lt T.H. Eyre was killed and 2. O.R. and 5. O.R wounded. A good deal of work done on wire in front of our front + support lines during the night. Lt. Col. G. le Mairis DSO went to Commanding Officers Conference to III Army School	DSC
"	17/7/17		Very quiet day, dark night + rain. Hostile trench mortars active on C Coy's front + support trenches about 2·30 AM. Our Stokes mortars and 4·5" Hows Howitzers retaliated	DSC
"	18/7/17		Quiet day. German trench mortars again active at night but were silenced by our Stokes mortars + ~~4·5~~ howitzers. The 2 platoons of 3/10th Middlesex Regt returned to their camp at St Nicholas during the night.	DSC
"	19/7/17		Capt W.H. Tickler commanding C. Coy was wounded in the foot by shrapnel about 3 AM. Arrangements completed for a small raid or battle patrol on WART trench in conjunction with 52nd Brigade to take place at 2 AM tomorrow morning. During the afternoon the ZERO hour for the raid was altered to 11 PM tonight. At 8 P.M. the ^XVII^ Corp postponed the raid ~~indefinitely~~. During the night beginning at 8 PM hostile T.Ms again active on our front line. The artillery + Stokes mortars silenced them each time they opened fire	Instructions + Battalion Orders for raid attached II DSC
"	20/7/17	1 AM.	An attack by the Divn on our left near GAVRELLE resulted in a heavy shelling of our	

A5834 Wt. W4973/M687 750,000 8/16 D. D. & L. Ltd. Forms/C.2118/13.

Instructions regarding War Diaries and Intelligence Summaries are contained in F. S. Regs., Part II. and the Staff Manual respectively. Title pages will be prepared in manuscript.

WAR DIARY

or

~~INTELLIGENCE SUMMARY.~~

(Erase heading not required.)

Army Form C. 2118.

7th (S) Battn Yorkshire Regt.

Place	Date	Hour	Summary of Events and Information	Remarks and references to Appendices
CADIZ. H.16.G.50.75	20/7/17	(cont'd)	front, + support lines and forward C.Ts. One man killed + 3 wounded by trench mortars in Cockburn. The German shells fell in front of our line + behind which accounts for so few casualties. Unoccupied + little used trenches were considerably damaged.	
"			During the day Pte Cuthbert went out several times from our front line in a camouflage snipers suit. He shot one man out of 4 in a German bombing post at I.8.a.25.00, located 2 hostile M. Guns shooting at aeroplanes at I.8.a.4.5 and 3.2. and also secured a shoulder strap numbered 463 from a dead German recently killed. There were no papers or documents on the dead man. Pte Cuthbert approached to within 20 yards of the German bombing post without being seen, but the remaining 3 threw bombs at him ~~..~~ after he fired.	
		11.15AM.	Orders recd from the Bgde to carry out the previously cancelled raid at 10.30 PM tonight before the Battn is relieved by 7th E. York Regt.	II O. Orders re attached.
		10.30PM.	The raiding party started. A full report of which is attached. Casualties in the raiding party 3 wounded + 2 others wounded in the trenches. No identifications secured.	" Raid report attached.
"	21/7/17	2.15AM.	Battn relieved by 7th Battn East Yorkshire Regt. The Battn less 2 Coys went back to the railway cutting H.7.d. arriving about 4.30 AM. C + D Coys accommodated in dug-outs in Fampoux - Gavrelle line in HERON trench (H.11.a). Total casualties Killed 1 Off + 2. O.R. Wounded 2 " + 9. O.R.	III
			Working + carrying parties from all 4 Coys. during the night.	
			Draft of 48 OR joined the Battn as reinforcements at the Rly Depot on 20th	
			Two men wounded + 2 mules killed in the transport at the Tank Dump H.11.a. at night.	
Railway Cutting. H.7.d.	22/7/17.		The result of the raid on Wart trench as published in Divisional Intelligence Summary states that 3 fighting patrols took part in it (7th Yorkshire Regt on the right and 2 patrols from 52nd Bgde). The centre patrol had no difficulty in getting into Wart trench, the enemy bolted. Patrol opened fire + several Germans seen to fall. One dugout shaft was bombed. The right + left patrols were unable to get through the German wire. No identifications were secured by any of the 3 patrols. During the Battn's tour in the trenches of 5 days	RE Map. 51 B N W Edition 6a

A5834 Wt. W4973/M687 750,000 8/16 D. D. & L. Ltd. Forms/C.2118/13.

Instructions regarding War Diaries and Intelligence Summaries are contained in F. S. Regs., Part II. and the Staff Manual respectively. Title pages will be prepared in manuscript.

WAR DIARY
or
~~INTELLIGENCE SUMMARY.~~
(Erase heading not required.)

Army Form C. 2118.

Place	Date	Hour	7th (S) Battn Yorkshire Regt — Summary of Events and Information	Remarks and references to Appendices
Railway Cutting	22/7/17	(contd)	A great deal of wiring was done on the front, support, & strong points "C" "D". The trenches we also improved, fire steps built & new C T to COAL deepened & widened. Several dead Germans were buried & the sanitation of the line greatly improved. Working & carrying parties from all 4 Coys out during the night.	gse
"	23/7/17		Relieved by 7th Battn Lincolnshire Regt in Railway Cutting & Fampoux - GAVRELLE line	gse
"	24/7/17	1.25AM	Relief completed. Battn marched back to St Nicholas Camp G.17. Battn bathing, Details at Bgde Depot, 2 Coys & HQ details fired on Moat Range G.20.a during the morning	Map Sheet 51B N.W. Edition 7
St Nicholas Camp G.17. Grimsby	25/7/17		Training 2 Coys on rifle range during the afternoon. Baths for Battn during the day.	
		6.P.M.	Lt Col G. deMariis D.S.O. returned and assumed Command of the Battn again. Transport & "B" Echelon camp moved to G.10.C.	gse
"	26/7/17 – 30/7/17		Training continued. Lecture by G.S.O.1 on WYTSCHAETE Ridge battle. 27/7/17. Battn shooting on range (Butte de Tir) 30/7/17	gse
"	31/7/17		Training, morning. Preparations for going into the line, afternoon. The Battn is taking over the trenches from 12th Battn Manchester Regt which is the left Battn of the Divisional front (Left sector left Brigade) 63rd Division on the left and, when relief is completed, 6th Dorset Regt on the right. Order of battle, front line from R to L. "B" Coy junction of COLIN-COKE to junction of COLIN CONRAD. "C" Coy continuing B Coys line to junction CONRAD-CIVIL (CIVIL inclusive) & bombing post at stop on road at I.1.b.6.1.. Support line along CORK, from its junction with CALEDONIAN, to I.1.a.6.2. D Coy prolonging A Coy's line to the left in CORK to junction of CORK & CIVIL. Battn H.Q. H.6.b.2.1. in CIVIL trench. Capt Bartrum in command of details at Bgde Depot consisting of 3 Offs + 28 O.R. Trench strength 15 Offs + 383 O.R. Ration strength 21 Offs + 513 O.R. Effective strength 22 Officers 626 O.R.	Map Marked I
		8.45PM.	Battn left for trenches	

A5834 Wt. W4973/M687 750,000 8/16 D. D. & L. Ltd. Forms/C.2118/13.

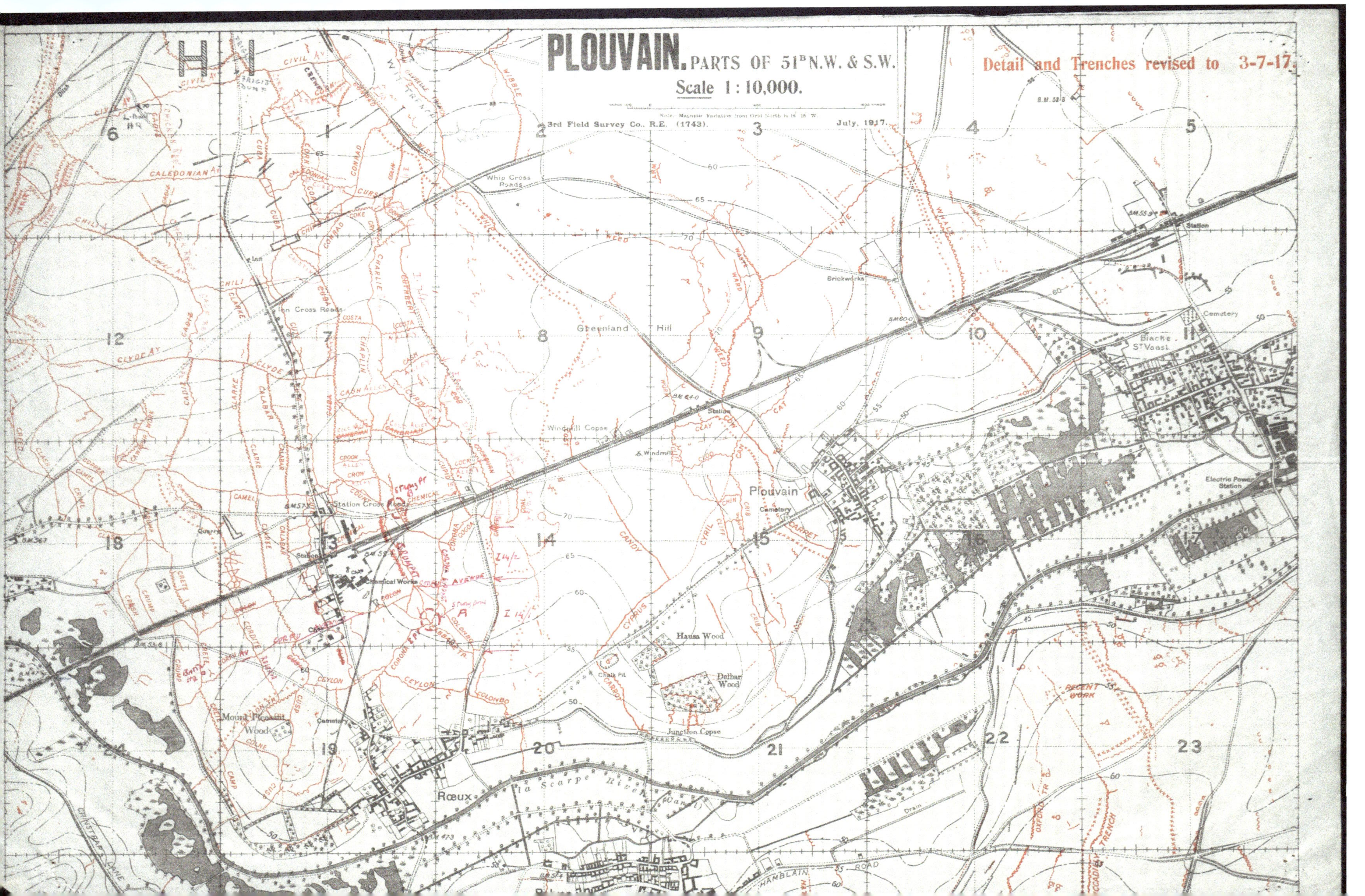

H I
PLOUVAIN. PARTS OF 51B N.W. & S.W.
Scale 1:10,000.
3rd Field Survey Co. R.E. (1743).
July, 1917.
Detail and Trenches revised to 3-7-17.
Whip Cross Roads
Greenland Hill
Windmill Copse
Station
Brickworks
Cemetery
Blache St Vaast
Electric Power Station
Plouvain
Chemical Works
Station Cross Roads
Hausa Wood
Delbar Wood
Junction Copse
Mount Pleasant Wood
Rœux
la Scarpe River
Drain
HAMBLAIN
ROAD
CALEDONIAN AV
CIVIL AV
CLYDE AV
CHARLIE
CUTHBERT
CHAPLIN
CUBA
CLARKE
CALABAR
CAMEL
CRETE
CRUMP
CASH ALLEY
CROOK ALLEY
CROW
CORONA
CEYLON
COLOMBO
CANDY
CYRIL
CYRUS
CARROT
CARPET
CRIB
CLAY
CAT
WEED
WARD
WASTE
WHALE
WIBBLE
COLNE
CUSP
CAMP
OXFORD TR
TRENCH
RECENT WORK

"A" Form.

Army Form C. 2121.
(In pads of 100.)

MESSAGES AND SIGNALS.

No. of Message..............

Prefix........ Code.............m	Words.	Charge.	This message is on a/c of:	Recd. at.........m.
Office of Origin and Service Instructions.	Sent		....................Service.	Date..............
	At..............m.			From..............
	To..............			
	By..............		(Signature of "Franking Officer.")	By..............

TO

Sender's Number.	Day of Month.	In reply to Number.	AAA
*			

after Zero and directly after capture of objectives.

? Hawkes Captain
York

From

Place

Time

The above may be forwarded as now corrected. (Z)

Censor. Signature of Addressor or person authorised to telegraph in his name.

* This line should be erased if not required.

(3198.) Wt. W 12952/M1294. 575,000 Pads. 1/17. H. W. & V., Ld. (E. 818.)

Instructions for Raid No 2

SECRET.

(1) Points of exit for parties tonight will be I 8 c 05, 70. Where four gaps will be cut through our wire after dark and tapes laid giving direction of advance. Gaps will be closed before day break.

(2) M.G. will fire from Zero plus 1 to Zero plus 4 on under mentioned targets:–

Nos 31, 32, 21, 23 to Barrage line I 8 D 00.50. I 8 b 90.00.

Nos 17, 18, 19, 20 to barrage line I 8 b 90.00 I 8 d 20 00.

Special attention being paid to COST Trench WINDMILL COPSE and MG at I 8 d 74 and 56 will intermittent bursts.

(3) M.G. Lewis rifles, and the Stokes Mortars of Right Battn will cooperate with brisk fire on their own front.

(4) Withdrawal. Men should be warned that 52 Bde will fire two golden rain rockets from CUTHBERT at Zero + 9 as a signal for withdrawal and to give direction.

over

Y/20Y

(5) Connecting files joined by holding a thin rope will maintain touch from front to rear.

(6) O.C. D Coy. will report the return of patrol by Fuller phone thus.

1 Equipment = Right covering party returned
2 Equipment = Right raiding party returned
3 Equipment = Left raiding party returned
4 Equipment = Left covering party returned.

Thus
"3 Equipment" 10.45 pm means "Left raiding party returned to our trenches at 10.45. pm."

a short account ~~[illegible]~~ by messenger will follow as soon as possible, via relay post ~~on~~ in C Coy H.Q.

(7) acknowledge.

[illegible] Capt
adjt [illegible]

IV

Secret

Operation Orders
by
Major R E Colton
Cmdg 7th Bn Yorkshire Regt

No

1 A miniature raid in conjunction with 52nd Bde will be carried out against WART trench on the night 19/20 July. By pushing fighting patrols close behind the creeping barrage the object being to secure identifications

2 The creeping barrage will be worked as shown in attached table

3 Boundary line between Brigades is junction CASH-CUTHBERT to I 8 b central.
Right limit of barrage I 8 c 16 to I 9 a 00

4 Zero hour 2 am.

5 OC D Coy will detail Lieut G W Bradley MC and 40 OR to carry out this raid

6. Formation for raid:—

(a) A party of 20 men in 2 sections under an officer with two flanking parties of 10 men and one N.C.O. each

(b) The centre party will advance in 3 groups of 10 men each, which will keep in sight of each other.

(c) The right flanking party will be composed of rifle grenadiers and a Lewis Gun team.

The centre and left flanking parties will only be armed with rifle + bayonet, no bombs will be carried.

(d) The role of the right and left flanking parties is to protect the flanks and cover the withdrawal.

The right flanking party only will keep up a steady fire with rifle grenades and Lewis Gun during the raid and withdrawal.

The left flanking party will only fire after the two centre parties have passed them and to their immediate front.

(e) Both flanking parties will take up a position 180 to 200 yards in front of our trenches and will not withdraw until centre party has passed through them.

7. During the night of the 19/20 gaps will be cut where necessary, in our own wire for the passage of the flanking and centre parties. O.C. D Coy. will arrange to close these gaps immediately after the raid.

8. At Zero hour when the barrage starts, the raiding party will get out of the trenches and move forward to our wire, pass through the gaps and line up on the other side. All four parties will then advance simultaneously keeping close up to our barrage, the flanking parties will halt when they reach the point above indicated.

9. On reaching the objective, prisoners or MG will be sent straight back to a point previously arranged by OC D Coy. O.C. D Coy will forward prisoners at once to Battn. HQ with a suitable guard.

Two Battn Observers will be attached to D Coy and will go forward with the centre parties, for the purpose of searching dead and bringing back shoulder straps, papers etc. This does not preclude the remainder from securing identifications, which is the chief object of the raid.

10. The idea underlying the whole scheme is to make a quick dash to the enemy line, secure identifications, M. G. etc and return.

In no case will the raiding party leave WART trench later than Zero + 9.

Order of withdrawal.

(1). Centre parties.

(2). Left Flank

(3). Right Flank

11. All ranks engaged in the raid will wear a band of white tape on both arms.

12. Short lengths of rope will be carried so as to bring enemy M.G. in quickly.

13. Raiding party will advance on a compass bearing, and arrangements will be made to prevent party losing direction.

14. A Report Centre will be

established at the junction CROOK-
and CINEMA in the Coy HQ there.

15. Acknowledge

18/7/17

Capt
Adjt 7 York R

Appendix I to OO No1. 7 York R

1. The raid will be supported
by Stokes Mortars, Lewis + M.G. Fire
Details will be issued later.

Capt
18/7/17 Adjt 7 York R

Issued to:-

1 Raid Coy
1 T.M. Battery
1 50th Bgde HQ
1 M.G. Coy
1 Adjt

III.

Secret

20.7.17.

To

58th Infantry Brigade.

Report on Raid

Observed from Battn. H.Q. CADIZ.
ZERO hour 10.30 PM.
Our barrage began at ZERO
Enemy " " " Z + 1½ and
became strong Z + 3½.
Our barrage ceased Z + 14.
Enemy " " Z + 20.
All quiet Z + 25 = 10.55 PM.

Lights observed

Enemy 2 red Verey lights Z + 1 on left of Batt
" 2 rockets bursting into 3 green
stars at Z + 2½.
52nd Bgd. Gold rain rocket Z + 7½ or Z + 7.

Enemy shelling

Steady shelling of 5.9 + 4.2 in howitzers on our C.Ts + Support trenches. CAMEL as far back as Battn. H.Q and 100 yards or so further back. Steadily shelled.

<u>Reports</u> from Coy. by wire.

Right party in at 10·38 PM } Written 10·58
2 Centre " " " 10·40 " } Recd 11·25.
Left party " " 10·43 " }

Delay seemingly caused by having to move telephone at Coy H.Q. reason not known.

Written report from Coy received at midnight sent off 11·15 PM. Apparently no success whatever.

Ronald E. Cotton.
Major
Commanding 7th Battn. Yorkshire Regt.

12·09 AM.

Secret.

21st July 1917.

To: 50th Infantry Brigade.

Raid night of 20th July.

Continuing my report dated 20th and sent off at 12.09 AM this morning Lt. Bilby laid a white tape on the bearing ordered from our front line almost to the German wire, before zero + the direction taken was therefore quite accurate.
All 4 parties were connected laterally by holding a light rope.

Artillery barrage very good and the raiding parties advanced close under it.

Three enemy machine guns opened fire as the men advanced

2/ The 2 flank supporting parties halted according to orders.

The machine guns appear to have fired high + only caused 3 casualties during the advance.
The ground was very cut up by shell fire + the men straggled a bit during the latter part of the advance.
Lt Bulby moving forward with some 16 men reached the German wire. Neither of the 2 parties could find any gap. Lt. Bulby, who reached the wire first with 4 men tried to get through at several points but he could find no gap anywhere.
The signal for the return went up on the left and the parties returned bringing in the 3 wounded men with them

3. The times of arrival of the parties back in our front trench were not quite as stated in my previous report. O.C. D. Coy reports that they arrive as follows 2 centre parties, right flank support, left flank support within a minute or two of each other.
Lt. Bilby, whose leadership was excellent, came in some minutes later.
Casualties in Raiding party
4 wounded (including 1 very slightly just before the raid began)
There was only 1 other man wounded in the Battn belonging to Right Coy in the front line.

German barrage. Very ineffective & not nearly so heavy as the previous night.
It was composed of 77 mm 5.9"

+ 4.2". No shells fell in the front line from which the raid started. CURLY + CUPID trenches were rather badly damaged especially the latter.
Result of the raid was nil. No identifications were secured + at no point was the German trench entered.
I attribute the failure to the fact that the wire was not cut + also to the short time in which to get to the German line + back. There was no time to cut gaps or force a way through.

Ronald E. Cotton.
Major
Commanding 7th Battn Yorkshire Regt

Time 5 AM. 21/7/17

SECRET

[illegible] additional orders for raid [illegible]

(1). The [illegible] flanking parties will not open fire unless attacked

(2). All [illegible] parties will leave our trench [illegible] [illegible] to be ready to move off from the front of our wire at Zero.

(3). The 2 Battalion [illegible] details [illegible] with the [illegible] centre parties will not be sent.

(4). Zero hour 11 p.m. tonight.

(5). [illegible] [illegible] [illegible] [illegible] [illegible] [illegible] [illegible] the attack

Copy

[illegible]

[illegible]

[illegible]

20th July 1917.

OC. D Coy.

The compass bearing on which the raiding party will assault tonight is 64° True from the point in C.O.D. fixed by the Bgde namely I. 8. C. 05. 70.

64° True = 77° Magnetic

This should take the raiders on to a located German M.G. emplacement at I. 8. C. 5. 9

Ronald E. Cotton.
Major
Commanding 7th Battn Yorkshire Regt

x

Secret

Barrage Table

(a) At Zero hour a barrage (A) will be placed 100 yards West of WART trench and a barrage (B) on WART Trench.

At Zero plus 2 minutes – Barrage (A) will lift back to WART.

At Zero plus 3 minutes – Barrages (A) + (B) will lift back to 150 yards East of WART where barrage (A) will remain.

At Zero plus 4 minutes – Barrage (B) will lift to a line 250 yards East of WART.

At Zero plus 5 minutes – Barrage (B) will lift to a line 350 yards East of WART.

At Zero plus 6 minutes – Barrage (B) will lift to a line 450 yds East of WART.

At Zero plus 7 minutes – Barrage (B) will drop to a line 350 yd East of WART.

At Zero plus 8 minutes – Barrage (B) will drop to a line 250 yds East of WART.

At Zero plus 9 minutes – Barrage (B) will join barrage (A).

150 yards East of WART
At Zero plus 13 minutes – Barrages (A) and (B) will drop on to WART Trench
At Zero plus 14 minutes – Cease Fire

(c) Between Zero & Zero plus 14 – 4.5" Hows. will barrage the following points –

1 Section – COST Trench
1 " – WINDMILL COPSE
1 " – I 8 a. 0. 3
1 " – MGs at I 8 a 5 6 + 7 4.
1 " – I. 8 b. 5 5
1 " – I 8 b 2. 5
1 " – I. 8 b. 3. 4
1 " – I. 2 c 8. 1 (lift to WHIP CROSS ROADS at Zero plus 3 and back to I 2 c 6. 1. at plus 10)
1 " – I 2 a. 05. 65

18/7/17 (Signed) S V C Hawker [illegible]
Capt 7 York R

SECRET 1/161

Instructions for Raid No1

A One Stokes gun on hostile T.M's near Rly cutting.

Two Stokes guns on hostile M.G. positions located in I 8 c.

B. Lewis Guns in Coal A Coy
- in front line C Coy -
will fire in short bursts to their immediate front during the raid.

C. Very lights will be fired at junctions of CASH & CAMBRIAN with front line at ZERO + 9 + continue until party returns.

D. A Stretcher manned by 4 men will follow close up behind the centre of each of the 2 raiding parties.

E. The wire in front of WART will be cut at the following points by the Artillery.

I.8.C.40.95

I.8.C.60.90

I.8.C.70.80

F. Wire cutters on rifles will be fixed so as to push and not to pull. At least 50% of the raiding parties should carry these on their rifles.

H. P. Bombs already issued will be carried by the two raiding parties to deal with any dug-outs that may be discovered.

R.E. Walker.

19/7/17

Capt

Adjt 7 Yorks R.

Instructions regarding War Diaries and Intelligence Summaries are contained in F. S. Regs., Part II. and the Staff Manual respectively. Title pages will be prepared in manuscript.

WAR DIARY
or
INTELLIGENCE SUMMARY.
(Erase heading not required.)

Army Form C. 2118.

Vol 23

Place	Date	Hour	7 (S) Battn Yorkshire Regt. Summary of Events and Information	Remarks and references to Appendices
Civil Trench H.6.b.3.3	1/8/17	1.20 AM	Relief of the 7th Battn East Yorkshire Regt completed. R. Naval Division on the left. 6th Battn Dorset Regt on the right. Front line Coys C & B sent out patrols but no information of any importance gained.	Distribution of Battn in trenches. See Diary 31/7/17
		5 AM	Enemy shelled CORK near junction with CIVIL. Killed 1 man & wounded another. Civil and Conrad near junction of Civil damaged by 5.9" shells. Trenches muddy & wet & falling in in places. CT especially bad. Day quiet	I PLOUVAIN Map attached see 1/10,000 Sec C of 51B N.W. & S.W.
"	2/8/17		In order to carry out instructions regarding cooking in the trenches to be done by platoons all 4 Coys began to construct dug-outs just behind the front & support trenches (2 per Coy). By day, work programme included repair of trenches, widening, deepening & revetting at night working parties engaged in, cutting grass to give better field of fire, wiring in front of front lines & continuing wire entanglement in front of new S.L. which is to be constructed later. General line of wiring in front of proposed immediate S. line. Course from junction Caledonian to I.1.a.50.05 to I.6.10.35 to I.1.b.15.50 & thence N.E. to CIVIL in front of CRETE. Hostile artillery again shelled Cork.	
	3/8/17		Work on trenches continued. Great progress made in wiring proposed new S.T. A patrol from B. Coy under 2/Lt Goodway with 5 O.R. reconnoitred "Wish" & moved on to enemy trench at I.2.c.10.60 to examine it up to I.1.d.90.45. It ascertained that the enemy did not patrol Wish. At I.1.9.5 enemy discovered holding bay about 10 strong bombs were thrown by the enemy & one hit 2/Lt Goodway on the chest but failed to explode. A hostile patrol was seen at I.1.d.8.7. & position of enemy M.G. & bombing post confirmed I.1.d.90.45 and 90.40 respectively. The trench seemed fairly strongly held. No casualties. Stokes Mortars dealt with this trench. C Coy's patrol gained no fresh information. Quiet night except for a few 5.9" shells near Cork & Civil junction.	

Instructions regarding War Diaries and Intelligence Summaries are contained in F. S. Regs., Part II. and the Staff Manual respectively. Title pages will be prepared in manuscript.

WAR DIARY
or
~~INTELLIGENCE SUMMARY.~~

(*Erase heading not required.*)

Army Form C. 2118.

Place	Date	Hour	7th (S) Battn Yorkshire Regt. Summary of Events and Information	Remarks and references to Appendices
Civil Trench H.6.b.3.3.	4/8/17		Intermittent shelling of CORK trench with 5.9" shells, 2 men went out from COLIN trench in camouflage suit & were killed accidentally by a man on sentry duty in COLIN, when returning. Progress made with Cookhouses in Support & front lines. Wire thickened in front of front line, trenches improved & duck boards laid. 2 men died of wounds from 5.9" shell that fell in Cork, 1 man wounded & 1 buried by the same shell.	R.S.C.
"	5/8/17	8 AM.	Lt. Col. G. Mairis D.S.O. took command of 50th Bgde during the absence of Brigadier on leave. Major Cotton took command of the Battn. Artillery asked to fire on hostile	
			Intermittent shelling of Cork with 5.9" shells. [working party on Greenland Hill + dispersed it.]	
		10-10.30PM.	Enemy shelled FRIGID Dump I.1.a.1.6 with 5.9" shells & gas shells.	
		10.30PM	In conjunction with a raid by 51st Bgde on the right all trench mortars Lewis & Machine Guns in the trenches held by the Battn fired for 14 minutes on selected targets. Rifle grenades were also fired. Enemy sent up rockets breaking into 2 green stars and retaliated on our lines with 4.2" & 5.9" howitzers. Trenches damaged but no casualties. Gas shells fired on the front of Naval Division on our left; gas drifted across our front & box respirators had to be worn most of the night.	R.S.C.
"	6/8/17		Quiet day. 7th E. York Regt began relief of the Battn about 11 PM.	R.S.C.
(HELFORD) HUMID TRENCH H.6.c.	7/8/17		Relief completed 1.15 AM., Battn went into Support in the FAMPOUX-GAVRELLE line & occupied HELFORD trench. Working parties for R.E. and repair of HOOD trench begun. At night, carrying & working parties.	R.S.C.
"	8/8/17 – 11/8/17		Working & carrying parties by day & night. Wiring in front of HUMID and CADIZ. The whole Battn working 4 hours by day & all night. 2 casualties wiring on night of 10th/11th.	R.S.C.

A5834 Wt W4973/M687 750,000 8/16 D. D. & L. Ltd. Forms/C.2118/13.

Instructions regarding War Diaries and Intelligence Summaries are contained in F. S. Regs., Part II. and the Staff Manual respectively. Title pages will be prepared in manuscript.

WAR DIARY
or
~~INTELLIGENCE SUMMARY.~~
(Erase heading not required.)

Army Form C. 2118.

Place	Date	Hour	7th (S) Battn Yorkshire Regt. Summary of Events and Information	Remarks and references to Appendices
(HELFORD) Humid trench H.6.c.	12/8/17		All trenches held by the Division re-named with few exceptions. Main CTs called "Avenues," subsidiary CTs "Alleys." Front line map References. Usual day working parties. Rain last night damaged HUMID + (Hood) NAVAL Tr. considerably	Note re names for trenches. Conrad = I.1.3, COLIN = I.1.2 in Left Battn Left B[illegible] front
		10 P.M.	Battn started from FAMPOUX-GAVRELLE line to relieve 7th Battn E. York Regt in the front line in the same sector held by the Battn 1st/6th inst. From R to L. A Coy + D Coy front line. B + C Coys immediate Support.	DC
CIVIL AVENUE H.6.b.3.3.	13/8/17	12.18 AM	Relief completed. Quiet night + day. A great deal of work to be done to maintain trenches in repair. CTs especially bad. Support line to be wired at once. About midnight an enemy party estimated at about 40 strong attempted to bomb the left of I.1.2 + simultaneously left of I.1.3 trenches under cover of a weak + ineffective barrage. The enemy did not get through our wire + was easily driven off with rifle + m.g. fire. A patrol on the left of A Coy was going out, as the attack started, under L/Cpl Rayner. This patrol broke up the enemy attack on that flank but lost 1 man missing + the rest, 3 OR including the L/Cpl, wounded. Patrols sent out to get identifications 3 or 4 dead were seen + the following day a wounded man was seen being carried in in front of W[illegible] trench.	
"	14/8/17 to 16/8/17		Working parties repairing + improving trenches by day + wiring front + support lines by night	DC
"			A fighting patrol from A Coy sent out on 15th just after midnight to capture any enemy in fortified shell hole in front of junction Conrad + I.1.3 failed to find any Germans. This shell hole was reported as occupied by a patrol the previous night.	DC
"	17/8/17	3.18 AM	Battn relieved by 7th Battn Border Regt and returned to camp at St Nicholas G 17 (Grimsby Camp). Day spent in rest + cleaning up. Casualties 4 wounded + 1 missing. Lt Col Mairis D.S.O. returned + took command of the Battn	DC

Instructions regarding War Diaries and Intelligence Summaries are contained in F. S. Regs., Part II. and the Staff Manual respectively. Title pages will be prepared in manuscript.

WAR DIARY
or
~~INTELLIGENCE SUMMARY.~~
(Erase heading not required.)

Army Form C. 2118.

Place	Date	Hour	Summary of Events and Information	Remarks and references to Appendices
GRIMSBY Camp.	18/8/17		Drafts received on 8th 4 Officers + 8 O R + on 15th 2 Officers + 8 O.R. The Brigade Depôt is somewhat changed. It will in future consist of 50 O.R. from each Batt to be trained in, bombing, bayonet fighting L. Guns &c with a proportion of Officers The instructors being composed of Officers + N C O's from the 4 Battns in the Brigade.	[illegible]
			Battn training + baths	
"	19/8/17		Baths + Church parades.	[illegible]
"	20/8/17 and 21/8/17		Usual training carried on — Patrols, drill, gas helmet drill etc. All Coy commanders went through a two day gas course and the "gas discipline" of the battalion is improving in consequence.	[illegible] Captadjt
"	22/8/17		A battalion working party 270 OR. under Captain H L Bartram went to dig out COHON C.T. from I 13 C 7 1 to I 13 D 4 3½. Party went up from St Nicholas to FAMPOUX by train and returned to camp without casualties about 5.30 am. 23rd. Trench was dug to average depth of left 6 inches and width of 3 feet. The road by the CHATEAU caused some difficulty and was only dug to a depth of one foot.	[illegible]
"	23/8/17		A flammenwerfer display arranged to take place at Bde. HQ in the afternoon was attended by all officers but the liquid failed to ignite in the strong wind. A better effect was achieved by Major P.B. O'Connor G.S.O. III Division who lectured to all company & platoon commanders at 5pm on "Patrol reports" —	[illegible]
"	24/8/17		Preparation for going to Trenches — Baths etc. In the evening the Brigade relieved the 52nd Brigade in the right subsector. Dispositions — Right Battn East York Regt.	[illegible]

A5834 Wt. W4973/M687 750,000 8/16 D. D. & L. Ltd. Forms/C.2118/13.

Instructions regarding War Diaries and Intelligence Summaries are contained in F. S. Regs., Part II. and the Staff Manual respectively. Title pages will be prepared in manuscript.

WAR DIARY

~~or~~

~~INTELLIGENCE SUMMARY.~~

(Erase heading not required.)

Army Form C. 2118.

Place	Date	Hour	Summary of Events and Information	Remarks and references to Appendices
Right support Chemical Works cuttings	24th August		Left Battn:- West York R - Right support 7th Yorkshire Regt with one company in CORDITE and ~~CRASH~~ CRASH, three companies in the GAVRELLE SWITCH just north of the ATHIES FAMPOUX ROAD and Battalion HQ in very fine German dugouts in the railway cutting at H14 A19 (51B N.W. 1/20000).	See [illegible] map attached. Chell
"	25th to 27th		In Brigade support and finding various RE Parties by night, carrying rations and RE stores for East Yorkshire etc. By day work on construction of shelters in GAVRELLE SWITCH and general improvements of Trench. The company in the forward area [CORDITE and CRASH trenches] was working on improvements to COLON AVENUE which dug out by the Battalion on the 22nd duckboarding etc.	
"	28th		Same as 25th to 27th. Battalion H.Q. moved to GAVRELLE SWITCH at H16 B99 to a large English built dugout. Coy commanders reconnoitred Trenches.	[51 B N.W. 1/20000] Chell
"	29th		Preparations for front line trenches etc during afternoon. In evening relieved 7th East York Regt in right Battalion front line. Relief complete 12.20 am. Distribution: Front line Right to left C.B.A. Coys with all Coy HQ in CORONA SUPPORT. In accordance with orders received from Bde just prior to relief the reserve (D) Coy moved forward a platoon to garrison strong points A & B at junctions CORONA CABBAGE and CHEMICAL CROW Trenches respectively - each with two sections. As this company already had one platoon in CUPID SUPPORT and COCOA Trench, this left no real reserve. Accordingly one company East York was moved from the GAVRELLE line into CRETE Trench where Battn HQ is situated (H24 B 88) and came tactically under command of Lieut Col [illegible]. On our right 3/10th Middlesex 4th Division on our left 10th West Yorkshire Regt	Chell

A5834 Wt. W4973/M687 750,000 8/16 D. D. & L. Ltd. Forms/C.2118/13.

Army Form C 2118.

War Diary
or
Intelligence Summary

Place	Date	Hour	Summary of Events and Information	Remarks and References to Appendices
Right front Battn Chemical works Sector	30th		Nothing special to report. Periodical Stokes and Trench Mortar bombardments are carried out on enemy's front and rear lines. One unfortunate 5.9 shell killed two men D Coy and wounded two	[illegible]
"	31st		Morning quiet. In afternoon at 2 p.m. enemy started a heavy bombardment of our front and support lines by T.M. 4.2 and 5.9. Considerable damage was done to trenches. Casualties OR. killed or wounded one	
			Effective Strength Officers 34 OR 622 — Ration Strength Officers 29 OR 509	[illegible]

I
Part of
PLOUVAIN. Map. Scale 1/10,000 51b NW + NE
Attached to July War Diary
Gavrelle
Cemetery
Hollow Copse
Railway Copse
Square Wood
B C
H I
Greenland Hill
Brickworks
Station
Windmill
Plouvain
Chemical Works
Hausa Wood
Delbar Wood
Junction Copse
Mount Pleasant Wood
Rœux
la Scarpe River (Canal)
Pelves
Pelves Mill
FUZE TRENCH
GRENADE
CROSS BOW STR.
ELBOW
CALEDONIAN
CHILI
CLYDE
CADIZ
CUBA
CORK
CONRAD
CHARLIE
CUTHBERT
WART
WEED
CEYLON
COLOMBO
CORONA
Div. Boundary.
Batt. "
Bgde "

I

July War Diary

Instructions regarding War Diaries and Intelligence Summaries are contained in F. S. Regs., Part II. and the Staff Manual respectively. Title pages will be prepared in manuscript.

WAR DIARY
or
INTELLIGENCE SUMMARY.
(Erase heading not required.)

Army Form C. 2118.

7 York Regt
Vol 24

Place	Date	Hour	7th (S) Battn Yorkshire Regt. Summary of Events and Information	Remarks and references to Appendices
Right front Battn CHEMICAL WORKS Sector H.Q. CORFU AVENUE.	1/9/17		Quiet day but a good deal of hostile TM fire at night. The artillery called on to retaliate on several occasions. A gas shell bombardment of the enemy lines. (Disposition of Battn in trenches see War Diary for Aug)	Trench maps I + II Greenland Hill Sector attached.
"	2/9/17.		Early in the morning C Coys H.Q. trench mortared + one entrance blown in. 2 men wounded in front line.	Marked I.
"	3/9/17.		Usual trench routine, Enemy quiet except at night.	
"	4/9/17	11.55PM	Battn relieved by 7th E. York Regt. H.Q. + 2 Coys went back to dug outs in the Fampoux Gavrelle line + the remaining 2 Coys under E. York Regt remained in Support. The whole Battn in Bgde Support. A large amount of work was done in the trenches + wire strengthened during the tour in the front line. Casualties Killed 2 O.R. Died of wounds 5 O.R. wounded 5 O.R.	
H.Q. PUDDING Trench	5/9/17. to		Battn employed on working + carrying parties + improvement of trenches held.	
H.16.b. GAVRELLE FAMPOUX	9/9/17.	10.30PM	Battn relieved by Sherwood Foresters 51st Bgde + returned to Grimsby Camp St Nicholas.	

A5834. Wt. W4973/M687 750,000 8/16 D. D. & L. Ltd. Forms/C.2118.

WAR DIARY
or
INTELLIGENCE ~~SUMMARY.~~
(Erase heading not required.)

Army Form C. 2118.

Instructions regarding War Diaries and Intelligence Summaries are contained in F. S. Regs., Part II. and the Staff Manual respectively. Title pages will be prepared in manuscript.

Place	Date	Hour	7(S) Batt^n Yorkshire Regt. Summary of Events and Information	Remarks and references to Appendices
Grimsby Camp G.17.c	10/9/17.		Batt^n resting, baths &c.	JEC
"	11/9/17. to 15/9/17.		Usual training carried out by the Batt^n while in Div Reserve. Football matches + Cross Country runs arranged. The German order of battle on 15/9/17 from R to L on Div^l front as follows:- 464th I.R. 463rd I.R both 238th Div^n and 363 I.R. of 214th Div^n	JEC
"	16/9/17		Church parades. Coy Commanders went up to the trenches to inspect the line to be taken over tomorrow. The Batt^n will be right Batt^n of left Brigade in the line.	JEC
"	17/9/17		Preparations for going into the line	
		7 PM	Battalion left for the trenches and relieved 3/4th Royal West Kent Regt. Dispositions in the trenches as follows. From Right to Left. D. B + A Coys with 1 platoon each in the front line + 1 platoon each in S. Line. Front trenches I.7/1 from Cash Alley exclusive + I.1/1 to CAB ALLEY exclusive. S. Line Charlie Support + City Support. "C" Coy in CALDRON with 1 platoon in E. Strong point. Quiet relief. H.Q in Chili Avenue. S. Staffordshire 51st Bgde on Right + 6th Dorset Regt on the left	JEC
H.Q. Chili AVENUE 4.12.b 2.9	18/9/17	12.15 AM	Relief completed.	
			Quiet day. At 8.30 P.M two hostile trench mortar shells fell in the sap leading to bombing post on the left + killed 2/Lt Freestone + Sgt Marsden D.C.M. M.M. 2/Lt	JEC

A5834 Wt. W4973/M687 750,000 8/16 D. D. & L. Ltd. Forms/C. 2118/12.

Instructions regarding War Diaries and Intelligence Summaries are contained in F. S. Regs., Part II. and the Staff Manual respectively. Title pages will be prepared in manuscript.

WAR DIARY
or
~~INTELLIGENCE SUMMARY.~~
(Erase heading not required.)

Army Form C. 2118

Place	Date	Hour	7th (S) Battn Yorkshire Regt — Summary of Events and Information	Remarks and references to Appendices
			Rolland, Stokes M. Battery was also killed + a Corpl wounded. Sgt Marsden who gained his M.M at Fricourt on 1st July/16 + the D.C.M. at Sailly Saillisel on 8th Feb 1917 is a great loss to the Battn.	
			Patrols went out as usual at night. A telephone wire was found tied to our wire + leading towards the German trenches.	
H.Q. Chili Avenue H.12.b.2.9	19/9/17		The Corps, Divisional + Bgd Commanders visited the trenches during the morning. At night a patrol from A Coy led by 2/Lt Bott + 2 O.R. entered the German trench in front of the bombing post at I.2.c.10.15 worked along the trench which is disused + is 7 ft deep by 1½ ft broad + found German dead, rifles &c. The patrol was fired at from about I.2.c.0.3 + returned to our lines without loss.	Copy of Information from Divl Intel. Summary attached marked II
"	20/9/17		Lt Col G. Mairis D.S.O. left to command the Bgde during the absence of the Bgd Genl + Major R.E. Cotton took command of the Battn. Quiet day. Usual work in + out side the trenches carried on.	
"	21/9/17		The Brigade is being relieved by 183rd Bgde 61st Divn in a few days. Representatives from this Bgde visited the trenches. Lt Col Bilton went round the Battn front (8th Batt Worcestershire Regt). The Corps Commander Sir Charles Fergusson came to say goodbye to the Battn and thanked all ranks for the good work they had done since April.	
		10.30 PM	Battn relieved by 7th E. York Regt and moved back to the Gavrelle Switch. Battn H.Q at H.11.b.6.8. Casualties during the tour of 4 days. Killed 1 Officer + 2 OR. Wounded 3 O.R.	

A5834 Wt. W4973/M687 750,000 8/16 D. D. & L. Ltd. Forms/C2118

Instructions regarding War Diaries and Intelligence Summaries are contained in F. S. Regs., Part II. and the Staff Manual respectively. Title pages will be prepared in manuscript.

WAR DIARY
or
~~INTELLIGENCE SUMMARY.~~
(*Erase heading not required.*)

Army Form C. 2118.

Place	Date	Hour	Summary of Events and Information — 7th (S) Battn Yorkshire Regt.	Remarks and references to Appendices
Gavrelle Switch Line H.Q. H11.c.6.5.	22/9/17 to 23/9/17		Working parties by day & night. Improvements carried out in the GAVRELLE Switch Line. Genl Sir Julian Byng Commanding the III Army has forwarded the following message from Sir Douglas Haig the Commander-in-Chief "The Commander-in-Chief congratulates you & your troops on the repeated successes gained in your local operations which show excellent spirit & skill. These successes help appreciably in the general plan"	JEC
"	24/9/17		Battn relieved by 2/7th Battn Worcestershire Regt. Battn marched to Billets in ARRAS.	JEC
ARRAS	25/9/17	2.P.M.	Battn marched to IZEL-LES-HAMEAU & went into billets. The march was about 12 miles & the Battn arrived just before dark. A draft of 178 O.R. joined	JEC
IZEL-LES-HAMEAU	26/9/17	10.30 AM	Battn continued march to LIGNEREUIL and arrived before noon & went into billets. Billets not particularly good & the Officers quarters bad. A draft of 149 OR arrived. The Division is now in 6th Corps area	JEC
LIGNEREUIL	27/9/17		Training in semi-open warfare, musketry &c	JEC
"	28/9/17		Battn practice attack.	JEC
"	29/9/17		The same attack repeated. Musketry on the range.	JEC
"	30/9/17		Church Parades, football &c. Effective Strength Officers 31, OR 953; Ration Strength Officers 27 OR 865.	JEC

A5834 Wt. W4973/M687 750,000 8/16 D. D. & L. Forms/C.2118

GREENLAND HILL TRENCH MAP TRENCHES CORRECTED TO 31.8.17.
SCALE 1/10,000
GREENLAND HILL SECTOR
CHEMICAL WORKS SECTOR
ROEUX SECTOR
COB
WINKLE
WHALE
WOE
WICK.
WAVE
WINE
WASH
WASTE
WARD
WEED
WET
WORM
WHACK
WHY
WAVY
WEAK
COUNT AVE
WOBBLE
WIBBLE
WEASEL
WHIP
WOOL
WHIP CROSS ROADS
WANT
WIT.
WART
WILLOW
WIG
COST
CUB
CRUST
CORN
CAT
CLAY
CLOD
CLIFF
CROW
CAN
CRIB
CHIN
CABIN
CAFÉ
CARPET
CANDY
CHARLIE SUPPORT.
CONRAD
COKE
COSTA ALLEY
CASH
CINEMA
COLD ALLEY
CROOK ALLEY
CROW
CURLY SUPPORT
CUPID SUPPT.
CHEMICAL ALLEY
CORFU AVENUE
COLOMBO
CABBAGE TR.
CORONA
CRUMPET
CALICO TRENCH.
CALDRON TRENCH
CIVIL AVENUE
CORK SUPPORT.
CREWE
CREAM ALLEY
CUBA TR.
CALEDONIAN AVENUE
CLYDE AVENUE
CALABAR TRENCH
CLARKE TRENCH.
CORDITE RES.
CHILI AVENUE
THE CROSS
SQUARE WOOD
GREENLAND
WINDMILL
HAUSA WOOD

MAP FOR WAR DIARY FOR 1st SEPT. - 9th SEPT. 1917

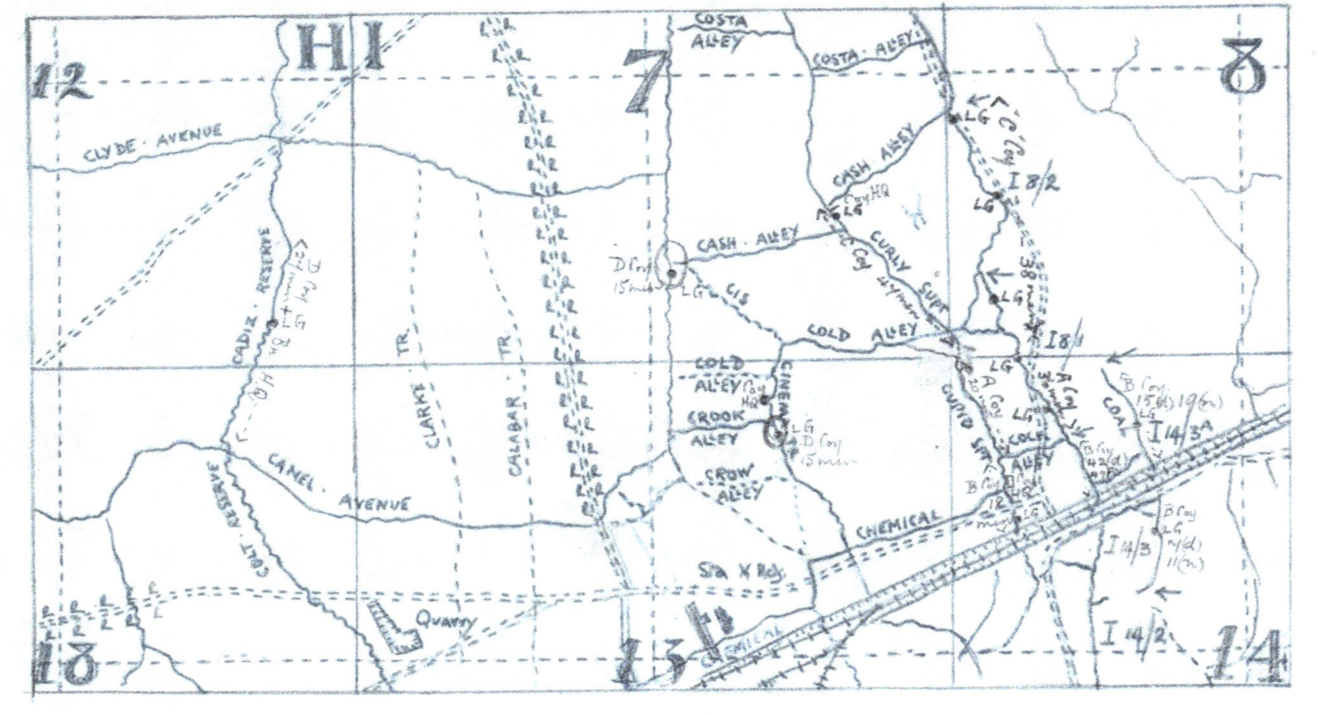

II

Copy of Information from Patrol report from Divisional Intelligence Summary dated. 20th Sept 1917. 8 AM.

Patrol leader 2/Lt. Bott
Patrol. 2 O.R.

"The enemy sap head at I·2·C·10·15 was entered & found to be unoccupied. It is sandbagged and about 7 ft. deep. Two German skeletons & a quantity of salvage were found in the saphead. The patrol then entered the German trench at I·2·C·15·25 and followed it for about 80 yards to approximately I·2·C·05·30, the trench is reported to be 18" wide and 5 ft. deep containing only enemy dead and salvage. At about I·2·C·05·30 the patrol encountered an enemy sentry post, & on returning to our lines was fired on by rifles & rifle grenades.

The Enemy wire in front of this section of trenches consists of 2 ~~sets~~ belts of barbed concertina wire close together & not supported by any fence. The inner belt is 8 ft from the trench. A few screw pickets hold the wire in position."

R.E.E. 27/9/17

War diary

H.Q.
No. 5/049
Date 26.9.17
50th INF. BDE.

COPY.

17th. Division.

On tho occasion of the Division leaving tho XVII Corps, I wish to express to all ranks , my appreciation of the fine soldierly spirit which has been conspicuous in the Division during tho last few months while serving on this front.

Its activity in patrolling, its keenness in Raids have both been admirable. But most conspicuous of all has been tho splendid spirit shown in the work done in consolidating the line. In spite of weakness in numbers and the absence of the Pioneer Bn., the work done has been remarkable; showing not only excellent organisation on the part of the Staff, but also energy and zeal on the part of Regimental Officers and men. All ranks may be proud of their record in this respect, R.A. and R.E. as well as Infantry.

I wish goodbye, and good luck to all in the Division, with every confidence that they will fully maintain the reputation they have gained wherever their duty may call them.

(Sgd) CHARLES FERGUSON,
Lieutenant-General.,
Commanding, XVII Corps.

24-9-17.

17th. Division.
........G.807.
25th. September 1917.

- 2 -

To all Units 17th.Division.

H.Q.
No. 5/049/2
Date
50th INF. BDE.

Forwarded for communication to all ranks.

West Yorkshire R.
East Yorkshire R.
Yorkshire R.
Dorsetshire R.

[signature]
Lieut.- Col.,
G.S., 17th. Division.

Forwarded.

27/9/17.

[signature]
Captain,
Brigade Major,
50th Infantry Brigade.

PDO

All Coy

Information

[illegible]

....Capt.

Adjt. 7th Yorkshire Regt.

2 8 SEP 1917

A WH

B [illegible]

C SC

D [illegible]

1:10 000

SCHAAP - BALIE

EDITION I.

Scale 1:10,000

TRENCHES CORRECTED FROM INFORMATION RECEIVED UP TO 4.10.17.

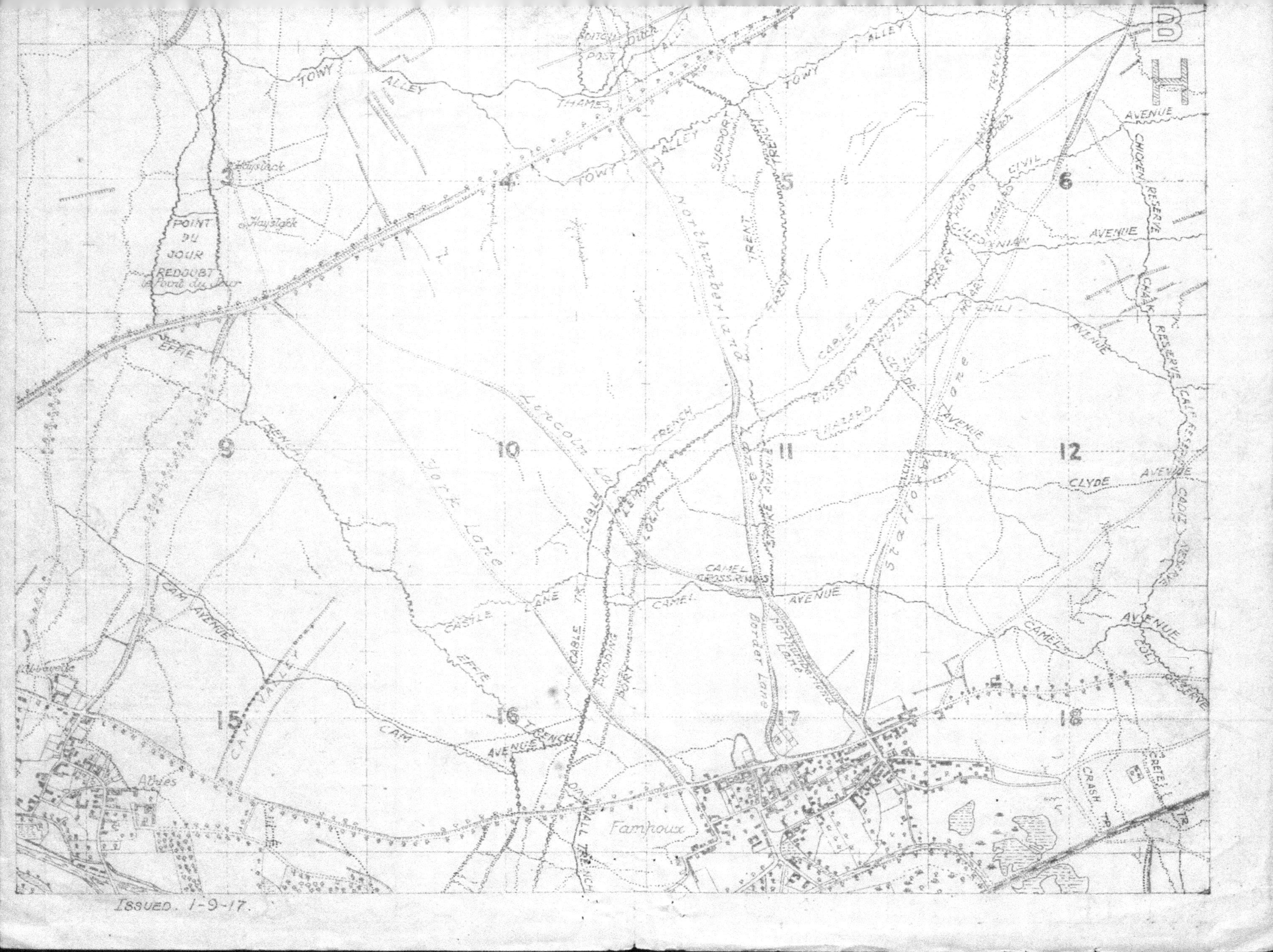
TOWY ALLEY
THAMES ALLEY
SUPPORT
TRENT
POINT DU JOUR REDOUBT
Haystack
EFFIE
Lincoln Lane
York Lane
CABLE TR.
CAMEL AVENUE
CLYDE AVENUE
CALEDONIAN AVENUE
CHICKEN RESERVE
CHALK RESERVE
CALF RESERVE
CADIZ RESERVE
COLT RESERVE
CAM AVENUE
CAM VALLEY
CASTLE LANE TR.
Border Lane
Northumberland Lane
DINGWALL TRENCH
CRASH TR.
CRETE TR.
Fampoux
Athies
ISSUED. 1-9-17.

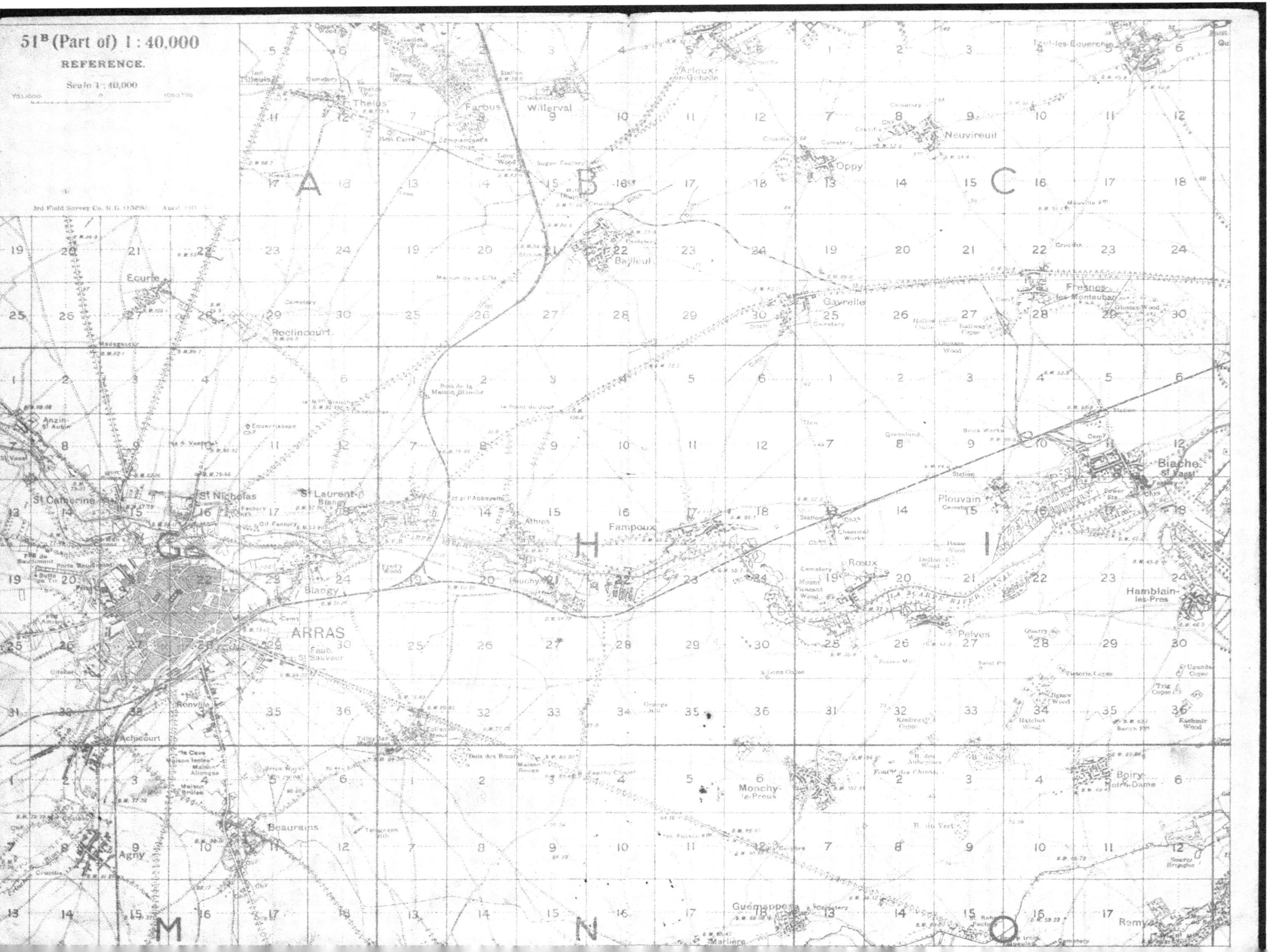
51B (Part of) 1 : 40,000
REFERENCE.
Scale 1 : 40,000
3rd Field Survey Co. R.E.
A
B
C
G
H
I
M
N
O
Thelus
Farbus
Willerval
Arleux-en-Gohelle
Oppy
Neuvireuil
Izel-les-Equerchin
Bailleul
Gavrelle
Fresnes-les-Montauban
Ecurie
Roclincourt
Anzin-St Aubin
St Catherine
St Nicholas
St Laurent Blangy
Athies
Fampoux
Feuchy
Roeux
Plouvain
Biache St Vaast
Hamblain-les-Pres
Pelves
ARRAS
Faub. St Sauveur
Blangy
Ronville
Achicourt
Agny
Beaurains
Monchy-le-Preux
Boiry-Notre-Dame
Guémappe
Remy
Marliere
LA SCARPE RIVER CANAL
Cemetery
Station
Sugar Factory
Long Wood
Maison de la Côte
Bois de la Maison Blanche
le Point du Jour
Greenland Hill
Brick Works
Chemical Works
Mount Pleasant Wood
Orange Hill
Quarry Wood
Jigsaw Wood
Hatchet Wood
Victoria Copse
Uganda Copse
Trig Copse
Kestrel Copse
Bois des Boeufs
Telegraph Hill
Tilloy Wood
Bois du Vert
Sart Copse
Vert
Maison Rouge
Fosse Farm
Ditch
Oil Factory
Crucifix

Instructions regarding War Diaries and Intelligence Summaries are contained in F. S. Regs., Part II. and the Staff Manual respectively. Title pages will be prepared in manuscript.

WAR DIARY
or
~~INTELLIGENCE SUMMARY.~~
(Erase heading not required.)

Army Form C. 2118.

7 Yorkshire Rgt
Vol 25

Place	Date	Hour	7th (S) Battn Yorkshire Regt — Summary of Events and Information	Remarks and references to Appendices
LIGNEREUIL	1/10/17		Lt Col Mavis D.S.O. assumed command of the Battn again. Draft 2/Lt Goodlass	
		3 PM.	Brigade practice attack with 3 objectives in conjunction with remainder of Bgde	
"	2/10/17	3 PM.	The same attack repeated	
"	3/10/17	9.45 AM	Practiced the same attack for the 3rd time. The Brigade was on a frontage of 2 Battns. First 2 objectives taken by the West York on right & E York on the left. The 3rd & final objective taken by Yorkshire Regt on the right & Dorset Regt on the left. Each Battn on a frontage of 2 Coys. Draft of 50 O.R.	
"	4/10/17		Preparations for moving from VII Corps Area to XIV Corps area V Army. All stores etc completed.	
"		8 PM.	Battn less B Coy & 1 cooker marched to Saulty & entrained with transport that had gone on in advance of the troops	MAP LENS
SAULTY Station	5/10/17	2.42 AM	Train left for Peselhoek and arrived about 2.30 PM. & marched to PIDDINGTON camp P1 Area PROVEN N.W. of POPERINGHE.	MAP HAZEBROUCK 5A 1/100000
PIDDINGTON Camp Proven	6/10/17		B Coy with cooker arrived about 7 A.M. & rejoined the Battn. Practice attack by Battn in the afternoon.	
"	7/10/17	9 A.M.	Practice attack & consolidation of a shell crater area on the lines at present employed against the Germans in Flanders.	
"	8/10/17		Afternoon practice attack 2 Coys at a time	
"	9/10/17		Preparations for move forward & relieve XXIX Divn	
"	"	9.15 PM.	Battn marched to PROVEN & entrained with a few men of E York Regt for INTERNATIONAL CORNER	

A5834 Wt. W4973/M687 750,000 8/16 D. D. & L. Ltd. Forms/C.2118/1

Instructions regarding War Diaries and Intelligence Summaries are contained in F. S. Regs., Part II. and the Staff Manual respectively. Title pages will be prepared in manuscript.

WAR DIARY
or
~~INTELLIGENCE SUMMARY.~~
(Erase heading not required.)

Army Form C. 2118.

Place	Date	Hour	Summary of Events and Information — 7(S) Batt^n Yorkshire Regt	Remarks and references to Appendices
	9/10/17	cont^d	at A.9.a about 11.40 P.M. From there, Batt^n marched to DRAGON CAMP situated in the wood at A 9.d + A 15.b. The men in bivouacks + tents, the Officers in huts.	Map. Trench Map Belgium Sheet 28 N.W. Edition 6^B 1/20,000.
DRAGON CAMP A.15.b.	10/10/17	2 AM.	Hostile aircraft bombed camp + neighbourhood wounding 3 O.R. Draft 18 O.R.	
		11.30 AM.	Batt^n + transport marched to HARROW Camp B.7.d.8.5. Bgde depôt formed at Dragon Camp. The usual compliment of Officers + men left out, extra transport men, butting section + stretcher bearers temporarily attached. MAJOR Acton in command of 50th Bgde Depôt. 50th Bgde is now Bgde in Support, 17th Bgde taking over the front line from 29th Div + 52nd Bgde in Div^nl Reserve.	
HARROW Camp B.7.d.8.5	11/10/17	8 AM.	XVII Div^n completes relief of XXIX Div^n. HARROW Camp shelled by hostile high velocity gun at 1 P.M. only one man wounded.	
		5.15 PM.	Batt^n less transport moved to Whitemill Camp ELVERDINGHE B.14.d. The 50th Bgde now in Divisional Support 51st Bgde holding the front lines.	
WHITEMILL Camp B.14.d.	12/10/17	3 PM.	The Batt^n moved to the ~~[illegible]~~ YSER Canal at B.12.d.1.2 near CACTUS PONTOON. Rained all day. There was no cover for the troops until the evening when a few bivouacks were procured. Trench strength 18 Officers 490 O.R.	
YSER CANAL	13/10/17		During darkness the Batt^n began to relieve 10th Batt^n Sherwood Foresters + portions of 7th Batt^n Lincolnshire Regt + 7th Batt^n Border Regt. The relief went on all night in the pouring rain. The guides frequently lost their direction but in spite of these difficulties the 2 Coys of the Border Regt were the only troops not relieved by daylight. Batt^n H.Q at OLGA HOUSES U.18.b.6.3. On the left the 10th W. Yorkshire Regt held the	

A5834 Wt. W4973/M687 750,000 8/16 D. D. & L. Ltd. Forms/C.2118/13.

Instructions regarding War Diaries and Intelligence Summaries are contained in F. S. Regs., Part II. and the Staff Manual respectively. Title pages will be prepared in manuscript.

WAR DIARY
or
~~INTELLIGENCE SUMMARY.~~
(Erase heading not required.)

Army Form C. 2118.

Place	Date	Hour	7th (S) Battn Yorkshire Regt — Summary of Events and Information	Remarks and references to Appendices
	21/10/17	(contd)	A B & C at LANDRETHUN-LES-ARDRES. Battn H.Q in the Chateau The men were very tired on arrival. The transport came by road via WATTEN distance about 25 miles.	MAP CALAIS 13. 1/100,000
LANDRETHUN-LES-ARDRES	22/10/17		Battn resting. Draft received of 40 OR & posted in equal numbers to B & C Coys.	
"	23/10/17		Coys practicing attacks near billetts	
"	24/26/10/17		Practice attacks on Bgde training area near GUEMY. Draft ~~4~~3 Officers & 8 OR.	
"	27/10/17		Bgde practice attack on a frontage of 2 Battns with 3 objectives. The 2 right battalions only being represented ~~The~~ Dorset Regt. taking the first 2 objectives & the Yorkshire Regt passing through the leading Battn & taking the final objective	
"	28/10/17		Church Parades. Draft 6. O.R. & 2/Lt E E Briggs	
"	29/10/17		Divisional field day. 50th Bgde practicing attack near GUEMY. Scheme with 3 objectives from R to left. 10th West York & 7th York Regt taking the 1st 2 objectives. 7th E York & Dorset Regt taking the final objective 10th West Riding Regt attached to the Bgde as counter attack Battn	
"	30/10/17		Practice attacks continued on 30th by Coys independantly & on 31st by the whole	
"	31/10/17		Battn. Practice after dark forming up on a tape line for assault.	
			Effective Strength: Officers 38, O.R. 973. Ration Strength: Officers 30, O.R. 848	

A5834 Wt. W4973/M687 750,000 8/16 D. D. & L. Ltd. Forms/C.2118/14.

The Adjutant Capt L.V.C Hawkes left the Battn, sick, 20/10/17

NOVEMBER 1917

Instructions regarding War Diaries and Intelligence Summaries are contained in F. S. Regs., Part II. and the Staff Manual respectively. Title pages will be prepared in manuscript.

WAR DIARY
or
~~INTELLIGENCE SUMMARY.~~
(Erase heading not required.)

Army Form C. 2118.

7 Yorkshire Rgt
Vol 26

7th (S) Battn Yorkshire Regt

Place	Date	Hour	Summary of Events and Information	Remarks and references to Appendices
LANDRETHUN-LES-ARDRES	1/11/17 to 3/11/17		Practice attacks carried out under Battn arrangements. Bgde practice attack on 3rd. Draft 26 O.R. arrived on 2nd	MAP. CALAIS 13 1/100,000
"	4/11/17		Church parades	
"	5/11/17		Training continued.	
"	6/11/17		Preparations for move to forward area in the Ypres Salient. Part of transport left by road.	
"	7/11/17	1.45AM	Battn less transport marched to AUDRUICQ station & entrained about 8 AM. Transport came by a later train starting at 2 P.M., 2 lorries containing blankets & officers kits to come by road. Battn detrained at ELVERDINGHE about 3 P.M. & marched to WOLFE Camp B 22.d SE of ELVERDINGHE. Camp consisted of tents & 1 hut for H.Q. Blankets & kits did not arrive. Hostile aircraft bombed the camp and neighbourhood during the night. No casualties.	MAP Belgium Sheet 28 NW
WOLFE Camp B22.d	8/11/17		Transport arrived about 1 AM. All ranks busy building protection against hostile bombs round the tents & huts. 2/Lts T.H. Morton and A.T. Dingle joined the Battn & Lt R.F.C. Scott attached.	
"	9/11/17		Continued work of protecting tents &c. Transport & QM stores at B.20.a.	

A5834 Wt. W4973/M687 750,000 8/16 D. D. & L. Ltd. Forms/C.2118/13.

November 1917.

Instructions regarding War Diaries and Intelligence Summaries are contained in F. S. Regs., Part II. and the Staff Manual respectively. Title pages will be prepared in manuscript.

WAR DIARY
or
~~INTELLIGENCE SUMMARY.~~
(Erase heading not required.)

Army Form C. 2118.

Place	Date	Hour	7th (S) Battn Yorkshire Regt — Summary of Events and Information	Remarks and references to Appendices
Wolfe Camp B22.d	10/11/17		Continued improvement of camp	Map Belgium Sheet 28 N.W. 1/20,000
"	11/11/17		Working parties &c. Major R.E. Cotter sent to command 50th Bde School at Dragon Camp A.15.b. Col Mairis went up to forward area to arrange about taking over the line	
"	12/11/17		Bde School formed at Dragon Camp. Parties detailed to attend courses in Bombing & bayonet fighting, Lewis Rifle, Vickers Gun, Signalling & Wiring.	
"	13/11/17		Trench strength 17 Officers 596 O.R. 3 Officers and 152 O.R. being left out of the line & made up as follows "B" Echelon (including transport) 5 Officers 100 O.R. Bde School 1 Officers & 38 O.R. Attached to 45th Sanitary Section 26 O.R., to 78th Field Coy R.E. 2 Officers & 55 O.R. Employed by the Division 36 O.R.	Map attached BROEMBEEK 1/10,000 marked
		2.30 PM	Battn moved from WOLFE Camp to the front line to relieve 2 Coys 10th Lancashire Fusiliers & 2 Coys of 12th Manchester Regt (52nd Brigade). Relief completed during the night. Battn H.Q. Olga Houses U.18.b. Owing to the state of the ground the troops could only move in single file along the duckboard tracks. In spite of considerable hostile shelling only 2 casualties occurred in the Battn. This is attributed to the fact that the Germans mainly used high explosive shells which exploded deep in the muddy ground.	

A5834 Wt. W4973/M687 750,000 8/16 D. D. & L. Ltd. Forms/C.2118/13.

November /17

Instructions regarding War Diaries and Intelligence Summaries are contained in F. S. Regs., Part II. and the Staff Manual respectively. Title pages will be prepared in manuscript.

WAR DIARY
or
~~INTELLIGENCE SUMMARY.~~

(Erase heading not required.)

Army Form C. 2118.

Place	Date	Hour	Summary of Events and Information — 7th (S) Battn Yorkshire Regt	Remarks and references to Appendices
	13/11/17	(contd)	Front line from Right to left D Coy holding posts in the neighbourhood of REQUETE FARM with B Coy on the left holding posts in the neighbourhood of BESACE FARM. 58th Division on the Right of the Battn + 10th W. York Regt on left. D Coy H.Q FERDAN House. B Coy H.Q near BESACE FARM. C Coy held a line of defended posts behind the front line + which was the main line of resistance. It extended across the whole Divisional front marked O on attached map. One platoon in each post. Coy H.Q at TAUBE FARM. A Coy was in reserve + detailed as the Counter attack Coy. It was grouped round the Coy H.Q at Millers Houses V.13.a. There was less shelling on the front line than on the support + reserve Coys during the night. The Division had one Brigade in the line on a frontage of 2 Battns, 1 Bgde Support + 1 Bgde Reserve	See map attached marked 1
OLGA HOUSES.	14/11/17	4	Relief completed at 4.30 AM. Enemy aircraft activity was very noticeable all day flying low + firing machine guns at any movement on our part. Slight gas shelling during the night. Our artillery carried out a gas shell bombardment during the night. 58th Div on the Right was relieved by 34th Div.	
	15/11/17		Enemy aircraft even more active than yesterday + registering for the artillery especially on the forward "duckboard" tracks.	

A5834 Wt. W4973/M687 750,000 8/16 D. D. & L. Ltd. Forms/C.2118/13.

November/17.

Instructions regarding War Diaries and Intelligence Summaries are contained in F. S. Regs., Part II. and the Staff Manual respectively. Title pages will be prepared in manuscript.

WAR DIARY
or
~~INTELLIGENCE SUMMARY.~~

(Erase heading not required.)

Army Form C. 2118.

7th (S) Batt. Yorkshire Regt

Place	Date	Hour	Summary of Events and Information	Remarks and references to Appendices
	15/11/17	cont.	6th Batt. Dorset Regt began the relief during the early hours of the evening. Relief completed at 1.30AM 16th. Batt. moved into Brigade Support A & C Coys in EAGLE Trench U 23. b and d. B & D Coys in MARSOUIN Camp C 8. b. Batt. H.Q DOUBLE COTTS U. 23. d. Considerable shelling during relief. Our batteries were also active. The Germans attempted a raid on the Corps on our left. Work in the line wiring + patrolling	
DOUBLE COTTS. U.23.d	16/11/17		Work on the improvement of EAGLE trench was carried out by A & C Coys. No hostile shelling	
"	17/11/17	5.30PM	Batt. moved forward again to the front line to relieve 6th Batt. Dorset Regt. Relief completed by 11.45PM. The dispositions of the Batt. was the same as on the previous tour. except that Batt. H.Q was at LOUIS FARM. U 24. c. There was not much shelling during the relief except crossing the STEENBEEK. Quiet night.	
LOUIS FARM U 24. c	18/11/17	7 AM	Our artillery opened a creeping barrage on enemy front system across the Divisional front with the result that A. & C. Coys came in for a considerable amount of hostile shelling which continued all the morning. Our aeroplanes showed considerable activity during the day. There was some gas shelling during the evening by the enemy	

A5834 Wt. W4973/M687 750,000 8/16 D. D. & L. Ltd. Forms/C.2118/13.

NOVEMBER 1917

Instructions regarding War Diaries and Intelligence Summaries are contained in F. S. Regs., Part II. and the Staff Manual respectively. Title pages will be prepared in manuscript.

WAR DIARY
or
~~INTELLIGENCE SUMMARY.~~

(Erase heading not required.)

Army Form C. 2118.

Place	Date	Hour	Summary of Events and Information — 7th (S) Battn Yorkshire Regt	Remarks and references to Appendices
LOUIS FARM U24.c	19/11/17		Fairly heavy enemy shelling during the morning. H.E. & gas shells between Frontline & Battn HQ continued for most of it. In the evening heavier shelling of Reserve Coy & the road behind it. Weather remained fine but foggy. Hostile aircraft not very active. During the night the Battn was relieved by 10th Sherwood Foresters 51st Bde and entrained at BOESINGHE at 1.45 AM (20th). Detrained at International Corner & marched to DRAGON CAMP A.14.b. Relief was completed by 1.30 AM (20th) only 2 casualties occurred.	
DRAGON CAMP A 14.b	20/11/17		Casualties during the Battn 2 tours in the front line from the afternoon 11th to arrival at Dragon Camp early this morning. No Officer casualties. O.R. 8 killed 34 wounded, 8 missing. Battn resting. Inspections & Baths. Bde in Divl Reserve	MAP BELGIUM Sheet 28 N.W. 1/20000
"	21/11/17		8 Lewis Rifles grouped round the camp for defence against hostile aircraft. Battn working on the improvement of the camp.	
"	22/11/17 to 24/11/17		Coy route marches, Drill & [illegible] carried on. Draft 6 O.R. received. Improvement of the camp continued. Lt Col [illegible] went on leave for [illegible] taking temporary command of the Battn. 2/Lt H Storch & 2/Lt [illegible] joined the Battn	
"	25/11/17	2.30 PM	Battn marched to Bridge Camp No 1. B.14.d. Bde in Divl Support. A Coy to CANDLE Trench C.8.b to provide working parties under R.E. Bde in Divisional Support.	
BRIDGE CAMP No 1 B14.d	26/11/17		Working party under R.E. supplied by the Battn	
"	27/11/17		Drill, inspections &c under Coy Commanders.	
"	28/11/17		Practically the whole Battn employed on a working party in the forward area. A Coy digging a new trench near EAGLE TRENCH U23.b	[illegible]

A5834 Wt W4973/M687 750,000 8/16 D. D. & L. Ltd. Forms/C.2118/13.

November 1917.

WAR DIARY
or
~~INTELLIGENCE SUMMARY.~~
(Erase heading not required.)

Army Form C. 2118.

Instructions regarding War Diaries and Intelligence Summaries are contained in F. S. Regs., Part II. and the Staff Manual respectively. Title pages will be prepared in manuscript.

7th (S) Battn Yorkshire Regt.

Place	Date	Hour	Summary of Events and Information	Remarks and references to Appendices
Bridge Camp No 1 B14.d.	29/11/17		Coys drilling, bayonet fighting &c.	RSC
"	30/11/17		12 Officers and 300 OR on a working party under RE in the forward area. Enemy long range H V guns active near this camp & transport lines during the night.	
			Effective Strength: Officers 42, OR 884. Ration Strength: Officers 27, OR 707	RSC
			Early this morning casualties were suffered by the party working at Ondank Dump A.S.C. under the RE resulting in 1 man being killed & 5 wounded from the Battn.	RSC

Ronald E. Cotton. Major

A5834 Wt. W4973/M687 750,000 8/16 D. D. & L. Ltd. Forms/C.2118/13.

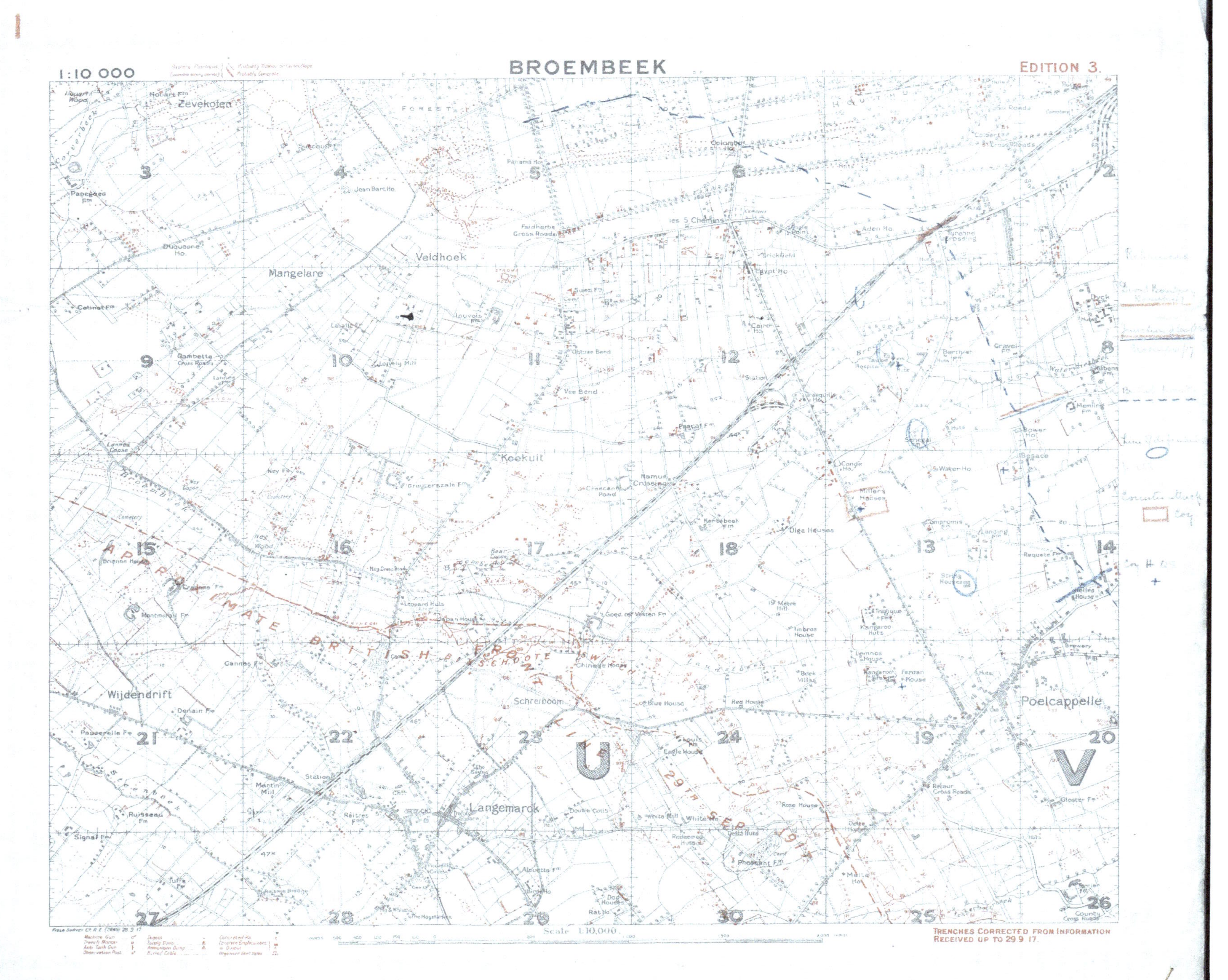

BROEMBEEK
1:10 000
EDITION 3.
Zevekoten
Mangelare
Veldhoek
Koekuit
Wijdendrift
Langemarck
Schreiboom
Poelcappelle
les 5 Chemins
Aden Ho.
Namur Crossing
Olga Houses
Miller's Houses
Station
Martin Mill
Cannes Fm
Montmirail Fm
Brienne House
Gambetta Cross Roads
Jean Bart Ho.
Duquesne Ho.
Papegoed Fm
Cabinet Fm
Hollart Fm
Panama Ho.
Fordhorbe Cross Roads
Louvois Fm
Lavalle Fm
Jolietly Mill
Yee Bend
Pascal Fm
Kerselaere Fm
Gruyterszale Fm
Crescent Pond
Ney Fm
Good ter Vesten Fm
Chinese House
Blue House
Red House
Eagle House
White Mill
Double Cotts
Alouette Fm
Rose House
Pheasant Fm
Rafael Fm
Gloster Fm
Taube Fm
Brewery
Louis Fm
Imbros House
Kangaroo Huts
Lemnos House
Fenian House
Compromis
Landing Fm
Requete Fm
Senegal
Water Ho.
Bower Ho.
Memling Fm
Gravel Fm
Conde Ho.
Signal Fm
Russeau Fm
Tuffs Fm
Denain Fm
Lannes Cross
Cemetery
Reitres Fm
Counter Cross Roads
Malta Ho.
3 Pig Huts
APPROXIMATE BRITISH FRONT LINE 29TH SEP. 1917
TRENCHES CORRECTED FROM INFORMATION RECEIVED UP TO 29.9.17.
Scale 1:10,000
U
V
2
3
4
5
6
8
9
10
11
12
13
14
15
16
17
18
19
20
21
22
23
24
25
26
27
28
29
30

December 1917

WAR DIARY
or
INTELLIGENCE SUMMARY.
(Erase heading not required.)

Army Form C. 2118.

7 Yorkshire Rgt

Vol 27

Instructions regarding War Diaries and Intelligence Summaries are contained in F. S. Regs., Part II. and the Staff Manual respectively. Title pages will be prepared in manuscript.

Place	Date	Hour	7th (S) Battn Yorkshire Regt — Summary of Events and Information	Remarks and references to Appendices
BRIDGE Camp No 1 B. 14. d.	1/12/17		Preparations for moving forward during the morning	TRENCH MAP Belgium Sheet 28 1/20,000
		12 15 PM	Battn marched to HUDDLESTON Camp C.7.d.1.4. and arrived at 2 PM. A Coy from Candle trench rejoined at 5 PM. B Coy in CADDIE trench C.7.d. accommodation in shelters the remainder of Battn in huts. Battn in Brigade Reserve.	RSC
HUDDLESTON Camp C.7.d.1.4	2/12/17		B Coy moved to CADDIE Trench. Battn supplied small working & carrying parties at night for R.E.	RSC
"	3/12/17		Major R.E. Cotton went up to SOUVENIR Farm, the H.Q. of left Battn in the front line (6th Dorset), to arrange about relief on the night of 4th–5th. Orders for relief of front line Battn subsequently cancelled. (Left Battn front from N bank of the WATERVLIET-BEEK to S bank of the BROEMBEEK)	SOUVENIR Farm V.18.c.45.55 Schaap-Balie Map Edition 1 1/10,000 RSC
"	4/12/17		Improvements made in the camp & Candle trench	RSC
"	5/12/17		Part of the transport left in the morning for the rest area near AUDRUICQ	Map Hazebrouck 5A 1/100,000
		3.30 PM	Battn relieved by 15th Battn Cheshire Regt 105th Inf Bgde XXXV Division & marched to Bridge Camp No 2. Accommodation Nissen huts. At night hostile aeroplanes active but no bombs dropped in the camp. The Lewis rifles engaged the aeroplanes.	
...2	6/12/17		Arrangements for moving to rest area	RSC
			In the afternoon all 4 Coy's inspected by C.O.	RSC
...d.	7/12/17	12 noon	Battn entrained at ELVERDINGHE for AUDRUICQ Station. Remainder of transport left by train 6 PM. Mens blankets &c by lorries. Battn arrived about 6.30 PM & marched to NORTKERQUE 3 miles away & went into billets. Part of C Coy in huts	RSC

A5834 Wt. W4973/M687 750,000 8/16 D. D. & L. Ltd. Forms/C.2118/13.

December 1917

Instructions regarding War Diaries and Intelligence Summaries are contained in F. S. Regs., Part II. and the Staff Manual respectively. Title pages will be prepared in manuscript.

WAR DIARY
or
~~INTELLIGENCE SUMMARY.~~
(Erase heading not required.)

Army Form C. 2118.

Place	Date	Hour	7th (S) Battn Yorkshire Regt — Summary of Events and Information	Remarks and references to Appendices
NORTKERQUE	8/12/17		Transport arrived in the early hours of the morning. Battn is comfortably billeted although the Coys are rather scattered. Inspections, refitting &c	Map Sheet Belgium HAZEBROUCK 5A 1/100,000
"	9/12/17		Church parades. Recreation room opened and football ground arranged	
"	10/12/17	9 AM.	Battn marched with transport to BAYENGHEM-les-EPERLECQUES and arrived about noon. Billets good on the whole.	
BAYENGHEM	11/12/17		Lt Col Mairis returned from leave & took over command of the Battn again. Orders received to be ready to move at 12 hours notice. Preparations made accordingly. Battn training. Platoons training under platoon commanders drill &c	
"	12/12/17		Lewis Rifle teams firing on the range near GUEMY. Remainder of Battn drill &c under Coy arrangements.	
"	13/12/17		The whole Battn musketry on range during the morning. Preparations for entraining during the afternoon consequent on the receipt of orders to move by train from ST OMER Station in 41 hours from noon today	
"	14/12/17		Brigade began entraining at 4 AM. One Coy of the Battn detailed for loading transport &c for the Bgde group entraining at St OMER. The Coy marched from billets yesterday 7 P.M	
"	15/12/17	4 AM.	Battn less 1 Coy marched with transport in advance to ST OMER and entrained for BAPAUME	Map LENS 11 1/100,000

A5834 Wt. W4973/M687 750,000 8/16 D. D. & L. Ltd. Forms/C.2118/13.

December 1917

Instructions regarding War Diaries and Intelligence Summaries are contained in F. S. Regs., Part II. and the Staff Manual respectively. Title pages will be prepared in manuscript.

WAR DIARY
or
~~INTELLIGENCE SUMMARY.~~
(Erase heading not required.)

Army Form C. 2118.

Place	Date	Hour	Summary of Events and Information	Remarks and references to Appendices
	15/12/17	(contd)	Detrained at 3.45 PM and marched to a camp ~~at~~ S. E of BEAULENCOURT near the Sugar factory, LE TRANSLOY Accomodation Nissen Huts. The Division is now in Third Army Reserve. at 2 hours notice to move.	[illegible]
BEAULEN-COURT	16/12/17		Heavy snow fell during the night 16/17. Church parades	[illegible]
"	17/12/17		Owing to the weather little training was done. It continued to snow on + off nearly all day	[illegible]
"	18/12/17		Companies training on ground near the camp during the morning. Recreational training afternoon	[illegible]
"	19/12/17		Training continued. Battn. practise attack morning of 20th.	
"	20/12/17		Frosty weather continues	[illegible]
"	21/12/17		Shooting on range. Xmas dinners for the Battn. C.O. reconnoitring forward positions	
"	22/12/17	2.PM	Marched to BERTINCOURT with the rest of the Brigade. Accomodation huts &c	[illegible]
		8.PM	Hostile aircraft dropped bombs in the village and killed one man + wounded 5 O.R.	
		8.30PM	The transport lines near RUYAULCOURT were bombed by German aeroplanes. 7 men were killed and 14 wounded (2 very slightly). The animals suffered many casualties killed 43. wounded 8	[illegible]

Instructions regarding War Diaries and Intelligence Summaries are contained in F. S. Regs., Part II. and the Staff Manual respectively. Title pages will be prepared in manuscript.

December 1917

WAR DIARY
or
~~INTELLIGENCE SUMMARY.~~
(*Erase heading not required.*)

Army Form C. 2118.

Place	Date	Hour	7th (S) Battn Yorkshire Regt — Summary of Events and Information	Remarks and references to Appendices
BERTINCOURT	23/12/17	9.20AM	Battn marched to trenches N.E. of HAVRINCOURT Wood & relieved 5th Battn Lincolnshire Regt. The Bgde is now in Divl Reserve with West Yorkshire Regt on the right of the Battn in HAVRINCOURT Wood & East York & Dorset Regts in BERTINCOURT village. Hard frosty weather continues	Map French 57c N.E.3 Edition 5A 1/10.000
HAVRINCOURT Wood K.31.b.6.1	24/12/17		The accomodation for the Battn is mainly shelters & tents & not good. The Division has 2 Bgds in the line 52 Bgde on the right & 51st Bgde on the left 50th Bgde Reserve. C.O. & Coy Commanders reconnoitring trenches N. & N.E. of HAVRINCOURT Village which the Battn will hold in the event of an hostile attack	
"	25/12/17		Xmas day. Improvement of trenches & bivouacks. Battn H.Qs moved to dugout vacated by Bgde H.Q. at K.32.c.7.9 during the afternoon.	
K.32.c.7.9	26/12/17		C.O. & Coy commanders reconnoitring trenches in the forward area with a view to relieving 52nd Bgde in the front line tomorrow. Arrangements made for relief of 10th Battn Lancashire Fuslrs holding the front line North of FLESQUIERES	Map MŒUVRES Special Sheet Ed. 5A Trenches Revised to 1/11/17
"	27/12/17		Preparations for moving forward to relieve Lancashire Fuslrs in the front line.	
		3.30PM	Battn began to march up to the trenches with usual intervals between platoons. No 4 Platoon B Coy came under shell fire 2/Lt J. Goodway & Sgt Kirk were killed and 2 O.R. wounded. Dispositions from Right to Left Front line A & C Coys in "Silver Street" from K.18.b.9.2 to FLESQUIERES – GRAINCOURT road exclusive. Support line B & D Coys. Battn H.Q under FLESQUIERES Church. On the Right of the Battn 10th West Yorkshire Regt and on the left 5th Border Regt.	Map attached with dispositions Marked I
			Relief completed 7 P.M. The Division is holding the line with a frontage of 2 Brigades. Each Bgde with 2 Battns in the front line. 1 Battn in Support & 1 Battn in reserve. Front line is a continuous trench narrow and shallow & held by posts. Wire in front good and an excellent field of fire is obtained from both front & support lines. Quiet night.	

A5834 Wt. W4973/M687 750,000 8/16 D. D. & L. Ltd. Forms/C.2118/13.

December 1917

Army Form C. 2118.

Instructions regarding War Diaries and Intelligence Summaries are contained in F. S. Regs., Part II. and the Staff Manual respectively. Title pages will be prepared in manuscript.

WAR DIARY
or
~~INTELLIGENCE SUMMARY.~~
(Erase heading not required.)

Place	Date	Hour	7th (S) Batt. Yorkshire Regt. Summary of Events and Information	Remarks and references to Appendices
FLESQUIERES	28/12/17		Quiet day. One man wounded. Snow drifted into the trenches and blocked all the CTs. Clearing & deepening trenches both day and night. Men in the front line have no accomodation except tarpaulins. Support Coys better off with a few dugouts in the Chateau grounds and sunken road K17 d. The present support lines being QUORN STRUB and LINCOLN SWITCH held in posts. Quiet night. RSC	Map attached I
"	29/12/17		Quiet day.	
		10.55PM	Chateau & neighbourhood shelled for 10 minutes. Wiring carried on after dark with the usual 2 patrols per night for each front line Coy. Nothing of importance was seen or heard by the patrols. Improvement of trenches continued. RSC	
"	30/12/17	6.15AM	A hostile attack on the 63rd Division on our right near La Vacquerie. At the same time our front & support lines were shelled with gas & 5.9 in ~~gas~~ shells. The village was also shelled. The fire soon died down after our artillery had retaliated. 2/Lt. BULLOCK slightly gassed and 5 O.R. During the night much work was done on improvement of the trenches assistance being given by 80 men of 6th Dorset Regt. Slight thaw during the day & night. RSC	
"	31/12/17		Quiet day. Began to freeze again in the afternoon.	
		7P.M.	Battn relieved by 6th Batt. Dorset Regt. Battn moved back to the old Hindenburg Support line. Batt HQ at K.24.a.90.25. Battn in Bgde Support with 52nd Bgde on the left and 9th Battn Royal Welsh Fuslrs 19th Divn on the right. Accomodation Dugouts, saps and shelters. During the 4 days tour in the trenches the weather was very cold. Snow lying on the ground the whole time. Ration Strength Officers 26. OR 631. Trench Strength Officers 23 OR 486. RSC	

Ronald E. Cotton. Major

A5834 Wt. W4973/M687 750,000 8/16 D. D. & L. Ltd. Forms/C.2118/13.

Attached to War Diary December 1917.

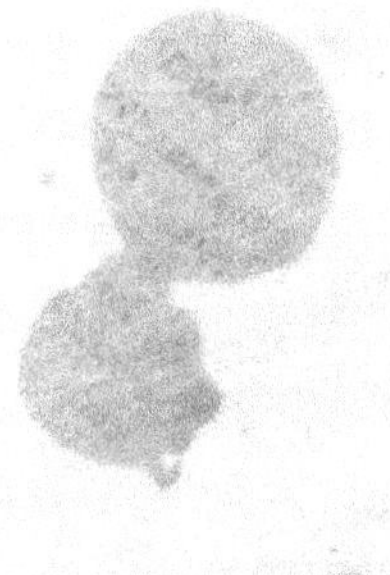

CORPS TOPO SECTION REFERENCE
Graincourt-lez-Havrincourt
Orival Wood
Flesquières
Havrincourt
Ribecourt
Canal Copse
Square Copse
Wigan Copse
Femy Wood
Water Copse
High Wood
Triangle Wood
LEFT DIV'L BOUNDARY
LEFT BDE
SHINGLER TRENCH
BRIGADE BOUNDARY
L. front Coy
R. front Coy
BATT. BOUNDARY
SILVER STREET
R Coy HQ
RIGHT DIVN'L BOUNDARY
BATT. HQ
RES Batt HQ

January 1918

Instructions regarding War Diaries and Intelligence Summaries are contained in F. S. Regs., Part II. and the Staff Manual respectively. Title pages will be prepared in manuscript.

WAR DIARY
or
~~INTELLIGENCE~~ SUMMARY.
(Erase heading not required.)

Army Form C. 2118.

7 Bn Yorkshire

Vol 28

Place	Date	Hour	7th (S) Battn Yorkshire Regt — Summary of Events and Information	Remarks and references to Appendices
Battn HQ. K24.a.90.25	1/1/18		Battn resting and improving accomadation in HINDENBURG Support line in L19.a. K.24.a and b. Lt Col Mairis went to command 50th Bgde during the absence of Brigadier	Trench Map MARCOING 1/10.000 Edition 5A
"	2/1/18		Improving trenches + wiring in front by transfering old German wire from S to N of the trench. Major R E Cotton in command of the Battn from yesterday.	
"	3/1/18		A few shells fell near the right + left Coys H.Q. B + A during the day. 2 working parties from A.C. + D Coys assisted the Battns holding the front line to dig out their trenches at night. New Year's Honours. "Lt Col G. Mairis, Major R Cotton + Lt G A. Tomlin" "Mentioned in despatches" also Coy S. M. Shaw. Capt S. Granswick + 2/Lt S. A. Mullaney awarded Military Cross	MOEUVRE Map Special Sheet 1/20,000
"	4/1/18	7 P.M.	Battn began moving up to the front line to relieve 6th Battn Dorset Regt in the same sector as occupied by the Battn at the end of December /17. Map showing trenches attached. From Right to Left B Coy front line in Silver trench. A Coy in Support in QUORN STRUE. D Coy in the front line in Silver trench on the left of B Coy with C Coy in Support in LINCOLN SWITCH. Battn HQ in HINDENBURG Support line S of the village of FLESQUIERES at K.24.a.4.4. the old Battn HQ under the Church not being suitably situated. Quiet relief. Relief completed at ~~7.15~~ 8.20 PM.	attached marked I
Battn HQ. K24.a.4.4	5/1/18		Hostile artillery rather more active than usual but no damage of note was done. Our patrols were very active but no hostile patrols encountered.	
"	6/1/18		C.Os of 17th + 18th Battns London Regt. 141st Brigade came to arrange the relief of the Battn tomorrow. Hostile howitzers of 22 cent: calibre fired at the Chateau + neighbourhood where A, B + D Coy H.Q.s are situated. No casualties + remarkably little damage done. Thaw began with rain all night. Trenches in a very bad state in consequence. Quiet night. Our patrols active.	

A5834 Wt. W4973/M687 750,000 8/16 D. D. & L. Ltd. Forms/C.2118/13.

January 1918

Instructions regarding War Diaries and Intelligence Summaries are contained in F. S. Regs., Part II. and the Staff Manual respectively. Title pages will be prepared in manuscript.

WAR DIARY
or
~~INTELLIGENCE SUMMARY.~~
(*Erase heading not required.*)

Army Form C. 2118.

Place	Date	Hour	7th (S) Battn Yorkshire Regt. Summary of Events and Information	Remarks and references to Appendices
H.Q. K.24.a.4.4	7/1/18		The relief by 141st Bgde tonight will effect the Battn as follow. Two platoons of B Coy on the right will be relieved by 4 sections of No 2 Coy 18th Battn London Regt. A Coy in Support will be relieved by half a Coy of 18th Battn London Regt. D Coy + the remaining 2 platoons of B Coy will be relieved by B Coy 17th Battn London Regt + C Coy by D Coy of 17th Battn. This Battn will relieve the H.Q. in this trench. (HINDENBURG Supp^t)	see
"	7/1/18	5.30PM	Relief began by 18th London Regt relieving 2 platoons of B Coy + the whole of A Coy. Entire relief completed 9.20 PM. Battn marched back to Phipps Camp on the BERTINCOURT – HAPLINCOURT Road O.6.d.2.2 Last Coy arrived 2 AM 9th. Roads very slippery. Only 6 men had to be carried in a G.S. waggon from HAVRINCOURT Wood to the camp. Accomodation Nissen + RE huts. Quiet relief no casualties the last 3 days in the front line. Total casualties during the 11 days tour in front + support lines from 27/28 Dec – 7/8 Jan Killed 1 Officer 2 OR Wounded 8 OR Gassed 1 Officer + 2 OR	Map 57c Edition 2 1/40000 see
PHIPPS Camp O.6.d.2.2	8/1/18 9/1/18		Battn resting. In Divl Reserve at 2 hours notice to move. Heavy snow early morning of 8th which drifted into most of the huts. During the evening 9th a thaw accompanied by rain began.	see
"	10/1/18	2PM.	Orders recd for Battn to move forward to J.35.d. 7th Battn E York Regt 10th Battn West York Regt moving at the same time. Battn moved at 2.50 PM + was held up at BERTINCOURT for 2 hours subsequently reaching its destination at 6.40 PM. Battn H.Q. in a shelter at J.35.d.2.5. An attack on the Divisional front was expected + at 8.30 PM our artillery	

A5834 Wt. W4973/M687 750,000 8/16 D. D. & L. Ltd. Forms/C.2118/13.

January 1918

Instructions regarding War Diaries and Intelligence Summaries are contained in F. S. Regs., Part II. and the Staff Manual respectively. Title pages will be prepared in manuscript.

WAR DIARY
or
INTELLIGENCE ~~SUMMARY.~~
(Erase heading not required.)

Army Form C. 2118.

Place	Date	Hour	7th (S) Battn Yorkshire Regt — Summary of Events and Information	Remarks and references to Appendices
	10/1/18	(contd)	heavily bombarded the enemy positions to which they replied energetically. The firing died down soon after 9 P.M. + the situation reported normal. The Battn remained all night with orders to move at short notice	see
H.Q. J25.d.2.5.	11/1/18		The morning was spent in improving the accomodation. Battn returned to PHIPPS Camp arriving shortly after 1 P.M.	see
"	12/1/18		Working party of 300 men laying buried cable nearly all day.	see Trench Map MOEUVRE Special Sheet 57c NW, NE SW + SE 1/20,000
"	13/1/18	1.50 PM	Battn moved forward to the Reserve line (Old British front line) + relieved West Riding Regt 52nd Brigade. Relief completed 5 P.M. Accomodation for the men extremely bad. in tents, + under tarpaulins in the trench &c. Froze during the night. Battn H.Q in the same dug out as it occupied 25th Dec last. Battn in Brigade Reserve. 50th Bgde relieved 52nd Bgde during the night. Frontline R to L 6th Dorset. 7th E. York. Support Battn 10th West York.	
H.Q. K32.c.7.7	14/1/18		Improving accomodation and clearing the trenches which are in a very dirty state + falling in. Coy Commanders reconnoitring route to Support Battn in TANK Trench + TANK Support (new names LONDON TRENCH + LONDON Support) 2 Coys working on DARWIN ALLEY K17.a. at night.	see Attached marked I
"	15/1/18		2 Coys working digging out DARWIN ALLEY at night. Heavy Rain. All trenches falling in. Making new accomodation for Reserve Battn in Spoil heap at K31.A. South of the Canal du Nord. C.O. reconnoitred as far as front Battn H.Qs in Whitehall in K15.d	see Divisional + Bgde Boundaries
"	16/1/18		Rain continued. Trenches getting worse + falling in as fast as they are dug out. Continued work on new accomodation S of Canal. Coy Commanders reconnoitring forward trenches both front + support	see map attached
"	17/1/18		Preparations for moving forward to front-line.	see II
		4.30 PM	Battn began moving up to the trenches to relieve the 6th Battn Dorset Regt in the front line.	see

A5834 Wt. W4973/M687 750,000 8/16 D. D. & L. Ltd. Forms/C.2118/13.

January 1918

Instructions regarding War Diaries and Intelligence Summaries are contained in F. S. Regs., Part II. and the Staff Manual respectively. Title pages will be prepared in manuscript.

WAR DIARY
or
~~INTELLIGENCE SUMMARY.~~

(Erase heading not required.)

Army Form C. 2118.

Place	Date	Hour	7th (S) Battn Yorkshire Regt — Summary of Events and Information	Remarks and references to Appendices
	17/1/18	(Contd)	Dispositions from Right to Left. Front line C Coy from the right Divisional Boundary in K 17. b road to GRAINCOURT inclusive to K11.c.7.4 in SHINGLER TRENCH. A Coy in OWEN TRENCH on the left of C Coy to K11.a.05.05. 10th Battn W. Yorkshire Regt on the left, which relieved 7th Battn E. Yorkshire Regt the same night. 17th Battn London Regt 47th Division on the Right. E. York Regt in Support and Dorset Regt in Bgde Reserve. Support line D Coy behind C Coy + B Coy behind A Coy in Hindenburg Support line in SEAL + SNAKE Trenches. Battn HQ in WHITEHALL K.15.d. Relief completed 8 PM. The trenches are in a very bad state + it is very difficult to get along the front line, the CTs being quite impassable. The night was very dark and patrols gained very little information.	Bgde + Divnl Boundaries see attached map. II
Battn H.Q. K.15.d.85.40	18/1/18		Quiet day	
		6.15 PM	Heavy enemy barrage put down on the whole of front line. SHINGLER + Owen. Roads, CT and approaches shelled with 5.9" shells + a few gas shells. Under cover of bombardment the enemy attacked posts Nos 6, 7, + 8 on the left of A Coy (No 9 being the extreme left hand post of the Battn) Posts are 50 - 80 yds apart + the Germans got into the front trench on the right of No 6 post and between 6, 7 + 8. The enemy had little difficulty in getting through the wire which, although continuous is weak throughout. No 6 post was attacked from the right + No 8 from the rear. The enemy withdrew in 3 or 4 minutes taking one prisoner + 2 Lewis Rifles. The S.O.S. signal was sent by wire from A Coy HQ in K.17.a.5.6. The light signal failed in the front line. Owing to the bombardment the Coys + even the posts on the R + L of those attacked did not know of the presence of the enemy. The night was dark and rapid communication through the trench was impossible owing to the mud. Our casualties amounted to 1 Killed 1 missing + 6 wounded. Pte Harris (wounded) was taken prisoner but escaped + got back to the West Yorkshire lines. Patrols sent out immediately found no sign of the enemy + it is doubtful if any loss was inflicted on him. About 30 Germans attacked.	

January 1918

Instructions regarding War Diaries and Intelligence Summaries are contained in F. S. Regs., Part II. and the Staff Manual respectively. Title pages will be prepared in manuscript.

WAR DIARY
or
INTELLIGENCE SUMMARY.
(Erase heading not required.)

Army Form C. 2118.

Place	Date	Hour	7th (S) Battn. Yorkshire Regt — Summary of Events and Information	Remarks and references to Appendices
Batt H.Q K15.d.85.40	19/1/18		Enemy artillery somewhat more active than usual. Quiet night. Large working parties from Reserve Battn. wiring front line. Patrols saw no sign of the enemy.	WE
"	20/1/18	1 AM	A + C Coys in the front line were relieved by B + D Coys. Very quiet night. Relief of 2 front Coys completed about 3 AM 21st.	WE
"	21/1/18		Hostile artillery active behind the front lines. 6th Battn. Dorset Regt relieved the Battn. Relief completed at 7.10 PM. Very quiet night. Battn. moved in Support in the old Hindenburg front line. See disposition map attached. Battn. H.Q at K21.a 7.7 in LONDON Trench. A Coy has 1 Platoon in SP in COLLINS Street at K.16.c 6.3	Map marked II WE
Batt H.Q London Trench K.21.a.7.7	22/1/18		Working on improvement of trenches occupied by the Battn. which are full of earth + water + collecting salvage. At night 2 working parties of 50 men each carrying RE material to the front line for the Right + Left Battns. in the front line. Quiet day except for hostile shelling in back areas. Night quiet on the whole	WE
"	23/1/18		A good deal of hostile gas shelling on the Havrincourt Flesquieres road in the morning. Mist and slight rain. Night carrying parties of 20s. for T.M. Battery + R + L front Battns.	WE
"	24/1/18		Work continued on the trenches which still require a lot of work to be done on them. Working + carrying parties at night considerably hampered by gas shelling. No casualties.	WE

A5834 Wt. W4973/M687 750,000 8/16 D. D. & L. Ltd. Forms/C.2118/13.

January /18

Instructions regarding War Diaries and Intelligence Summaries are contained in F. S. Regs., Part II. and the Staff Manual respectively. Title pages will be prepared in manuscript.

WAR DIARY
or
~~INTELLIGENCE SUMMARY.~~
(Erase heading not required.)

Army Form C. 2118.

Place	Date	Hour	7(S) Battn Yorkshire Regt — Summary of Events and Information	Remarks and references to Appendices
H.Q.			Continued work on the trenches occupied by the Battn.	Map attached marked I
K 21. a. 7. 7.	25/1/18	8.30 PM	Battn relieved by 10th Battn Sherwood Foresters (51st Bgde). Battn marched to a camp composed of Nissen huts &c at the Spoil Heap in J. 34. c. The whole Brigade relieved during the night & came into Divisional Reserve. Total Casualties while in the line from 13th inst O.R. 1 killed, 2 Died of Wounds, 6 wounded, 1 Missing Total 10. No casualties to Officers. Hostile aircraft active dropping bombs during the night.	
Spoil Heap J 34. c	26/1/18		Battn resting & making bomb protection to huts. Lt Col Mauns D.S.O. took over command of the Battn again.	
"	27/1/18		Working party of 200 men burying cable under R.E. Work continued on the protection of huts. Coy Commanders reconnoitring Support line S. & W. of Canal on front where wiring party will be employed tomorrow night.	
"	28/1/18		Continued work on camp. All 4 Coys wiring in front of proposed new Support line from K 16. b. 0. 7 to Divisional boundary K. 8. c.	
"	29/1/18		Baths, work on camp continued.	
"	30/1/18		Working party under R.E. burying cable. Work discontinued early owing to hostile balloons overlooking the ground where they were working.	
"	31/1/18		Preparation for moving up to the front line to relieve 52nd Brigade in	

A5834 Wt. W4973/M687 750,000 8/16 D. D. & L. Ltd. Forms/C.2118/13.

January 1918.

Instructions regarding War Diaries and Intelligence Summaries are contained in F. S. Regs., Part II. and the Staff Manual respectively. Title pages will be prepared in manuscript.

WAR DIARY
or
~~INTELLIGENCE SUMMARY.~~
(*Erase heading not required.*)

Army Form C. 2118.

Place	Date	Hour	7th (S) Battn Yorkshire Regt — Summary of Events and Information	Remarks and references to Appendices
	31/1/18	(contd)	The Left Brigade Sector Dispositions of the Battn at the end of relief as shewn on attached map Battn H.Q. at K.9.c.30.15. Modification of these dispositions will be made tomorrow.	See attached map marked I
		6. P.M.	Battn started to march to the trenches	
			Relief completed 10.30 P.M.	
			Effective Strength — Officers 35, OR 761 Ration Strength — Officers 28, OR 509 (Including Chaplain & Medical Officer) Trench Strength — Officers 18, OR 504	
			Ronald E. Cotton Major	

A5834 Wt. W4973/M687 750,000 8/16 D. D. & L. Ltd. Forms/C.2118/13.

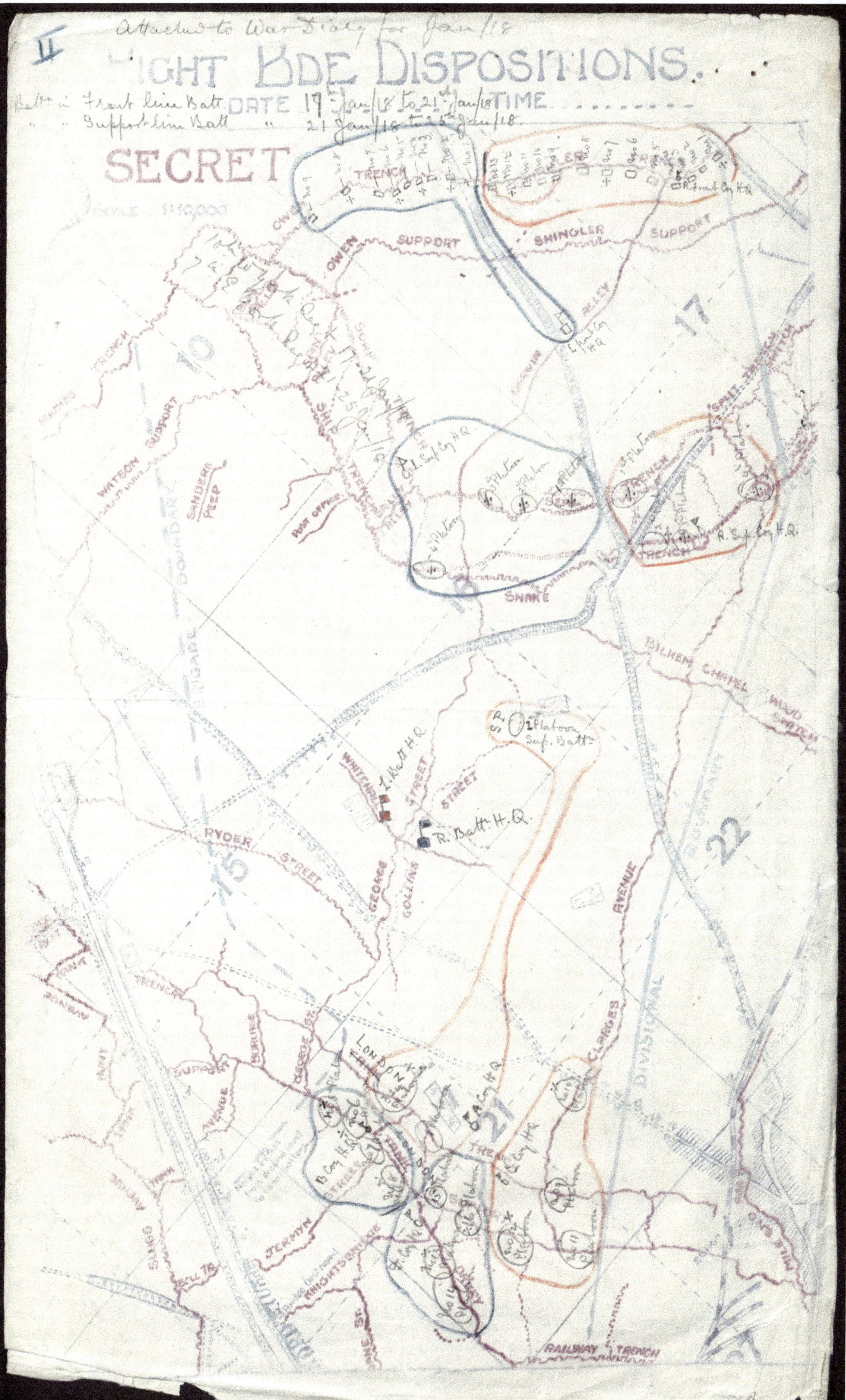

II
Attached to War Diary for Jan/18
RIGHT BDE DISPOSITIONS
DATE 17th Jan/18 to 21st Jan/18 TIME
Battn in Front line Batt.
Support line Batt. 21 Jan/18 to 25th Jan/18
SECRET
SCALE 1:10,000
TRENCH
SUPPORT
SHINGLER
SUPPORT
OWEN
SNAKE
BILHEM CHAPEL
WOOD SWITCH
WHITEHALL
STREET
R. Batt H.Q.
L. Batt H.Q.
RYDER
STREET
GEORGE
COLLINS
AVENUE
BOUNDARY
DIVISIONAL
BRIGADE
BOUNDARY
CLARGES
LONDON
JERMYN
KNIGHTSBRIDGE
RAILWAY TRENCH
SUPPORT
AVENUE
HUNT
SLAG
10
15
17
18
21
22
R. Sup. Coy H.Q.
L. Sup. Coy H.Q.
R. Front Coy H.Q.
L. Front Coy H.Q.
B Coy H.Q.
2 Platoon Sup. Batt.
SANDERS KEEP
WATSON SUPPORT
POST OFFICE
SPLIT TRENCH SWITCH

February 1918

Instructions regarding War Diaries and Intelligence Summaries are contained in F. S. Regs., Part II. and the Staff Manual respectively. Title pages will be prepared in manuscript.

WAR DIARY
or
~~INTELLIGENCE SUMMARY.~~
(Erase heading not required.)

Army Form C. 2118.

7 Yorkshire Regt. Cased 29

Place	Date	Hour	Summary of Events and Information — 7th (S) Battn. Yorkshire Regt.	Remarks and references to Appendices
Battn. H.Q. R.9.c.30.15	1/2/18		Battn. relieved 9th Battn. Duke of Wellington's Regt last night (see diary for Jan). Actual numbers in the trenches 18 Officers 363 O.R. Day quiet. Hard frost. Usual improvement of trenches carried on by day & wiring at night. On the right of the Battn. 8th S. Staffordshire Regt was in the front line and on the left.	RC
"	2/2/18		Hostile artillery inactive. No special incidents occurred.	RC
"	3/2/18		Quiet day. Artillery inactive. Patrols had nothing of interest to report.	RC
"	4/2/18	6.45 AM	An enemy raid on the front of 8th S Staffordshire Regt, the Battn. on our right was preceded by a heavy T.M. bombardment. "A" Coy coming in for a good deal of it, but suffered no casualties. Our artillery retaliated.	
		11 PM	Battn. relieved by 6th Battn. Dorset Regt and went into Bgde Reserve at the Spoil heap J.35.c & d. Accomodation huts & shelters. Casualties during the tour in the line 3 OR wounded. This is the last tour of the Battn. in the line. Preparations for disbandment of the Battn. necessitated by the reduction of Brigades to 3 Battns instead of four.	Memo & map attached marked 'X'
Spoil heap J.35.c.	5/2/18 to 8/2/18		Working parties found daily by the Battn. varying from 150 to 230 O.R.	RC

A5834 Wt. W4973/M687 750,000 8/16 D. D. & L. Ltd. Forms/C.2118/13.

February 1918

Instructions regarding War Diaries and Intelligence Summaries are contained in F. S. Regs., Part II. and the Staff Manual respectively. Title pages will be prepared in manuscript.

WAR DIARY
or
~~INTELLIGENCE SUMMARY.~~
(Erase heading not required.)

Army Form C. 2118.

Place	Date	Hour	7th (S) Battn Yorkshire Regt. Summary of Events and Information	Remarks and references to Appendices
Spoil Heap J. 35. C	9/2/18		C + part of D Coys moved back to Phipps Camp. O. 6. d. 2. 2	Map 57 C 2nd Ed.
	10/2/18		Disbandment of the Battn begins. The Officers + men posted as follows. 12th Battn Yorkshire Regt 12 Officers 250 OR. 13th Battn Yorkshire Regt 10 Officers + 200 OR. both these Battns are in 40th Division III Army. 6th Battn Yorkshire Regt 12 Officers + 250 OR. 11th Division I Army. C Coy + part of D Coy posted to 6th Battn A Coy + " " " " " 12th " B Coy + " " " " " 13th " The first drafts entrained for 6th Battn + consisted of 6 Officers + 167 OR. the H.Q with A. B + remainder of D Coy moved to Phipps Camp near BERTINCOURT in the afternoon	List of Officers attached
PHIPPS Camp O. 6. d. 2. 2	11/2/18		Major Genl P. R. Robertson. C.B. C.M.G commanding XVII Division paid a farewell visit to the Battn + to say goodbye to the Officers. Coys handing in stores.	
"	12/2/18		A Coy + part of D Coy 7 Off 154 OR } B Coy + " " " " 7 Off 159 OR } left to join the 12th + 13th Battns respectively by motor busses	

A5834 Wt. W4973/M687 750,000 8/16 D. D. & L. Ltd. Forms/C.2118/13.

February 1918.

Instructions regarding War Diaries and Intelligence Summaries are contained in F. S. Regs., Part II. and the Staff Manual respectively. Title pages will be prepared in manuscript.

WAR DIARY
or
~~INTELLIGENCE SUMMARY.~~
(Erase heading not required.)

Army Form C. 2118.

Place	Date	Hour	Summary of Events and Information — 7th (S) Battn Yorkshire Regt	Remarks and references to Appendices
Philippe Camp O.6.d.2.2	12/2/18		Battn H.Q. and the few details remaining joined Transport 200 yds near Bertincourt on the HAPLINCOURT – BERTINCOURT Road at P.1.c	Map 57.C.
	~~/2/18~~			RCL
H.Q. P.1.c	13/2/18		The disbandment of the Battn is now practically completed although not all the Officers + men have as yet gone to their new units. The H.Q. Staff still awaits disposal by G.H.Q.	
	15/2/18		Lt Tomlin + all transport + horses transfd to 50th Inf Bgde H.Q.	
	22/2/18		The Adjutant Capt. L.V.C. Hawkes joined 7th Entrenching Battn a new formation under Corps.	RCL
	23/2/18		Court of Enquiry on deficiencies in mobilisation Stores, held under Bgde arrangements. Major R.E. Cotton returned from leave + H.Q. moved to billets in the village of BERTINCOURT.	RCL
BERTINCOURT	24/2/18		Col. Maires, Major Cotton + 8 O.R still await instructions as to disposal	RCL
"	25/2/18		QM Lt Asbrey posted to 7th Entrenching Battn Regt S.M. Staines " " 6th Battn Yorkshire Regt	RCL RCL

A5834 Wt. W4973/M687 750,000 8/16 D. D. & L. Ltd. Forms/C.2118/13.

February 1918

Instructions regarding War Diaries and Intelligence Summaries are contained in F. S. Regs., Part II. and the Staff Manual respectively. Title pages will be prepared in manuscript.

WAR DIARY
or
INTELLIGENCE SUMMARY.
(*Erase heading not required.*)

Army Form C. 2118.

Place	Date	Hour	7th (S) Battn. Yorkshire Regt. Summary of Events and Information	Remarks and references to Appendices
BERTIN-COURT	28/2/18		Commanding Officer Lt Col. G. B. de M. Marris D.S.O. appointed to command 6th (S) Battn. Dorsetshire Regt. 50th Inf. Bgde. Major R E Cotton remaining attached to XVII Division. The Battn. ceased to exist officially on 10th inst. There still remain unposted 9 NCO's + men. The Battalion has been on service in France for 2 years + 7 months from 13th July 1915 with XVII Division. The Battn. was formed in Sept. 1914 at WAREHAM Dorsetshire + commanded by Lt Col. R. D'A. Fife C.M.G. D.S.O. + formed part of 50th Inf. Brigade XVII Division from that date to the present time. It has taken part in the principal engagements since the opening of the British Offensive on the Somme on 1st July 1916. + has throughout its existance upheld the honour + traditions of The Green Howards. The Diary finishes. [signature] Lt Col. Comdt. 7/ Yorkshire Regt.	List of officers of the Battn. on disbanding attached

A5834 Wt. W4973/M687 750,000 8/16 D. D. & L. Ltd. Forms/C.2118/13.

SECRET.

10th West Yorkshire Regt.

Copy No. 13

Operation Order No. 53.

28-2-17.

Refer. Maps ALBERT combined sheet and LENS 11.

I The Battalion will march to billets in the WARLOY area at 9.45 a.m. to-morrow.

(i) ROUTE. Road junction E.16.a 9.1 - ALBERT - ALBERT = AMIENS road to cross roads D16. b. - LAVIEVILLE - HENENCOURT - WARLOY.

(ii) ORDER OF MARCH. Headquarters, A, B, C & D Coys. An interval of 200 yds. will be maintained between Companies.

(iii) DRESS. Marching Order with pack. Greatcoats will not be worn. Steel helmets will be carried on the packs.

Officers will parade in the proper order of dress.

(iv) TRANSPORT. The following Transport will march in rear of each Company.

1 Lewis Gun limber.

1 Cooker.

1 Pack Mule.

The remainder of the Transport (less 2 S.A.A pack mules, with Headquarters) will follow in rear of the Battalion at 200 yards interval in the following order:-

Tool Limber

Bomb "

3. S.A.A. "

Forage "

Water carts.

Mess cart.

Maltese cart.

2 G.S. wagons.

(v) DRUMS. The Drums will commence the march at the head of B Company changing to the head of C Company at the second ha[lt]

(vi) REAR PARTY. a straggler party of 10. O.R. (to be detailed by the Regtl. Sergeant Major)

7th YORKSHIRE REGIMENT

LIST OF OFFICERS prior to the disbandment of the Battn

Lt. Col. G.B. de M. Mairis. D.S.O.	~~B. Ech.~~	Posting
Major R.E. Cotton	~~Leave.~~	of H.Q.
Capt. L.V.C. Hawkes. to 7th Entrenching Battn	~~B. Ech.~~	Officers
Lt. and Q.M. E. Asbrey " " " "	~~B. Ech.~~	not yet
Lieut. G.A. Tomlin. to 50th Infantry Bgde	~~B. Ech~~	known.
Lieut. L.G. Collins.	13 Bn	
2/Lt. A.H. Strong.	6 Bn.	
Capt. W.D. Wilkinson. D.S.O. M.C.	12 Bn.	
2/Lt. G.H. Royce.	12 Bn.	
2/Lt. S. Bott.	12 Bn.	
2/Lt. C.L. King.	Leave. (12 Bn)	
2/Lt. J. Bywell.	12 Bn.	
2/Lt. R.A. Mullaney. M.C.	Bde H.Q.	
2/Lt. J.H. Morton.	12 Bn.	
2/Lt. J. Binns.	12 Bn.	
Capt. R.G. de Quetteville M.C.	B. Ech. (13 Bn)	
2/Lt. C.S. Hill.	13 Bn.	
2/Lt. F.W. Hudson.	13 Bn.	
2/Lt. H. Storch.	13 Bn.	
2/Lt. T.W. Tunnicliffe.	13 Bn.	
2/Lt. E.E. Wood.	13 Bn.	
Capt. S. Cranswick M.C.	6 Bn.	
Capt. F.A. Foley.	Base. (6 Bn)	
2/Lt. E.E. Briggs.	Hosp. (6 Bn)	
2/Lt. C.J. Stanton.	Hosp. (6 Bn)	
2/Lt. L.H. Barker.	6 Bn.	
2/Lt. W. Bullock.	6 Bn.	
Capt. F.R. Milholland.	6 Bn.	
2/Lt. W.J. Lucas.	13 Bn.	
2/Lt. E.C. Sharpington.	6 Bn.	
2/Lt. C.W. Goodlass.	6 Bn.	
2/Lt. A.W. Tovell.	6 Bn.	
2/Lt. E.L. Downs.	12 Bn.	
2/Lt. M. Wilkinson.	Hosp. (12 Bn)	
2/Lt. A.V. Deans.	12 Bn.	
Capt. R.C. Driscoe. R.A.M.C.	E. York Regt.	
Capt. J. McPolin. R.C. Chaplain.	Leave.	

X Attached to War Diary [illegible]

MŒUVRES. Ed. 7 Detail and Trenches revised from information received to 3-1-18.

SPECIAL SHEET. PARTS of 57c N.W. N.E., S.W. & S.E.

Scale 1 : 20,000.

MŒUVRES

HINDENBURG

SUPPORT

Bourlon

Bourlon Wood

Graincourt

Orival Wood

Beaumetz

Doignies

Hermies

Havrincourt

Ribécourt

Lebucquière

Morchies

Lagnicourt

Havrincourt Wood

DIV BOUNDARY

INTER BATTN BOUNDARY

DIV BOUNDARY

DIVN BOUNDARY

ENEMY ORGANISATION. 3-1-18

ORGANISATION.

RAILWAYS (Gauge Written). Shown broken where damaged.

OVERHEAD CABLE JUNCTIONS.

SUPPLY DUMPS. Boundaries of Large Dumps Hatched.

AMMUNITION DUMPS.

BALLOONS.

TRACKS.

TELEGRAPH CENTRES.

H.Q. (Name Written).

H.Q. (Divisional).

57c N.E.

57c S.E.

www.ingramcontent.com/pod-product-compliance
Lightning Source LLC
Chambersburg PA
CBHW080923230426
43668CB00014B/2185
9781474510479